GLORIANA

EXPLORING THE REIGN OF ELIZABETH I

GLORIANA

EXPLORING THE REIGN OF ELIZABETH I

BERTRAM FIELDS

MARMONT LANE
BOOKS

Marmont Lane
BOOKS

Gloriana: Exploring The Reign Of Elizabeth I

For information address Marmont Lane Books
139 South Beverly Drive Suite 318
Beverly Hills, CA USA 90212

www.marmontlane.com

First Printing

Publisher: Bobby Woods/Marmont Lane Books

Design: ♡x☕=⚡

Engravings: Paul Rogers

ISBN 13: 978-0-9905602-9-6
ISBN 10: 0-9905602-9-5

ALSO BY BERTRAM FIELDS

Royal Blood: Richard III and the Mystery of the Princes

Players: The Mysterious Identity of William Shakespeare

Destiny: A Novel Of Napoleon & Josephine

Shylock: His Own Story

AS D. KINCAID

The Sunset Bomber

The Lawyer's Tale

To

ENGLAND,

my lifelong friend

GLORIANA

EXPLORING THE REIGN OF ELIZABETH I

BERTRAM FIELDS

MARMONT LANE
BOOKS

In the year following the defeat of the Spanish Armada,
the first three books of Edmund Spenser's epic poem

THE FAERIE QUEENE

were published.

Literate Englishmen recognized that Gloriana,
the magnificent queen whose bold knights
went forth seeking love and glory,
was Spenser's idealized portrait of Elizabeth I.

Contents

INTRODUCTION

ELIZABETH I may have been England's greatest monarch. With its centuries of colorful history, dueling dynasties and warrior kings, can that nation's "greatest monarch" have been a woman? A good case can be made for it.

Elizabeth was not England's first female ruler. Matilda, in the twelfth century, and Mary Tudor, in the sixteenth, preceded her. But Matilda's reign is generally considered a disaster, marked by years of civil war; and Mary's was marked by extreme cruelty, poor decision making and the loss of vital English territory. Elizabeth's reign — indeed, her life — was fundamentally a triumph and a triumph over fearsome adversity.

Elizabeth faced and, for the most part, dealt successfully with, grave political and personal challenges that threatened the nation and herself. For decades during her reign, England faced the ominous threat of invasion by more powerful adversaries. They viewed Elizabeth as a dangerous heretic and schemed to take her throne and her life. Meanwhile, in England itself, religious conflict simmered just beneath the surface and sometimes boiled over into rebellion and open warfare.

Elizabeth faced each of these crises with remarkable skill and intelligence, plus a complete grasp of the facts, personalities and motivations involved and the valuable ability to remain breathtakingly unpredictable. Lord Burghley, who watched her work her magic for decades, said she "was the wisest woman that ever was, for she understood the interests and dispositions of all the princes in her time and was so perfect in the knowledge of her own realm, that no councillor she ever had could tell her anything she did not know before."

Elizabeth faced a constant problem of financing the administration and defense of the realm. This was a personal, as well as political problem. At that time, the burden of providing normal financing for the government fell primarily on the monarch, rather than on parliament or the people. Before her reign ended, Elizabeth had sold most of her jewelry and much of her land to meet England's needs. But she paid her bills and met those needs with remarkable success.

Sixteenth-century England was, in every sense, a man's world. Elizabeth had the added difficulty of trying to rule as a woman, surrounded by ambitious, aggressive and often vainglorious men — some of whom may (or may not) have been her lovers.

Her unique way of dealing with serious problems involved creating ambiguity and uncertainty as to what she really intended. She altered, then re-altered her decisions to the point that she was seen as "capricious" by the men who advised her or were dependent on what seemed her ever-changing moods. Her tactics could be irritating, even infuriating, but they succeeded time after time.

She endured years of extreme pressure to marry and produce an heir. She considered and encouraged one suitor after another, ultimately rejecting them all. Probably, she never intended to marry; but her behavior in that regard, like so much of her life, remains highly ambiguous.

These and other aspects of Elizabeth's conduct have generated centuries of controversy on the part of historians and biographers. In many ways, she was an enigma. She still is.

Elizabeth was physically attractive — at least until her later years. She was also highly intelligent, well educated and multi-talented. At least one book claims, in what seems an unwarranted stretch of the evidence, that she was the real author of Shakespeare's poems and plays. She did write well; but not *that* well. Still, she was highly articulate and able to stir a crowd with her eloquence. To use a modern term, she had "charisma."

Elizabeth dealt with the problems that faced her like a brilliant acrobat walking a tightrope high above the crowd, always working without a net. When, at times, she appeared to stumble, she always regained her balance, never falling, always finishing, arms raised high in triumph, cheered by the crowd below.

I'll try to create a coherent picture of the tall, slim, regal "Gloriana," as she was sometimes called. It's not my intention to include every act and event of her life. Instead, Part One will be an overview of her reign and of the Tudor monarchs who preceded her. Part Two will analyze the specific questions about Elizabeth that have intrigued and bedeviled historians for centuries. The answers have remained her secrets — secrets she took to her grave.

Was she truly the "Virgin Queen" of legend or the promiscuous, lust-crazed woman portrayed in gossip and in European diplomatic reports? Was she complicit in the murder of her lover's wife? Why did she never marry? Why come close from time to time, always to back away? What were her real attitudes toward religion? Toward torture? Toward slavery? How did those attitudes affect her policies? Was she driven by one fancy after another, unable to make up her mind, or were her changes of mood and mind carefully contrived policy? And was she a penny-pinching miser or a careful head of state, recognizing the need for fiscal prudence, when the enormous national and international needs of her subjects threatened bankruptcy?

Through a separate and comprehensive analysis of each such issue, we may discern patterns not evident in a chronological study. In the end, you'll draw your own conclusions about this extraordinary woman and her place in history.

PART ONE
ELIZABETH — AN OVERVIEW

O
N A SUMMER DAY IN 1485, the Wars of the Roses — the long running series of vicious battles between the great houses of York and Lancaster — finally came to an end. Betrayed by the peers on whom he relied, Richard III, the reigning king, was defeated by Henry Tudor at Bosworth Field, significantly altering the history of England and the Western world. Richard, the last Plantagenet King, died, fighting ferociously against overwhelming odds. Henry Tudor, whose claim to the throne was comparatively weak, took the throne as Henry VII, founding the Tudor dynasty.

Henry's mother, Margaret Beaufort, was a direct descendant of the Duke of Lancaster, one of the sons of Edward III. She married Henry's father, the Duke of Richmond, when she was twelve and gave birth to the future king when she was thirteen. She became the wealthiest woman in the kingdom. On Richmond's death, she married Lord Thomas Stanley and apparently pressured him and his brother William into betraying Richard III at Bosworth Field, making her son England's king.

During his reign and even that of his son, Henry VIII, Margaret Beaufort was a highly influential and outspoken presence. She frequently occupied rooms adjoining those of her son and never hesitated to express her strongly held opinions.

Henry VII became a shrewd and practical king. He married Richard's niece, Elizabeth, the daughter of Richard's deceased brother, Edward IV. She was quite beautiful. More importantly, she was the daughter of a Yorkist King, and Henry was founding a dynasty. Their Tudor heirs would carry the blood of both York and Lancaster. They would be descendants of the Plantagenets; and their claims to the throne would be strong ones — certainly stronger than Henry's.

Sometimes described as a miser, Henry VII was more than fiscally prudent. After an early and unsuccessful raid into France, he avoided war at any cost, considering it an enormous waste of money.

A shrewd trader, Henry managed some ingenious financial coups. For example, he was able to dominate the market for alum, then a commodity in great demand. Dealing with the Venetians and even the Turks, he successfully circumvented the Pope's attempts to monopolize the lucrative alum trade.

Later in his reign, Henry added to his wealth by a form of extortion. His agents would falsely accuse noblemen and wealthy merchants of crimes, threatening them with imprisonment or worse if they failed to "confess," pay a massive fine to the Crown and post an equally large bond against future "misconduct." The legendary Thomas More was one of those falsely accused. Refusing to "confess," he left England, ostensibly to "study" in France, but presumably to avoid imprisonment. Ultimately, Henry became quite rich. Among other things, he used his wealth in attempts to bribe other rulers, a policy that had only mixed success.

Elizabeth, Henry's queen, was intelligent, gracious and widely beloved by the people. Although Henry had married her for dynastic reasons, it became a loving relationship; and Henry was heartbroken when she died in childbirth at 37. She bore him six children, including Prince Arthur, his younger brother Henry, who became Henry VIII, Princess Margaret, who married the King of Scotland, and Princess Mary, who married the King of France.

As Henry VII grew older, it seemed that the kingdom would be secure in the hands of his son, Arthur, who, in 1501, married the Spanish princess, Catherine of Aragon. They had been "betrothed" at three and married when they were both fifteen. Catherine was the daughter of Ferdinand and Isabella, the famed Catholic monarchs who completed the re-conquest of Spain from the Moors, sent Columbus on his voyages and fostered the Spanish Inquisition. Catherine was attractive, intelligent and well educated.

But Arthur died after only six months of marriage, and the heir to the throne became his energetic younger brother, Henry. Since their mother, Elizabeth, had also died, the aging Henry VII seemed inclined to marry Princess Catherine himself. Her parents, apparently mortified, refused their consent. Catherine was consigned to years of waiting in England while Henry VII and her parents fought over her dowry. In the end, the Spanish never paid.

Meanwhile, Prince Henry developed into a handsome, athletic young man, who had long been attracted to Catherine. In 1509, on the death of his father, he took the throne; and, having received a papal dispensation, he married his brother's attractive widow. He went on, of course, to become the legendary Henry VIII, a monarch of enormous intelligence, vast appetites and a mercurial and ferocious will.

Henry soon came to trust Catherine's intelligence and judgment. In 1513, when he undertook an ill-advised campaign in France, he appointed Catherine to govern the kingdom in his absence. She successfully managed the logistics and planning that led to the crushing defeat of a Scottish army at the Battle of Flodden. She had prevented a Scottish invasion and had won the hearts of the English people.

In 1516, Henry and Catherine had a daughter, the Princess Mary. Although Catherine was pregnant six times, Mary was her only surviving child.

Catherine was six years older than Henry and, by the time she reached her forties, she had grown heavy in body and spirit. Her inability to produce a male heir led Henry to explore the possibility of ending their marriage. Finally, his growing obsession with the sensual and cunning Anne Boleyn moved Henry to take action.

Anne was the daughter of the fiercely ambitious Sir Thomas Boleyn. She was tall and slim with large dark eyes and lustrous raven hair. Well educated and bilingual, she had spent years in the French court, where she acquired European sophistication and served as a lady in waiting to Henry's sister Mary, who had married the French king.

When Anne returned to England, so different from the other available girls, she soon caught the eye of the king — and held it. This created a problem. Anne had seemed headed for marriage to Lord Henry Percy. But Percy's father, the Earl of Northumberland, was aware that Anne had become the object of the king's desire. He rushed from his Northern estates, threatened to disinherit the young man and put an end to the romance.

Before his fascination with Anne, Henry had carried on a long affair with her younger sister, Mary, who was married at the time to Sir William Carey. During her affair with the king, Mary bore two children, a daughter, Katherine, and a son, perhaps significantly named Henry. Out of deference to Sir William, the children were given the name Carey. Their father was probably Henry VIII.

We cannot be sure of Carey's true feelings; but there is no record of his objecting to his wife's relationship with the king, and he was handsomely rewarded. Mary's father, Thomas Boleyn, who encouraged the affair and schemed to bring it about, received even richer rewards.

There were rumors that, in their younger days at the French court, both Boleyn sisters were promiscuous. This may have been true of Mary, but probably not of Anne. It is possible that Anne and Henry Percy slept together before his father put an end to their relationship, but it is unlikely. While it has also been suggested that Anne was the lover of the poet, Thomas Wyatt, she claimed to have been a virgin when Henry met her, and she probably was.

Mary Boleyn was not Henry's only mistress. There had been several. He had even fathered a son with his one-time mistress, Bessie Blount. But Anne was different. Perhaps realizing from her sister's case that the mistress relationship was an ephemeral one, leading nowhere, Anne refused to sleep with the king until he married her or at least publicly committed to do so. There was, of course, one problem – the King was already married.

Utterly smitten with Anne and frustrated by her refusal to enter his bed, the King sought an annulment of his marriage to Catherine on the ground that she had been his brother's wife. This led to a thorny issue of canon law. In 1509, the Pope had issued a dispensation permitting Henry to marry Catherine, despite her prior marriage to his brother. Now, Henry argued that no papal dispensation could override what he claimed was a biblical injunction against such a marriage. After all, he argued, Leviticus 20:21 provides that "if a man shall take his brother's wife, it is an unclean thing...They shall be childless." Since Henry and Catherine had a daughter, Henry argued that the biblical reference to being "childless" was a mistranslation, that the correct translation was "they shall have no sons." Evidently, Henry ignored the contrary dictum in Deuteronomy that it is a man's *duty* to marry his brother's widow.

In any event, Catherine adamantly refused to agree to an annulment. She swore that, because of Arthur's youth and ill health, their marriage had never been consummated. Despite her deeply held religious beliefs — or perhaps because of them — Catherine's claim may have been untrue. Catherine loved Henry deeply and had been his wife for 18 years. She desperately wanted to avoid their daughter Mary being branded illegitimate. Possibly, in these circumstances, she lied.

If Catherine's marriage to Henry was valid, Mary was heir to the throne. The princess had been raised a devout Catholic, certain to remain true to her faith and loyal to the Pope. By contrast, Anne may already have been suspected of holding the reformist views on religion that became evident later. Who knew how that could affect the views of Anne's children should she become queen? Catherine's spiritual advisors may have considered Mary's legitimacy and right to the succession crucial to the Church. They may have assured Catherine that, given the circumstances, God would forgive a lie about the consummation of her marriage, even if told under oath.

Henry turned to Pope Clement, expecting a timely decision in his favor. Probably, the Pope would have preferred to see the marriage remain intact and staunchly

Catholic Mary remain heir to the throne. On the other hand, Henry was a powerful and aggressive monarch, whose aid Clement might need in fending off the French and the Empire. It would be wise not to displease him.

But another factor necessarily affected the Pope's conduct. The Holy Roman Emperor was Catherine's nephew, Charles V. Charles had won significant battles in Italy, and his troops had sacked Rome. The Pope was virtually his prisoner. Anxious not to outrage Henry, but under constant pressure from the Emperor, Clement employed scheme after scheme to delay any decision on Henry's petition. Ultimately, it became clear he would never decide.

But Henry was not one to accept defeat when his personal desires were at stake. Cardinal Wolsey, the Lord Chancellor, was charged by the king with obtaining a papal decree ending the royal marriage. Wolsey was an intelligent, capable man, but one filled with self-importance. He lived like an emperor, in grand, lavishly furnished residences, including Hampton Court Palace. When Wolsey failed to bring about a favorable decision from the Pope, Henry suddenly removed him from office, seized Hampton Court and Wolsey's other valuable properties and dispatched the Cardinal to the provinces, where he died, a broken man.

Henry began to rely on a brilliant and decisive lawyer, Thomas Cromwell, who had previously been counsel to Wolsey. The tough, burly son of a provincial blacksmith,

Cromwell had been a mercenary soldier. He was widely traveled and worldly cynical. Returning to England, he became a highly successful lawyer and trader. Having observed Cromwell's work for Wolsey, Henry recognized his unique abilities and realized how helpful he might be in finding a way to solve the king's "great matter." Cromwell was appointed to the Privy Council and, ultimately, became Henry's Principal Secretary. And Cromwell had some very aggressive ideas — ideas that changed England and the world.

Encouraged by Cromwell and disgusted with the Pope, Henry brought about what is often called the "English Reformation." This was a severance of all ties between England and the Church of Rome. Henry placed himself at the head of the new Church of England, as "Defender of the Faith." Neither he nor England remained subject to papal dictates.

A Protestant reform movement grew during Henry's reign, fueled, to a significant extent, by an extraordinary group of Protestant scholars at Cambridge University. But Henry was not a leader or even a part of that movement. At an earlier time, he had even signed his name to a tract vituperously attacking Lutheranism as an abominable heresy. Even after its ties to Rome were severed, England remained essentially Catholic, although a reform movement took hold. Most of the time, Henry considered himself Catholic, although the king's views on religion, as on most subjects, could be subject to sudden and dramatic change. In any event, the Latin Mass continued to be said, although, in many churches, priests began reading from the Bible in English, rather than Latin.

Henry VIII was a profligate spendthrift. Unlike his father, he embarked on unnecessary and costly military adventures. This, plus his lifestyle and feverish construction of monumental palaces, severely depleted the royal treasury. In short, Henry faced a perilous financial problem. The ingenious Cromwell had an answer.

For centuries, Catholic monasteries had existed throughout the country. In many instances, they had accumulated vast land holdings and had substantial income. Following Cromwell's advice, Henry appropriated virtually all of that property and revenue. The monastic leaders were visited and "requested" to deliver over their holdings to the king. It was quickly perceived that those who refused were imprisoned and, in some instances, executed. Soon there were few who declined Cromwell's "request."

The mass appropriation of monastic property greatly increased the royal wealth. It also allowed Henry to grant or sell some of the newly acquired lands to powerful and influential men. Cromwell understood that this gave the new owners a powerful incentive to support and defend Henry's "reform." If it failed, they might have to give back their lands.

In 1533, Henry appointed a new Archbishop of Canterbury, Thomas Cranmer. Cranmer had been a Cambridge scholar and lecturer and was an advocate of the reform movement that had begun with Martin Luther in 1517. That movement was carried forward in Geneva, where John Calvin established a Protestant theocracy, and it spread to France and much of Northern Europe. Cranmer and Cromwell became something of a team. Both appeared to advocate the king's relationship with Anne Boleyn, who, like them, favored religious reform.

By this time, Cromwell had begun to make enemies. To powerful noblemen, he was an overly ambitious commoner — a ruffian from the gutter. To conservative Catholic prelates, he was a dangerous heretic.

But the King became more and more reliant upon Cromwell's ingenious and aggressive counsel. In January 1533, when Anne became pregnant, Henry married her in a private ceremony without even waiting for a divorce or annulment. In May of 1533, Archbishop Cranmer decreed Henry's marriage to Catherine void, validating his marriage to Anne and making Princess Mary illegitimate. When Catherine continued to claim she was the rightful queen, she was banished from the court.

We are accustomed to think of Anne Boleyn as a shallow and selfish courtesan. She was hardly that. A member of the notoriously ambitious Boleyn family, she had a fierce temper and could be arrogant. But, while quick to make enemies, she was highly intelligent and knowledgeable about matters of religion, as well as foreign and domestic politics. She was a staunch supporter of religious reform; and this, in itself, had the potential to create significant enmity.

It was not too long before Henry began to tire of Anne. Perhaps, after years of waiting, he found her a less exciting bed-mate than her sister or his longtime mistress, Bessie Blount. After radically changing the religious and political order to marry Anne, he was now publicly involved with other women. But, being pregnant, Anne had a powerful card to play. Astrologers predicted the arrival of the male heir for whom the King had waited so many years.

In September 1533, the day finally came. But the much anticipated child was not the male heir for whom Henry hoped. It was the Princess Elizabeth. Female or not, bells rang out all over London. Most Englishmen were thrilled at the birth of the new princess, particularly those who favored the reformed Church. She would be free of the Pope's dictate; and she was pure English, unlike her half-sister, Mary, who was half Spanish and staunchly Catholic.

The King, however, was less enthusiastic. He treated Elizabeth with honor as a royal princess; but he was deeply disappointed that she was not male.

His older daughter, Mary, who was eighteen at the time, was certainly not pleased with the new child. She was humiliated at being forced to call the infant "Princess Elizabeth" and to serve as her maid in waiting. Being illegitimate now, she was simply called "Lady Mary."

But Mary displayed the stubborn courage that was evident throughout her life. Often, at table or on trips, if assigned a position inferior to Elizabeth's, she had to be dragged forcibly to her place. Even when she complied without compulsion, she would write a letter of protest or recite a quiet incantation to the effect that she was not acquiescing in her placement or status.

Despite the change in his feelings toward Anne, Henry had Parliament pass the Act of Succession. This required every Englishman to swear that the children of their marriage were the legitimate heirs to the throne. Refusal to take this oath was punishable by life imprisonment.

Unlike France, England did not follow the Salic law, which barred women from the succession. However, its only experience with a female ruler had not been a happy one. In the 12th century, Matilda, the daughter of Henry I, took the throne. Her rule led to civil war and brutally difficult times for her subjects. Improvement only came with the ascension of her son, Henry II, an intelligent and effective ruler and the first Plantagenet king.

Nevertheless, under the Act of Succession, Princess Elizabeth was Henry VIII's heir and destined to be the first female ruler of England since Matilda — unless Anne Boleyn could give Henry a son.

Henry also had Parliament pass the Act of Supremacy. This required all Englishmen to swear that Henry was the Supreme Head of the Church of England. Refusal was a capital offense. Sir Thomas More, the brilliant and popular Lord Chancellor, had long been a friend and close advisor to the king. A committed Catholic, More would not take the oath. He was taken from his family home in Chelsea, imprisoned, and, ultimately, when he continued unwilling to take the oath, he was executed. Later, he was made a saint for his stand and his martyrdom. When Henry heard that More's execution had been carried out, he shouted at Anne "It is because of you the honestest man in the kingdom is dead."

In a sense, this was true. But for Anne, there would have been no separation from Rome, Henry would not have become "Supreme Head of the Church of England" and there would have been no Act of Supremacy. Henry and More could have remained friends.

By this time, Anne certainly recognized the peril in her situation. At any time, Henry might cast her aside, as he had Catherine. To avoid that, Anne desperately sought to provide the male heir for whom Henry yearned. It was not to be. Anne became pregnant again — more than once. Each time, her pregnancy ended in miscarriage.

By this time, Henry had lost physical interest in Anne. He had come to resent her meddling in politics, government and religion, matters he did not consider the proper realm of women. He continued to have widely known affairs with other women — women apparently wise enough to keep their opinions to themselves, if they had any. The French Ambassador reported that the king's "regard for the queen is less than it was and diminishes every day."

From the beginning, Anne was probably ill suited to be the wife of this selfish and tyrannical monarch. Unlike most queens, she was not prepared to acquiesce quietly in the king's open infidelities. She objected — strenuously.

Others had suffered from her temper. But she had the bad judgment to unleash it on Henry. He responded with rage, shouting that she must shut her eyes to his conduct, just as others had. He had raised her up, he threatened, and he could just as easily bring her down.

Two factors deterred Henry from ending his marriage to Anne. One was that Catherine of Aragon was still alive. If his marriage to Anne was annulled, it would revive the claims that he was still married to Catherine. The second factor was the possibility that Anne might still conceive a male heir.

In January 1536, both factors changed radically. Catherine suddenly died, still professing her love for Henry and the validity of their marriage. At the end, she questioned whether she had made the wrong decision in resisting Henry's determination to end their marriage. If she had not — if she had retired gracefully and in comfort to a provincial residence or even to a nunnery — would England have remained tied to Rome and totally Catholic? Probably not; but Catherine couldn't know that, and it must have troubled her greatly.

But Henry didn't question his decision. Hearing of Catherine's death, he shouted "God be praised!" Then, dressed in yellow satin, he led celebratory dancing and revelry.

Three weeks later, Anne bore another stillborn child — this time a boy. To Henry, it now seemed plain she would never produce a male heir.

At this point, Cromwell had enormous influence with the king. He had been allied with Anne in urging Henry to sever his marriage to Catherine, and he tended to agree with Anne in favoring religious reform. Now, however, grasping how the situation had changed, Cromwell turned against Anne and began planning her downfall. As he put it to the Imperial Ambassador, he "thought up and plotted" Anne's demise.

Whether or not it was Cromwell's doing, it was reported to Henry that Anne had joked to others about his sexual inadequacy — that he was impotent. That was the last straw — that and the fact that Henry had fallen in love with Jane Seymour, one of Anne's maids of honor. Apparently, this too had been planned by Cromwell.

The King decided to act; and, characteristically, he acted with swift and draconian measures. His marriage to Anne was pronounced invalid on the ground that he had previously had sexual relations with her sister, which, of course, was true. Probably on Cromwell's advice, he also arranged for Anne to be charged with treason. In May 1536, she was conveyed to the Tower of London.

Among the "treasonous" acts of which Anne was accused were multiple instances of adultery, including incest with her brother George, now Lord Rochford. She was also accused of adultery with Mark Smeaton, her young music teacher, as well as with Sir Henry Norris, Sir Francis Weston and Sir William Brereton, all members of the Privy Council allied with the Boleyn family. An added charge was conspiring with her lovers to kill the king.

It's most unlikely that Anne plotted Henry's murder. She tended to be a realist. It would have been nice to believe that, on the king's death, the infant Elizabeth would peacefully become queen, with Anne governing as regent. But Anne would not have believed that. She surely realized that, despite their quarrels, Henry was her only protection against dangerous enemies, and that, with his death, she would never be allowed any position of power — if she was even allowed to live.

Nor is it likely that Anne and her brother were lovers. Sexual relations between siblings were rare, even if not unknown. And, although married, George was probably homosexual. Could one or more of the other accused men have shared her bed? It's doubtful Anne had any feelings of love or loyalty for the king. And he really may have become impotent — at least with Anne. Possibly, desperate to become pregnant, she had turned to other men. But it seems unlikely she would have taken the enormous risk inherent in conducting such an affair. Probably, she was innocent of all the charges.

Smeaton was sent to the Tower, where he was thrown in a dungeon. He was questioned for twenty-four hours, probably under torture. Ultimately he "confessed" to adultery with the queen and provided evidence against his four co-defendants. Being of the upper class, the other four were given more comfortable accommodations in the Tower and were not tortured. Each vigorously denied the charges.

Nevertheless, Norris, Weston, Brereton and Smeaton were tried and convicted. They were sentenced to be "hanged, drawn and quartered, their members cut off and burnt before them, their heads cut off and [they be] quartered." Later, these brutal sentences were commuted, so that the three Privy Council members, and even Smeaton, were "mercifully" beheaded on Tower Green.

Given their higher rank, the queen and her brother were tried separately by a jury of their peers. At her trial, Anne vigorously denied all the charges, and gave "to each a plausible answer." But, of course, the outcome was foreordained from the moment she was charged. Anne was found guilty. It was widely assumed that Henry would force her to agree to an annulment of their marriage and send her to a nunnery. He did not. Her sentence was to be burned or beheaded at the king's pleasure.

George Boleyn's trial followed shortly after Anne's. His wife, Lady Rochford, testified against him, supporting the crown's charge that he had committed adultery with his sister. It was a striking act of disloyalty; but Lady Rochford apparently despised both her husband and Anne. Moreover, by testifying, she probably saved her position, if not her life.

To prevent spreading the rumor that the king was impotent, the question of whether Anne had made that embarrassing claim was never to be asked openly in court. Instead, it was written out on a piece of paper that was handed to the witness. The witness was directed to read the question *to himself* and then answer simply "yes" or "no." But George Boleyn, probably believing he had nothing to lose, read the humiliating question aloud from the witness box. The king and his officials were furious, and, instead of beheading, George was sentenced to be hung, drawn and quartered.

Following the trial, Archbishop Cranmer visited Anne in the Tower. We do not know what was said; but they may have struck a deal. Anne would consent to an annulment of her marriage, and the deaths of her brother and herself would be as painless as possible. Whether or not this occurred, Cranmer did issue a decree that Henry's marriage to Anne was invalid, apparently on the ground that Henry had previously had sexual relations with Anne's sister Mary.

Ironically, with her marriage invalidated *ab initio*, i.e., from its inception, Anne would seem unable to have committed adultery, since, by the decree, she had never really been married. The inconsistency may have troubled the lawyers. It troubled Henry not at all.

George Boleyn's sentence was also commuted. He was beheaded, rather than hung, drawn and quartered. Possibly, this was part of a deal struck by Anne and Cranmer.

Moments before her execution, Anne swore her innocence "on the damnation of her soul." It was not a likely time to lie. This was an age in which virtually all Englishmen believed themselves threatened with the fires of hell.

Despite her oath of innocence, Anne was promptly beheaded. This was not done in the customary English way, with the victim's head on a wooden block severed by the downward blow of a heavy axe. That method of beheading sometimes required two or three blows before the head was completely severed. Sometimes, even a saw was required to sever stubborn tendons. Instead, Anne's execution was carried out in the French manner. Kneeling, she was decapitated by the sidearm stroke of a razor-sharp sword. It was wielded by an expert imported from France specifically for the occasion. This had been Anne's request, and it had been granted. It may also have been part of a deal with Cranmer.

All of these events had moved swiftly — the arrests, the trials, the annulment and the executions. Anne was beheaded on May 19, 1536, just two weeks after her arrest. That same day, she was buried beneath the chancel in the Chapel of St. Peter ad Vincula within the Tower grounds. Anne's daughter, Elizabeth, was not yet three. Like her sister Mary, she was now illegitimate.

So far as we know, for the rest of her life, Elizabeth never referred to her mother's death or even mentioned her name. Yet, after she became queen, Elizabeth commissioned a ring that opened to reveal miniature portraits of herself and her mother. She wore the ring for the rest of her life. It was removed from her finger at her death.

Elizabeth's new illegitimacy left something of a dilemma as to succession to the throne. Mary had priority over Elizabeth by reason of age. But, even though a female could rule, males took precedence; and the King's illegitimate son, Henry FitzRoy, the Duke of Richmond, had priority over both of Henry's daughters. Fitzroy, the child of Bessie Blount, had been acknowledged by Henry to be his child, as, of course, had Mary and Elizabeth. Since all three were now illegitimate, it was possible that none of them would succeed to the throne. Henry had not acknowledged his paternity of Mary Boleyn's two children. They remained officially the children of Sir William Carey and were not included in the line of succession.

Only a day after Anne's execution, Henry and Jane Seymour were betrothed. Ten days later, they were secretly married, probably with Cromwell's encouragement. With both Anne and Catherine dead, there was no impediment to the marriage.

In 1537, when Elizabeth had just turned four, Jane Seymour produced the male heir for whom Henry had yearned. Her son was later to become king as Edward VI. But Jane died within days of giving birth. The newborn Prince solved the problem of the succession. Before his birth, that problem had become even more troubling, because Henry FitzRoy had died, leaving fiercely Catholic, half Spanish Mary the apparent heir to the throne.

Despite her mother's execution and the birth of a male heir, Elizabeth was well cared for. She was placed in country manors under the supervision of a governess. At first this was Lady Bryan, who had been Mary's governess as well. Later, it was Kat Ashley (before marriage, Katherine Champernowne), an intelligent and literate woman, who, for years, played a significant role in Elizabeth's life.

Elizabeth received a superb education. Tutored by distinguished Protestant scholars from Cambridge, she naturally acquired Protestant views. After initial schooling by Kat Ashley, she was taught by Prince Edward's tutors, Richard Cox and John Cheke, one of the greatest scholars of the age. Later, she had her own tutors, William Grindal, followed by Roger Ascham, another renowned Cambridge scholar. Ascham had been Cheke's star pupil at Cambridge; and, when Ascham taught there, Grindal had been his star pupil. All had a hand in shaping Elizabeth's learning and ability to reason, write and speak. All were Protestants.

Elizabeth excelled as a student. At an early age, she acquired fluency in languages, as well as a thorough grasp of classical and medieval history. When she was only five and a half, she presented her brother Edward with "a shirt of cambric of her own making." The next year, she made him a needlework sampler. At six, she wrote letters in Italian with exquisite penmanship.

At eleven, Elizabeth translated into English the French work *Le Miroir de l'âme Pécheresse* as a New Year's gift to the queen. This was a religious poem by Margaret of Angoulême, Queen of Navarre, a sister of the French king and a leader of the reform movement in the French Court. Elizabeth not only translated the poem, she wrote a prefatory note succinctly describing the poem's theme, which was the Protestant doctrine of "justification by faith," that man achieves salvation through faith, rather than through good work. Elizabeth's translation of the French poem was so well done it was published for general consumption.

The following New Year, her gift to the queen was a translation into English of Calvin's *Institution de la Religion Christienne*, accompanied by a letter in formal French. Her gift to her father was a triple translation of the queen's prayers and meditations from English into Latin, French and Italian, with an embroidered cover she made by hand. She was twelve at the time. Those who viewed her accomplishments were astounded at her intelligence and skill.

Following the death of Jane Seymour, there arose the question of a new wife for the king. Cromwell pressed Henry to seek a match with Anne, sister of the Duke of Cleves. Cromwell argued that Cleves was a strategically important Lutheran Duchy, famous for its skilled mercenary soldiers and a member of an increasingly powerful Protestant alliance. He posed the match as the means to offset what then loomed as a potential alliance of France and the Empire and to improve England's leverage in dealing with those menacing Catholic powers. Henry had only seen Anne of Cleves in a flattering portrait by Hans Holbein. He had also heard that she was indeed lovely, a report possibly instigated by Cromwell. Henry gave his approval. After difficult negotiations with Anne's brother, agreement was reached, and the match was made.

When the King learned that his betrothed had arrived in England and was on her way by coach, he hit on the idea of surprising her en route. Filled with romantic enthusiasm, he rode hard to the provincial inn where Anne was spending the night on her way to London.

Bursting into her room, Henry stopped cold. This was not the lovely girl in the portrait. Not at all. He saw a rather plain young woman, stiff, awkward and wearing a most unbecoming Germanic costume. From that first moment, Henry found her physically repulsive. That never changed.

The King groped desperately for an out. According to Cromwell, there was none. He said there was no impediment to the marriage, and that simply cancelling it would be a grievous insult to the powerful Duke of Cleves, risking the enmity of the entire Protestant alliance.

Dutifully, the angry and disappointed king went through with the wedding. But the marriage was never consummated. Henry could not bring himself to consummate it. Evidently, the bride didn't mind.

Six months later, she raised no objection to an annulment on the ground that she had previously entered into a binding pre-contract to marry a son of the Duke of Lorraine. Such an agreement was considered tantamount to a prior marriage. Seeking to keep her marriage to Henry alive, Cromwell urged Anne to renounce the pre-contract, an act directly contrary to the result Henry desperately sought. Anne, however, had sound judgment, as well as intelligence. She ignored Cromwell and acceded to the wishes of the mercurial king.

When the annulment was granted, Anne was rewarded with valuable estates and permitted to live freely, as an unmarried woman. Her wise decision to acquiesce probably saved her life. Although no longer queen, Anne of Cleves remained for years a respected friend of the king and was treated by succeeding rulers as an honored member of the Royal Family.

Meanwhile, the circle of Cromwell's enemies was closing in. It included influential anti-reform bishops, as well as powerful noblemen. They realized that Cromwell's urging the match with Anne of Cleves and then scheming against the annulment had made him vulnerable.

That vulnerability was increased because the feared alliance of France and the Empire had collapsed, leaving Henry far less dependent on the Protestant League and more inclined to believe that Cromwell had used poor judgment in his assessment of the Franco-Imperial threat and had been influenced to side with the Protestant states by his own reformist views. Sometimes, Henry appeared to tolerate and even support those views. Other times not. No one could be sure of just where the king stood on this critical issue.

Determined now to destroy Cromwell, his enemies played on all of these themes with the angry and vindictive king. They convinced Henry that Cromwell had been pursuing his own religious and political goals, rather than those of his king. In 1540, with Henry's concurrence,

Cromwell was suddenly charged with treason, "convicted" without a trial by a bill of attainder, and promptly executed.

As the years passed, Henry may have felt that he'd made a mistake. Frustrated by events, he was heard to lament that he "lacked a Cromwell."

But that was in the future. Now, with Cromwell's protection removed, some Protestant preachers were burned, typically at the direction of Bishop Bonner, a Catholic prelate determined to root out all vestiges of reform.

At the time of Cromwell's execution, Henry's attention had been diverted by a beautiful teenager, Catherine Howard. Possibly she was brought to the king's attention by Cromwell's enemies, just as Cromwell had pointed Henry in the direction of Jane Seymour as a means of destroying Anne Boleyn. Smitten once more, the king showered Catherine with gifts and caresses. Then he married her. Eighteen months later, he executed her for adultery with her handsome cousin, Thomas Culpepper. This time, the charge appeared quite true.

Ironically, young Catherine's affair with Culpepper had been abetted by George Boleyn's widow, Lady Rochford. She had testified against her husband at his trial for committing adultery with his sister, Anne Boleyn. Now, she was executed for her part in the commission of a similar crime. Why had she taken the extreme risk of aiding young Catherine's trysts with Culpepper? Like Catherine, she was a member of the powerful Howard family. Perhaps she hoped that Catherine would become pregnant, bearing a child Henry would consider his own, creating a Howard heir to the throne. Perhaps. Or perhaps she was just being foolish.

On the scaffold, Lady Rochford clarified at least one issue. "God has permitted me to suffer this painful doom" she said, "As punishment for having contributed to my husband's death. I falsely accused him of loving, in an incestuous manner, his sister, Queen Anne Boleyn. For this I deserve to die."

Later, when Henry married his sixth and final wife, Catherine Parr, Elizabeth and Mary were often brought to court, along with their half-brother, Edward. Elizabeth's education was furthered under Queen Catherine's guidance, and she added dancing, riding and musicianship to her accomplishments.

By this time, Henry had become hugely fat and suffered from ulcers on his leg that were extremely painful and emitted a loathsome smell. Yet Queen Catherine was kind and caring with him. Whether she was more than that is questionable.

Archbishop Cranmer sought to move the English Church in the direction of reform. But he was too cautious a man to pressure the king. Instead, he tried to move Henry only slowly and carefully, always giving the appearance of yielding to the king's views. Despite his efforts, significant Catholic practices remained, generally supported by the king.

The new Queen was committed to the Protestant cause. But she was well aware of Henry's views on religion and that, while he considered himself and the realm free from the Pope's dictate, he still counted himself a Catholic and considered most reform views heretical — at least most of the time. Generally, she had the good judgment to speak tactfully and lovingly in discussing religious issues with her volatile and unpredictable husband.

On one occasion, however, Catherine narrowly escaped a charge of heresy, when her staunchly Protestant views came to the attention of a pro-Catholic faction at court. Evidently, they subtly suggested that Henry seemed unable to control his wife's heretical views; and, predictably angered, the king signed a warrant for Catherine's arrest.

By this time Henry was regularly ordering arrests and executions for what he deemed a lack of conformity to the royal views on religion, as well as for other seemingly innocent acts that were, or were described to the king as, a failure to conform to his own views or wishes. Even the arrest of the queen could mean her imprisonment or even death. She could hardly overlook the fate of her predecessors, Anne Boleyn and Catherine Howard.

Learning of the warrant before it could be served, Catherine quickly and profusely apologized to the king. She assured him that, while she may have voiced religious opinions from time to time, Henry was her guide and mentor in all such matters and she would obediently follow his instruction. His ego stroked, Henry ordered the warrant quashed. He was genuinely fond of Catherine, but, in anger, he had ordered her arrest. Would he have ordered her execution? We'll never know.

Henry's signing of the warrant is evidence of what were generally his anti-reformist views. Yet, there remained a remarkably anomalous fact. Elizabeth and even Prince Edward, the heir to the throne, were being raised as Protestants and tutored by Protestant scholars from Cambridge. Henry must have been aware that his son, the future king, as well as his younger daughter, were being taught and trained as dedicated Protestants by well-known Protestant scholars. Yet, he did nothing to change this or even slow it down. Indeed, he evidently approved of it and paid for it.

How can we square Henry's willingness to see the next King of England shaped as a committed Protestant with ordering his wife's arrest for espousing Protestant views? It's not easy. Perhaps he was ready to accept that England would become a Protestant realm upon his death, but was determined to remain a Catholic and see England remain Catholic as long as he lived. If so, he may have considered his wife's conduct more an embarrassing personal betrayal than an act of heresy.

In any event, in 1544, at Henry's direction, Parliament passed a new Act of Succession. It provided that Edward, Mary and Elizabeth, in that order, and their heirs, would succeed to the throne on Henry's death. Although Mary and Elizabeth were theoretically "illegitimate," they were given priority over the children of Henry's sisters. His sister Margaret and her heirs were completely excluded from the succession. But, if Edward, Mary and Elizabeth all died without heirs, the heirs of Henry's other sister, Mary, were to take the throne. This order of succession, established by Act of Parliament, was also confirmed in Henry's will, a provision generally considered to have legal force in itself.

In 1544, Henry commissioned "The Family of Henry VIII," a painting now hanging at Hampton Court. The work must have been a hurtful surprise for Queen Catherine. Henry is enthroned in the center of the scene. Beside him, however, is not Catherine Parr, Henry's queen when the painting was made. Instead, it is the deceased queen, Jane Seymour. Her son, Prince Edward, stands on the other side of his father, while Mary and Elizabeth stand farther to each side. Unquestionably, the subjects and their placement had been dictated by the king.

That same year Henry started a needless war against France and led a large English army across the Channel, successfully taking the port city of Boulogne. Henry returned a conquering hero. But the cost of that war and of rebuilding the fortifications of Boulogne was staggering and severely depleted the royal treasury.

Even before this, Henry's extravagance had created a financial crisis, leading him to "increase" the supply of money by mixing England's silver coins with copper and lead. This created even further problems, since merchants on the Continent and even in England were unwilling to accept the coins at face value or anything near face value.

Ultimately, the English agreed to sell Boulogne back to the French, in effect allowing the French to ransom the town.

In 1547, Henry died. He was 56. The royal treasury was empty. It has been reported that, five months before his death, the king remarked that he was inclined to abolish the Latin Mass and replace it with the Protestant Communion service. If so, it would have been a radical change of position. It seems unlikely. Yet, there was the Protestant education of Edward and Elizabeth; and, in his last days, Henry had appointed a Regency Council dominated by Cranmer and others the king certainly knew were advocates of reform. Did he intend a Protestant future for England? It remains a mystery.

Henry's proclivity to order sudden arrests, attainders and executions had increased in his last years. Shortly before his death, he accused the Duke of Norfolk's son, Surrey, of "treason" for including on his coat of arms an emblem of Edward the Confessor, a Saxon, and thus a pre-Norman, king. This had been a family tradition for centuries. Norfolk, himself, was accused of treason for failing to report his son's "crime." Surrey was executed, and Norfolk was attainted. All of his extensive property passed to the Crown. On January 26, 1547, Henry signed an order for Norfolk's execution, but he died that night. The Duke was destitute, but alive.

Before the king's death was announced, Edward and Elizabeth were brought together, so that they would receive the news at the same time. Although hardly a normal father, Henry had been a powerful and forceful figure their entire lives; and, in their limited times with him, he had apparently been kind and approving. Both children wept uncontrollably for a time. Ultimately, however, they bore the matter with the resolute courage they had been taught.

Henry's death began a series of difficulties and dangers for the young Elizabeth. Edward was only nine years old. Theoretically, he became king, as Parliament and Henry's will had provided. But, given his age, England would, in reality, be ruled by a "Protector," who would govern in the young king's name. In this case, the Protector was the king's uncle, Edward Seymour, a brother of the late queen. A dedicated Protestant, haughty and opinionated, Seymour was a renowned military commander and a hard, ambitious man.

To secure his position as Protector, Seymour and his allies kept Henry's death a secret for three days while they maneuvered to eliminate any opposition. When the king's death was announced, Seymour reported that, on his death bed, Henry had insisted that oral promises he was then making be enforced as a part of his last will. These oral "promises" included a provision of enormous lands and wealth for Seymour, as well as the title Earl of Somerset. That title was conferred on Seymour at young Edward's coronation.

The new Earl quickly consolidated his position, making all decisions of the Regency Council subject to his approval. In this way, Seymour — now "Somerset" — would effectively rule England in the name of the boy king.

The young King was openly and militantly Protestant, and his accession to the throne led to a full scale Protestant reformation. The heresy laws, under which outspoken Protestants had been burned, were repealed. Archbishop Cranmer now felt free to express his views (and to disclose his secret wife). Cranmer promulgated and, to a significant extent, wrote a Protestant *Book of Common Prayer*. This took the pre-existing Latin liturgy used for centuries by Catholic priests and converted it into an English prayer book for use by parishioners, employing much of Cranmer's own phraseology. The Catholic Mass was replaced by the Protestant Communion Service based on Cranmer's *Book of Common Prayer*.

The congregation could now partake of the bread and wine of the Eucharist, previously available only to the priest saying the mass. The Catholic doctrine of transubstantiation was also gone. This was the belief that the bread and wine are actually changed into the body and blood of Christ and that, when the holy wafer, or "host," is held aloft by the priest, Christ is literally present in the room — the "Real Presence." Protestants rejected this concept, treating the bread and wine as merely symbolic of the body and blood of Christ.

In addition, Protestant Englishmen could now pray directly to God, rather than asking for the intercession of the Pope, the Virgin or the Saints. Priests could now marry, and altars, crucifixes, relics and candles were eliminated from English churches.

A report that Henry VIII had intended these fundamental changes was circulated to justify them to a public that was still primarily Catholic.

Undoubtedly, the doctrinal changes pleased both Edward and Elizabeth, since both had been raised as Protestants. Occasionally, Elizabeth came to her young brother's court. Their positions were naturally altered now that Edward was king, but they shared their religious views, and their relationship continued to be a cordial one, unlike Edward's relationship with the stubbornly Catholic Mary.

A portrait of Elizabeth as a teenager shows a tall, slim, graceful girl with red hair, dark eyes and a light complexion. Her countenance shows restraint, but radiates intelligence. At court, she dressed in a modest, highly conservative style, wearing simple black gowns and shunning the elaborate head dresses and brightly hued, jeweled creations favored by the older women. As her tutor put it, "In adornment she is elegant rather than showy."

But, intelligence and modesty aside, Elizabeth was still a teenager, and one already capable of passion. At first, she resided peacefully enough in Chelsea with the widowed queen, Catherine Parr. Catherine's inherited wealth from two previously deceased husbands was now vastly increased by what Henry left her. She was now one of the wealthiest women in the kingdom. That attribute was not lost on Thomas Seymour, the Lord Admiral. Seymour, a strikingly handsome man, was the brother of

Protector Somerset and of the late queen, Jane Seymour. Thus, like Somerset, he was the young king's uncle.

But Admiral Seymour lacked the judgment and stability of his siblings. Having tried and failed to obtain the Council's permission to court Princess Mary, he turned his romantic attentions to the widowed and wealthy Queen Catherine. Catherine had been desperately in love with the bold and handsome Seymour before she caught the attention of Henry VIII. Given the mores of the time, however, she had felt unable to reject the king's proposal. Now, she was thrilled to resume the relationship with Seymour; and, soon thereafter, they were married. It was a secret ceremony, since they doubted that the Council would approve the match.

The dashing, reckless Admiral became part of Queen Catherine's household. Soon, he began to flirt outrageously with the attractive teenage princess. He had keys made to her quarters; and he seized every opportunity to enter her bedroom to tickle, fondle and kiss her — and, according to gossip, perhaps do more. She appeared to be totally infatuated with him.

Finally, Catherine came upon Seymour holding Elizabeth in his arms, passionately kissing her. There is some ambiguity as to Catherine's reaction, which is discussed in a later chapter. But the situation could not continue. The princess was sent away to the country manor of Sir Anthony Denny, an ally of Somerset, whose wife was Kat Ashley's sister. Despite the move, Catherine continued to show concern for Elizabeth's welfare.

In her new home, Elizabeth's education progressed and was expanded. It was here that she was tutored by the renowned scholar, Roger Ascham, who commented a number of times on her high intelligence and scholastic aptitude. Ascham wrote to a fellow scholar that the teenage princess "talks French and Italian as well as she does English, and has often talked to me readily and well in Latin, moderately in Greek. When she writes Greek and Latin, nothing is more beautiful than her handwriting. She delights as much in music as she is skillful in it." The letter went on extolling Elizabeth's qualities; and, at the end, lest his friend think he was exaggerating, Ascham added "I am inventing nothing . . . there is no need."

While residing with Catherine Parr, Elizabeth first met William Cecil, who was to play an important role in her life. Cecil was highly intelligent and a Cambridge graduate from the same college as Cheke, Ascham and Grindall. He seemed destined for a bright future. At twenty-seven, he was already Secretary to Protector Somerset and a member of Parliament. Later, Elizabeth retained Cecil to manage her properties.

Catherine Parr died in childbirth, leaving her wealth to Admiral Seymour, who was suspected of poisoning her. Following her death, he behaved rashly and foolishly. He schemed to marry the teenage Elizabeth, making indiscreet inquiries into her property and income. Even Kat Ashley sought to persuade Elizabeth to consider the match. Surprisingly, however, Elizabeth proved much too sensible. And, in any event, the Council would never have given its approval.

But the Admiral's rashness went far beyond his marital scheming. Feeling that he had not been given the recognition he deserved, he had long resented the power, honors and the riches acquired by his brother, the Protector. Now, the Admiral planned to overthrow his brother, if Somerset and the Council opposed his plans. He secretly passed money to his nephew, young King Edward, seeking to win his support in what he increasingly viewed as a battle to the death with his own brother. He raised a body of men to fight that battle, and took steps to raise even more. He arranged for a corrupt official of the Royal Mint to provide funds to pay his forces, and he traveled to the ports in an attempt to persuade the fleet to support his "cause."

As if that were not enough, the Admiral tried to kidnap the king. Evidently he patronized an ingenious London locksmith. Just as he had obtained a key to young Elizabeth's door in Chelsea, he had acquired keys that fit the entrance to King Edward's quarters. In a rash and bizarre act, the Admiral invaded the young king's apartment at night, accompanied by accomplices. He brandished a gun, with which he shot Edward's pet spaniel. Possibly, Seymour only intended to persuade Edward to back his cause and was angered by the dog's barking. But, given the time and manner of his entry, the men who accompanied him and that he was bearing arms, his plan was probably to take physical control of the young king and, thereafter, to rule in his name.

Admiral Seymour was arrested, confined in the Tower and charged with several counts of treason. The charges included raising men to take the realm by force, attempting to seize the king, murdering Catherine Parr and plotting to marry Princess Elizabeth.

Just fifteen at the time, Elizabeth was interrogated repeatedly by the devious and skillful Sir Robert Tyrwhitt, who reported to Protector Somerset, "I do assure your grace she hath a very good wit, and nothing is gotten of her but by great policy."

But no amount of "policy" could induce the young princess to confess wrongdoing of any sort. On the contrary, she wrote directly to the Protector that "there goeth rumours abroad which be greatly both against my honour and honesty (which above all other things I esteem) which be these: that I am in the Tower and with child by my Lord Admiral. My Lord, these are shameful slanders."

Elizabeth sought permission to come to court to clear her name and reputation before her brother, the King. It proved unnecessary. No action was taken against her.

At Christmas 1548, Elizabeth was permitted to establish her own household at Hatfield, twenty miles from London. There, under Roger Ascham's guidance, a university-like atmosphere provided advanced learning, and the days were filled with erudite discussions.

In March 1549, based on the order of his brother, the attractive, but reckless Admiral Seymour was beheaded. Later, Elizabeth described him as "a man of much wit and very little judgment."

In the view of many Englishmen, however, Protector Somerset had too eagerly signed his brother's death warrant. Even though legally justified, Somerset's act was unpopular with the people and even with some of the Council. The Protector was also blamed for harsh economic times, fueled by a seriously debased currency and bad harvests. In addition, the increasing demand for wool had led to the enormously unpopular "enclosure" movement, by which common lands farmed by the people for centuries were enclosed for the private and profitable raising of sheep.

A rebellion began, but was outmaneuvered by royal forces led by John Dudley, a skilled military leader and a highly intelligent, devious and forceful man. Dudley's father, Edmund, had been executed by Henry VIII for supposed treason. But Dudley had energetically worked his way back into a position of political power. Somerset had never been well liked, and was blamed for the nation's problems. His career began to decline, and the popular Dudley's to rise.

Soon, Dudley schemed successfully to remove Somerset as Protector and to replace him as *de facto* ruler in the name of the young king. Dudley flattered Edward and gained effective control of the government without even using the title "Protector." He was able to charm, bribe or bully others into supporting the measures he favored, especially measures for his own advancement. Edward followed Dudley's advice in virtually everything, even making him Duke of Northumberland. Somerset had been made an Earl. Now Dudley surpassed him by becoming a Duke, the only English Duke not of the blood royal.

Meanwhile, the Protestant views held by the young king and the men surrounding him were laid down as law of the land. A new, thoroughly Protestant prayer book was written; and, by Parliament's Act of Uniformity, it was made the only lawful form of worship. Mary quietly refused to abide by this law; and tension grew between Edward and her over the religious issue.

Edward and the Council wanted to force Mary to obey the Act of Uniformity. But, although London and English youth tended to favor the Protestant cause, there was still significant Catholic sentiment throughout the realm. Moreover, Mary was the Emperor's cousin, and there was a threat of war with the Holy Roman Empire if she was denied religious freedom. These factors led Edward and the Council to refrain from any precipitous action concerning Mary's religious practices.

In 1553, the young king, who had been physically ill for some time, was diagnosed as having severe tuberculosis. This may or may not have been a correct diagnosis. Whatever the cause, however, he was grievously ill.

Soon it became clear to Northumberland that Edward was nearing death. But the Duke schemed to keep the severity of the king's illness a secret. He had a bold plan for the succession that was very different from that intended by Henry VIII. It did not involve Mary or even Elizabeth becoming queen. Obviously, his plan had a better chance of succeeding if Mary and her potential supporters remained unaware that the young king's illness had reached the terminal stage.

Perhaps Northumberland would have had a stronger case if he had chosen a male to take the throne on Edward's death. England had not had a female ruler since the Empress Matilda centuries earlier. Matilda was the granddaughter of William the Conqueror and the daughter of Henry I. She had been married at an early age to Heinrich, the Holy Roman Emperor. In the Imperial Court, she learned the ways of world politicians. On Heinrich's death, Matilda married Geoffrey "Plantagenet," called that because he wore a yellow flower, the "planta genesta," in his helmet. On the death of Henry I, Matilda was heir to the throne. But, as a female, there was resistance to her rule, and, while Matilda was away in France, her cousin Stephen seized the throne. There followed decades of civil war that finally ended with a settlement. Stephen would be "King for life" but Matilda's forceful, intelligent son, Henry, would be his heir. On Stephen's death, Matilda's son became Henry II, a strong and effective ruler and the first Plantagenet king. He was advised by Matilda, who even counseled him not to appoint his friend, Thomas Beckett, Archbishop of Canterbury, a decision he regretted for the rest of his life.

Now, with Edward VI about to die, Northumberland might have considered the turmoil caused by the prospect of a female ruler. He might have sought a reliable Englishman to be designated as heir, rather than Mary, who was Catholic as well as female. But the Duke had something quite different in mind, and he moved swiftly to carry out his scheme. He pressed the dying Edward to sign a document excluding both Mary and Elizabeth from the succession and naming Lady Jane Grey as heir to the throne.

Jane Grey was of the blood royal. Henry VIII's younger sister, Mary, had married the French king. On his death, she was to be escorted back to London by a handsome nobleman, Charles Brandon, the Duke of Suffolk. During the reign of Henry VII, the young Brandon had been something of a rake. Having promised to marry a young lady, he married her wealthy aunt instead. The bride was 20 years his senior. Brandon sold her lands, pocketed the money and then divorced her. Now, somewhat, but not totally reformed, Brandon found Henry's sister Mary (or her money) quite attractive. In Paris or on the trip back, the two fell in love. Soon, they were secretly married.

At first Henry was furious. Later, he forgave them. Ultimately, their daughter, Frances Brandon, married Henry Grey. Grey became the Duke of Suffolk through his wife's title, which she had inherited from her father. Their daughter was Jane Grey. Thus, Jane was the grandniece of Henry VIII and the great-granddaughter of Henry VII, the first Tudor King.

Although a slight, freckled teenager, Jane was already known for her intelligence and scholarship. She was a devout Protestant who, like Elizabeth and Edward, had been tutored by Cambridge scholars. Unlike Mary and Elizabeth, however, she was clearly legitimate. Most importantly, Northumberland considered Jane firmly under his control.

The Duke's scheme was devious and self-serving. With the eager complicity of Jane's voraciously ambitious parents, Northumberland intended to marry Jane to one of his own sons, Guilford Dudley. He aimed to make Guilford and Jane King and Queen of England. And, of course Northumberland would be the power behind the throne.

To carry out this plan, Mary and Elizabeth had to be excluded from the succession. That Edward would sign a document excluding Mary is not surprising. They were never close; and she was a militant Catholic, while Edward was a staunch Protestant. But Edward was fond of Elizabeth, whom he knew to be a fellow Protestant and liked to call "sweet sister temperance." Why would he exclude her?

Probably Northumberland convinced the dying king that the only effective argument to exclude Mary was her being illegitimate, and that same defect necessarily applied to Elizabeth. And the Duke may have argued that, as queen, Elizabeth would be forced to marry a foreign Catholic prince who would effectively rule the nation, or that, even if she did not make such a marriage, being subject to the claim of illegitimacy, she would probably be unable to hold the throne against the claim of Catholic Mary Stuart. That young woman, known to history as

"Mary Queen of Scots," was great-grandchild of Henry VII, the grandchild of Henry VIII's sister Margaret and the daughter of the Scottish King, James V. Her mother was Mary of Guise, a member of a powerful and rigorously Catholic French family. And, while she was barred from the succession by the will of Henry VIII, Mary Stuart was betrothed to the Dauphin, heir to the French throne, so that the might of France was available to support her claim to the English throne.

Moreover, knowing Elizabeth, Edward may have been persuaded that, if he excluded only Mary, Elizabeth might refuse to usurp what she considered her sister's title, creating a potentially disastrous uncertainty as to the succession.

Northumberland may have persuaded the young King that the soundest alternative was leaving the crown to Jane Grey. She was legitimate, Protestant, of the blood royal and would be married to a reliable Englishman (who just happened to be Northumberland's son). Unlike the heirs of Henry's sister Margaret, the heirs of his sister Mary, who was Jane's grandmother, were not excluded from the succession by Henry VIII's will. Thus, Jane could succeed to the throne if Edward, Mary and Elizabeth all died without heirs. Mary and Elizabeth hadn't died, but they were illegitimate and could arguably be excluded on that ground. Whatever the reason, the terminally ill Edward signed the document pressed upon him by Northumberland.

But the Duke's plan required Jane's mother, Frances Brandon, to relinquish her own claim to the throne. As the child of Henry VIII's sister Mary, her claim was, of course, superior to her daughter's. But Northumberland could not be sure of controlling the strong-willed Frances and had no interest in putting her on the throne. What he was after was crowning his son as king. Frances, recognizing Northumberland's power and content to see her daughter queen, agreed to relinquish her own claim. With that done, and with Jane now Edward's designated heir, all Northumberland needed was the young king's death; and he may even have hastened that event with discreet doses of arsenic.

Guilford Dudley, Northumberland's son, was a tall, rather handsome weakling, who was delighted at the prospect of becoming king. Jane Grey, however, realized the potential consequences of Northumberland's scheme and preferred a private life immersed in her books. She wanted no part of seizing the crown. Initially she refused to marry Guilford. Then, she refused the throne. In both instances, she was unable to stand against Northumberland and her own furious parents.

Their pressure was partly verbal — that this was the only way to preserve England as a Protestant country. But it was also physical. Jane was brutally whipped by her mother until she relented. She reluctantly married Guilford and, finally, consented to accept the crown. Apparently, however, she had little respect for Guilford. Even when she agreed to be queen, she insisted that, while he might be her consort, he could not be king. Furious, Northumberland continued adamant on the point; and it remained unresolved.

Elizabeth knew none of this. Fearing that her brother's condition was more serious than Northumberland was letting on, she wrote Edward letter after letter. Her letters were intercepted by Northumberland, who, of course, kept them from the dying king.

Finally, Edward died, having wasted away to a hairless skeleton, covered with foul smelling ulcers. Northumberland kept his death a secret for two days, while he mobilized men at arms to defend the claim of Jane and Guilford. His hope was that Mary would remain unsuspecting and unprepared and that his plan would be a fait accompli before she could organize any action to oppose it.

At last, when he felt it was time, Northumberland announced the young king's death and publicly proclaimed Jane Grey queen, disclosing Edward's signed revision of the order of succession.

Because the grotesque appearance of Edward's body might have aroused suspicion, it has been speculated that the Duke buried Edward secretly in an unmarked grave, placing another corpse in the elaborate coffin seen at the royal funeral. We do not know if this was true. Today, DNA testing would tell us.

Learned judges and respected lawyers considered the document Edward had signed to be void. It violated not only Henry VIII's will, but also Parliament's Act of Succession. Moreover, they opined that, as a minor, Edward could not make a valid testamentary instrument.

But Northumberland was a powerful and ruthless man. He "persuaded" the legal scholars to retract their views.

Mary had been warned of Northumberland's scheme even before his public announcement of the young king's death. She immediately realized that she was in serious danger. Northumberland could not afford to leave her free — or, for that matter, alive. At liberty, she would almost surely attract many followers who would recognize the validity of her claim. They would include not only the multitude of Englishmen who remained Catholic, as well as Northumberland's many enemies, but also a vast number of citizens who simply considered Mary the lawful heir, regardless of her religion.

Mary knew that, at all costs, she must avoid falling into Northumberland's hands. Traveling as rapidly as possible, sometimes in disguise, she raced from town to town. Finally, she took refuge in the redoubtable Framlingham Castle, with its 40 foot walls and multiple towers.

Elizabeth was aware that she too was in danger. As a Protestant daughter of Henry VIII, Northumberland might have considered her at least as dangerous as Mary, even though she was not asserting any claim to the throne. When the Duke summoned Elizabeth to join him at Greenwich, she pleaded illness and remained at Hatfield, her country estate, where she had staunch local supporters.

At Framlingham, Mary was surrounded by a large body of men enthusiastically loyal to her and ready to give their lives to protect her. Day after day, their ranks increased to a growing army prepared to fight for her cause. There were noblemen, who brought hundreds of their own retainers, as well as "innumerable companies of the common people" who, even if Protestant, believed that Mary was the rightful heir to the throne and that she should have it.

Northumberland had dispatched a force led by his son, Robert Dudley, in a futile pursuit of Mary. Now, the Duke set out to take her himself with what men he could muster in a deeply divided London. Before the battle was joined, however, the Council took the matter into its own hands and decided it — at least as a legal matter. They were aware of Mary's readily growing support among the people and had received reports that even the sailors on Royal Navy ships had announced for Mary. They undoubtedly realized, in addition, what fate would be in store for them if they backed Jane Grey and Mary won. With these factors in mind, the Council officially proclaimed Mary the queen and offered a reward for Northumberland's arrest.

The Duke's men, aware of the growing forces arrayed against them, began to desert in great numbers. Realizing that he faced a hopeless situation, Northumberland surrendered.

Elizabeth sent an immediate message of congratulations to Mary and joined her in a triumphal entry into London. As Elizabeth passed through the city she was enthusiastically greeted by the people. Still, she tried not to eclipse her sister. It was Mary's day.

Northumberland was attainted. That is, he and his heirs were divested of his title and his property. He,

Guilford and Jane Grey were confined in the Tower, as were four of Northumberland's other sons, John, Ambrose, Robert and Henry Dudley. Northumberland — now just John Dudley — was executed. Jane and Guilford were tried for treason, convicted and sentenced to death.

Despite the urging of others, however, Mary had no intention of executing Jane. She was well aware that the girl had been coerced into accepting the crown. Mary's plan was to keep Jane in the Tower for a time and then pardon her. Jane's father was briefly imprisoned and then freed. Her mother, Frances Brandon, was never even imprisoned.

After 18 months, John Dudley's sons were released, subject, of course, to the attainder imposed on their father. One son, John, soon died. But another, Robert Dudley, went on to play a major role in Elizabeth's life.

At Mary's coronation, Elizabeth was given a place of high honor, and naturally became a focus of attention. Her red hair, white skin and regal bearing were accentuated by a splendid silver gown. When she was younger, there had been cruel rumors that she was not Henry's child. Even Mary remarked cattily that Elizabeth resembled Mark Smeaton, the musician convicted of having an affair with Anne Boleyn. But there was no mistaking the paternity of the tall, regal young woman with the flaming hair. Elizabeth's resemblance to Henry VIII was obvious and far greater than Mary's.

Like Edward, Mary had inherited a royal treasury that was empty and a nation facing serious economic problems. Although intelligent and well educated, she had no understanding of how those problems could be solved.

Of course, Mary intended to restore Catholicism as the established religion. But doing so created serious problems. Reform had been spreading for twenty years and was widely accepted in London and by younger Englishmen in most of the realm. Moreover, a substantial number of influential men had acquired former monastic properties and were by no means ready to give them back. And there were priests who had married and would have to choose between their wives and the priesthood.

At first, Mary spoke of the need for understanding and civility, asking her subjects to avoid such inflammatory terms as "papist" and "heretic." Soon, however, she moved forward to re-establish Catholicism and preclude dissent. She forbad Protestant teaching and imprisoned a number of Protestant clergymen who violated her decree. Open criticism of Catholicism or advocacy of religious reform was punished. Printers who espoused such views found themselves out of business, their presses smashed or confiscated by the Crown. Still, Mary delayed restoring the supremacy of the Pope. Essentially, she re-established the Pope-less Catholicism generally followed by her father. But it was a different England now, an England that had lived under a militant Protestant regime.

Fearing persecution, imprisonment or even death, many dedicated Protestants left the kingdom seeking safer places to ride out Mary's reign. Among these Protestant refugees was Katherine Carey Knollys, the daughter of Mary Boleyn, born during her long affair with Henry VIII. Katherine was Elizabeth's cousin and close friend. Probably she was Elizabeth's half-sister as well, since it is likely she was Henry's child.

Ironically, this would also have made Katherine the half sister of Mary, the new queen from whose policies she was fleeing. But Katherine, like her brother Henry, had been given the name Carey; and, even if she believed she was the daughter of Henry VIII, she would not have said so. Her claiming to be the love child of the Queen's father would almost certainly have evoked in Mary fury, rather than favor.

Elizabeth wrote Katherine Knollys in her new home abroad that "the length of time and distance of place separates not the love of friends." She signed her note "Your loving cousin and ready friend, Elizabeth, cor rotto" [broken hearted].

After Mary's accession, Elizabeth wisely appeared reconciled to the "old religion." According to the Venetian Ambassador, "she concealed her religion and comported herself like a good Catholic." She had no choice. For the heir to the throne to have rejected Catholicism during Mary's rein would probably have resulted in her death by assassination, if not by a royally ordered execution.

Mary was what was then considered middle-aged. She was not looking for romance. But no woman had ruled England since Matilda, and no one wanted to repeat that unhappy experience. Nor did Mary. She had been raised by those who believed that only a man could truly rule a kingdom and that, if a woman inherited a throne, she should have a husband who could actually rule.

Mary relied heavily on the advice of her powerful cousin, the Emperor Charles V, who had even threatened war to preserve Mary's religious freedom during the reign of Edward VI. Typically that advice would be communicated through Simon Renard, the Imperial Ambassador, who also became Mary's confessor.

The Emperor considered marrying Mary himself, but ruled it out. He could accomplish even more with a different idea. Based on his advice, Mary announced her betrothal to his son, Prince Philip of Spain, then a widower and Regent of that Catholic nation.

The Emperor viewed the match strictly in terms of international politics. He saw it as a way to tie England to Spain and the Empire, striking a blow at France, his rival for European hegemony. This would offset the Franco-Scottish alliance formed by the betrothal of Mary Stuart to the French Dauphin, heir to the throne of France. Sharing the English throne would also give Philip a strong base from which to control the Netherlands, which Charles considered a rightful part of his Empire. And, unlike the Emperor, Philip was young enough to bring all of these benefits to fruition.

The English public was extremely hostile to the match. Not only was Philip a foreigner and a staunch Catholic, he was Spanish, and that seemed to generate particular anger among the common people. But, Mary was unswayed. She would follow her Imperial cousin's advice. Soon, it became more than that. Despite her age and previous disinterest in romance, Mary fell in love with a miniature portrait of her intended groom, and developed an obsessive desire to marry him.

Meanwhile, Mary harbored the suspicion that Elizabeth's religious conversion lacked sincerity. Her concerns were heightened by the fact that Elizabeth was enormously popular and that virtually every Protestant plot aimed at deposing Mary sought to place Elizabeth on the throne. And such plots seemed to be everywhere, often founded on Mary's Catholicism, but also fueled by violent opposition to her Spanish marriage.

In 1554, one such plot eventuated in an uprising led by Sir Thomas Wyatt. The plot began as an attempt to prevent Mary's marriage to Philip. As it progressed, however, replacing Mary with Elizabeth seemed to become another goal of the rebels.

Elizabeth had probably been aware of this plan, but there was no evidence that she encouraged it. Still, when Royal forces intercepted a French diplomatic pouch, it was found to contain a copy of a letter from Elizabeth to Mary. The letter itself was innocuous, but Mary reasoned that Elizabeth must have given it to the French. The Imperial Ambassador had warned Mary of a report that a French fleet was being assembled on the coast of

Normandy; and Mary believed the French were preparing to invade England in support of Elizabeth. Under the circumstances, Elizabeth's giving any document to the French was alarming.

Even though France was ruled and controlled by Catholics, Mary would have been ready to believe that the French would invade England, even if it meant putting a Protestant princess on the throne. Sixteenth-century rulers frequently placed greater importance on international power and prestige than on furthering the cause of their religion. France and Spain were each determined to prevent the other from gaining ascendancy in Europe. During the reigns of Edward and of Mary, France was actually at war with Spain and its ally, the Empire. The French Ambassador desperately tried to prevent Mary's Spanish marriage, urging that, instead, she marry an Englishman, Edward Courtenay.

With Mary betrothed to a Spanish prince, it was conceivable that the French would invade England to replace her with Elizabeth, after which they would marry Elizabeth to a French prince. The reasoning was that the French would consider it more important to frustrate their principal European rival, than to retain a Catholic queen on the English throne. The Emperor, who was pressing for an Anglo-Spanish alliance, may have held that view of French intentions when his Ambassador told Mary of the reported French fleet. In any event, Mary seems to have considered a French invasion a realistic possibility and, for that reason, was particularly concerned at what seemed evidence of Elizabeth's complicity in a French plot.

The French invasion did not materialize. Neither did much support for the planned rebellion. Most of its expected leaders opted out, remaining on their estates. But Thomas Wyatt pushed on. The aged Duke of Norfolk led a small force from London to confront him. But most of Norfolk's men went over to the rebel side, shouting "A Wyatt! A Wyatt!" Now Wyatt's rebel forces, probably 5,000 strong, entered London itself, threatening not only Mary's proposed marriage, but her life.

Despite the imminent danger, Mary made a courageous and impassioned plea to a huge crowd of Londoners gathered at the Guildhall. She told them that she would never marry outside the realm without her Council's consent and unless "all her true subjects be content." The latter assurance was certainly misleading, if not an outright lie. But this was a crisis, and, evidently, Mary considered it essential. On the positive side, she told Londoners that she would live and die with them in the streets, ending with the exhortation "And now, good subjects, pluck up your hearts, and like true men face up against these rebels, and fear them not, for I assure you, I fear them not at all." Her speech was greeted with a roar of approval.

Stirred to action by Mary's personal bravery, thousands of Londoners quickly volunteered to join Mary's existing troops in resisting Wyatt's invading army. Thus, reinforced, the loyal forces fought and defeated the rebels in the streets and parks of the Capitol. Wyatt was captured and imprisoned in the Tower. The rebellion was over.

Now, Mary came under enormous pressure to execute Jane Grey. Jane's father, the Duke of Suffolk, had been an active supporter of Wyatt's rebellion, foolishly announcing his intention to restore Jane to the throne. And, even more significant from Mary's point of view, the Emperor advised her that, so long as Jane lived, he could not permit his son Philip to come to England for their marriage. This was a form of pressure Mary could not withstand. Reluctantly, she signed the death warrant, and seventeen-year-old Jane was beheaded after her father and the hapless Guilford. Not one to be thrown off stride by personal tragedy, Jane's domineering mother, Frances Brandon, plunged quickly into a scandalous affair with her handsome young stable master, whom she later married.

With the rebellion defeated, Mary turned to the problem of Elizabeth. Under suspicion, the princess was summoned to report immediately to Court. Although ill, she slowly made the journey from Hatfield to the capital, fearing what was in store for her. Mary was certain that Elizabeth had been complicit in the recently defeated plot; but her Council was divided as to whether Elizabeth should be charged with treason.

There seemed to be no proof. Repeated interrogation of Wyatt and other conspirators produced no evidence of Elizabeth's complicity. On the contrary, even as Wyatt was about to die, he stated from the scaffold that Elizabeth was completely innocent. Such statements in the face of imminent death carried great weight, since it was believed that, by lying, the speaker would be imperiling his immortal soul. Elizabeth, herself, vehemently protested her innocence and denied giving her letter to the French, although she could not explain how a copy got in their diplomatic pouch.

In this state of uncertainty, Mary was prepared to leave London for the Easter holidays and, thereafter, to attend a session of Parliament in Oxford. With the Queen away from the Capitol, the danger of another rebellion centering around Elizabeth was considered too great. Renard, the Imperial Ambassador, advised Mary that she could never be safe while Elizabeth lived. Here was an opportunity to eliminate that danger by executing her. As a compromise, however, Mary decided that, even without evidence of treason or a charge of any crime, Elizabeth should be confined in the Tower.

When a deputation of Council members arrived to tell Elizabeth of the Queen's ominous order and to deliver the Princess to the Tower, she pleaded for a chance to speak with her sister. This was not allowed. Then she pleaded for time to write Mary. This was permitted. Elizabeth wrote the letter, leaving most of one page blank. Fearing that someone would forge a treasonous entry in the blank space, she filled it with diagonal lines.

Elizabeth was probably aware that no letter would change Mary's mind. But, by drafting the letter ever so slowly, the tide in the river turned. The boatmen could no longer shoot safely under London Bridge to reach the Tower. The dreaded trip had to be postponed until the tide was favorable.

We might wonder why Mary's representatives did not take Elizabeth to the Tower by land, without waiting for a favorable tide. Probably they feared that, traveling through the narrow London streets, they could easily be attacked by a mob supporting the popular princess.

In any event, the delay gained Elizabeth only a few hours. Not surprisingly, Mary did not change her mind; and, the next morning, Elizabeth made the trip down the river to the Tower. The commonly reported story, from John Foxe's *Book of Martyrs*, is that she landed in the rain at the Traitor's Gate, wet, frightened, reluctant to enter, tearfully protesting her innocence and expecting that her life was nearing its end. That would be understandable. She was only 20; and, however she entered the Tower, she probably believed she would never leave it alive. But the morning tide would have made landing at the Traitor's Gate impossible. It is probable that she landed at Tower Wharf and crossed the westerly drawbridge into the Tower, and that the dramatic scene at the Traitor's Gate never happened.

Elizabeth was lodged in the royal apartments of the Tower. This was hardly a dungeon. But it was the part of the Tower in which Anne Boleyn had been held before her execution. Elizabeth must have feared that what lay ahead for her was a similar fate. She was held in the Tower for two months, probably in a continuous state of fear.

In that period, however, the tide of opinion had significantly shifted in Elizabeth's favor. Mary's judges had advised her that there was insufficient evidence to convict Elizabeth of treason. Perhaps more tellingly, Philip, Mary's betrothed, urged her to relent. Displeased by the opinions of her judges, but anxious to please Philip, Mary reluctantly ordered her prisoner released. Escorted by a troop of guardsmen, Elizabeth triumphantly made the trip up river accompanied by resounding cheers of Londoners and even the firing of guns in an expression of popular support for the newly freed princess.

Still, Elizabeth was not entirely free. She was to be under house arrest. Renard, the Imperial Ambassador, suggested sending her to Pontefract Castle, where Richard II had reportedly been murdered. Probably he intended the same fate for Elizabeth. But the Council had other plans.

Elizabeth was sent to Woodstock, an ancient and dilapidated manor in Oxfordshire. There, she was placed under the strict surveillance of Sir Henry Bedingfield, a narrow-minded, poorly educated and stubborn Catholic knight. Ironically, Bedingfield's father had been the custodian of Catherine of Aragon during her last years, after she had been sent away from court. Now, Catherine's daughter Mary had chosen his son as custodian of Elizabeth.

Bedingfield did not want the assignment and tried to avoid it. But, commanded by the Queen's Council, he did his duty as he saw it. He allowed Elizabeth few liberties, even restricting her reading material.

Elizabeth was resentful, and, as the months passed, she still considered herself a prisoner, albeit in a place far less menacing than the Tower. Legend has it that, using a diamond, she scratched her feelings in the glass of a window:

Much suspected by me,

Nothing proved can be

Quoth Elizabeth, prisoner

The legend is supported by Elizabeth's embroidery on the silk cover of a book that has been preserved. She wrote: "Vicit omnia pertinax virtus. E.C," "Firm virtue conquers all." The "E.C." stands for "Elizabetha Captiva," "Elizabeth the captive."

In July, 1554, Mary married Philip of Spain. Notwithstanding those who believed that only a man could rule, the marriage treaty provided that, although Philip could be called "King," Mary would govern as the true ruler and that, on Mary's death, Philip would have no claim to the English throne. Although Mary had fallen desperately in love with the idea of her Spanish prince, Philip was less romantic. He confided to the Spanish courtiers who accompanied him to England that Mary was not attractive to him. Nevertheless, he remained considerate to her and, at least in public, acted as a loving husband.

Having maintained the proper public appearance, Philip sought to leave England after a few weeks to lead an Imperial army against the French. He even had a ship standing by to carry him to Flanders. But his father, the Emperor Charles, insisted that he remain in England with his wife. Philip obeyed — at least for a time. Ultimately, he left and was away from England more than he was there.

Following her marriage, Mary brought about the religious change she had desired, but delayed. The breach between England and the Pope was ended. The Pope forgave England for its earlier separation and issued a bull giving up any claim to English lands that had been taken from the Church. Given these papal concessions, Parliament made England once again subject to Rome; and the ancient heresy laws that had been abolished under Edward were restored.

After her marriage, Mary's policy toward Elizabeth softened somewhat. First, she allowed Elizabeth classical books that Bedingfield had denied her. Then, she allowed Elizabeth to write to her, another thing Elizabeth's keeper had refused. Their correspondence, however, was hardly a warm one. Elizabeth wrote, still professing her innocence and pointing out that there was no evidence of her encouraging the rebellion. Mary responded that Elizabeth obviously knew about the plot and added bitingly that treason was rarely proved by direct, as opposed to circumstantial, evidence. Elizabeth feared that the price of her freedom from Bedingfield might be an admission of guilt and a plea for mercy. That was a price she was not prepared to pay.

However, the restrictions on Elizabeth were soon eased, even without such an admission. There may have been more than one reason for this. It was announced that the Queen was pregnant, and, according to the midwives, her child would be born before May 9, 1555. This happy news may well have caused Mary to put aside her suspicions concerning her sister.

It is also likely that Philip persuaded Mary to adopt a more liberal policy toward Elizabeth. Probably, Philip had begun to realize that, if his wife died in childbirth and the baby was stillborn, Imperial and Spanish interests would be better served with Elizabeth on the throne than Mary Stuart, the Scottish Queen. Putting aside the will of Henry VIII that would have excluded her as an heir of his sister Margaret, the young Scottish queen had a solid claim to the English throne as the great-granddaughter of Henry VII. Although she was Catholic, Mary Stuart posed serious problems for Spain and the Empire. Betrothed to the French Dauphin at an early age, she had been sent to live at the French Court. Her French mother, Mary of Guise, had become Regent of Scotland, ruling for her young daughter. Clearly, Mary Stuart had strong French ties and pro-French views. It is likely that, at this point, Philip feared her succeeding to the English throne and gave greater consideration to his intense rivalry with France than to the Pope's struggle against Protestantism. Probably, this led to his advocating Elizabeth's cause to his new wife.

Apparently, the same factors altered Renard's stance as well. Changing his position dramatically, the Imperial Ambassador now advocated that Elizabeth succeed to the throne should Mary die in childbirth, lest pro-French Mary Stuart become the successor, vastly expanding French power at the expense of Spain and the Empire. In any event, probably because of the views of both Philip and Renard, Mary's attitude toward Elizabeth appeared to soften.

At this same time, however, the Queen may have wanted to show her husband and her confessor the depth of her feelings for the True Church. Or perhaps it was expecting their child that awakened in her a more militant attitude concerning religion. Whatever the reason, in February 1555, the Queen began the practice of cruelly burning Protestants that led to her historical sobriquet "Bloody Mary."

Mary's victims were tied to a stake atop a pile of kindling and were burned alive, suffering excruciating pain. Their immolation was intended to teach the public the fundamental error of rejecting Catholicism and to remind them that the fires of hell awaited them if they did. Convinced that publicly burning Protestants would act as a deterrent to other heretics, Mary had some 300 of them horribly immolated. Sixty were women. Since those barbarities took place in East Smithfield, just beyond the Tower of London, the unfortunate victims were called the "Smithfield Martyrs."

Sometimes it would rain, or a sadistic official would wet the wood. When this occurred, the fire burned slowly and the victim's agony was prolonged. Other times, a sympathetic official would fasten a small sack of explosive to the martyr's body, so that his suffering would end quickly when the flames reached the sack.

There were instances in which the immolations were particularly cruel. In the summer of 1556, a young pregnant woman was burned as a heretic. Possibly she had denied the "Real Presence," or some other aspect of Catholic doctrine. The intense heat caused her to give birth prematurely, and her baby fell into the fire. A sympathetic spectator quickly pulled the infant to safety. But a royal official ordered it thrown back into the flames. As the crowd gasped, the order was obeyed. Would Mary have sanctioned that particular act of cruelty? Probably not; but her rigorous policy of burning Protestants alive necessarily led to grotesque brutality.

Along with ordinary "heretics," Mary burned Protestant Bishops, including even Thomas Cranmer, Henry VIII's Archbishop of Canterbury, who had written the Protestant *Book of Common Prayer* and had decreed Henry's marriage to her mother invalid. When Mary ordered Cranmer to be burned, he sought to avoid that fate by signing a statement recanting his Protestant beliefs. Not one to forgive what Cranmer had done to her mother, Mary ordered him burned despite his recantation. Hearing this, Cranmer determined to reverse himself again. When he was about to be burned, he was expected to make a public statement of contrition for his former heretic views. Instead, he defiantly proclaimed his Protestant beliefs. Then, when the fire was lit, he thrust his right hand into the flames, since that was the hand that had signed the false recantation.

And, when Mary sent John Rogers to be burned at Smithfield, he calmly chanted as he approached the pyre. Rogers had been the Vicar of St. Sepulchre Church in London. As his body began burning, Rogers reached down into the fire appearing to wash his hands in the flame. Then, smiling, he raised his flaming hands to God.

Mary burned other churchmen as well, including Bishops Gardiner, Lattimer and Ridley. As Lattimer and Ridley were about to be subjected to the flames, Lattimer told Ridley "Be of good comfort, Master Ridley, and play the man. We shall this day light such a candle by God's grace in England as I trust shall never be put out." In a sense, they did.

Philip and other advisors counseled Mary that the hideously cruel practice of burning at the stake was actually harmful to the Catholic cause. They feared the public would blame Philip and the Spanish, who were still seen as the architects of the inquisition and the inventors of the *auto da fe*, the burning of Spanish "heretics." The French, Imperial and Venetian ambassadors also deplored Mary's burning of Protestants. But, certain she was doing "God's work," Mary would not relent.

Years later, in 1563, Foxe's *Book of Martyrs* provided horrifying accounts of the torture and burning of Protestants in Mary's reign. In those later years, Foxe's work was to fuel significant and sometimes extreme anti-

Catholic sentiment, just the kind of sentiment Mary believed she was suppressing.

At the end of April, 1555, as the time neared for the birth of Mary's child, Elizabeth was allowed to return to court to be present at the delivery. This was a time of great concern for Mary's councilors and for Philip as well. The burning of Protestants, plus the potential birth of a Catholic heir, were inflaming the passions of Protestant Englishmen. The birth of a healthy baby would eliminate Elizabeth as the heir, shatter the dreams of a Protestant succession and perhaps continue for decades the brutal immolation of Protestants. There was significant danger that outraged Protestants, about to lose their chance of ending this Catholic reign of terror, would now rebel.

Philip, always prudent, continued his cautious view of the matter. Yes, Elizabeth posed a threat. But returning her to the Tower or worse would almost surely invite an immediate and perhaps unstoppable rebellion. And, if Mary and the baby did not survive — a frequent occurrence in the 16th century — Philip would want to work out a *modus vivendi* with a friendly Elizabeth — perhaps even marry her. After all, she was much nearer his own age than Mary and considerably more attractive and witty. And whether or not he married Elizabeth, Philip probably continued to consider her vastly preferable to pro-French Mary Stuart.

From Elizabeth's point of view a successful birth of Mary's child significantly increased her peril. Once Mary delivered a healthy baby, Elizabeth would be considered a dangerous rival to the infant — possibly too dangerous to survive. Elizabeth did what she could to mitigate the danger. She used her poignant good looks, sharp wit and sensual femininity to charm Philip and his Spanish courtiers.

Meanwhile, Mary had "taken her chamber." After a religious ceremony, the Queen, by tradition, was accompanied to the door of her bed chamber, at which point the men were excused. Once she and her women entered, no man was allowed until 30 days after the birth of the child.

In Mary's case, however, May and even June came and went without her delivering a child. So did July. By August, it was obvious there would be no child and that Mary had never really been pregnant. The many nobles who had been at Hampton Court for months awaiting the royal birth were permitted to return to their homes.

In August, Mary's problems increased. Philip left for the fighting in Flanders, assuring Mary his absence would be a few weeks. It was, of course, much longer; and, there were rumors of his involvement with other women.

In October, 1555, Elizabeth was allowed to return to her own estate at Hatfield. She was joined there by her old tutor, Roger Ascham, with whom she expanded her education. By this time, Elizabeth spoke seven languages and was thoroughly familiar with the Latin and Greek classics. She had also learned much about statesmanship, not only from her comprehensive study of history, but also through shrewd observation of the reign of Edward

VI and of the errors made by Mary in governing and even in marrying.

In the Winter of 1555-1556, however, another plot arose to overthrow Mary and put Elizabeth on the throne. The plot was uncovered; and, although the principal leaders were in France, other plotters were captured including Francis Verney, a young aide to Elizabeth. This time there was more serious evidence against Elizabeth. Kat Ashley's rooms in Elizabeth's London residence were searched, revealing materials attacking Catholicism and insulting Philip and Mary. Kat and three women servants in Elizabeth's household were arrested and questioned. Evidently, the women, and possibly even Kat, implicated Elizabeth in the failed plot.

Mary was urged to send Elizabeth to the Tower once again. But this was not a decision she was prepared to make herself. Instead, she sent a courier to Brussels to inquire as to Philip's wishes in the matter.

His answer as swift and unambiguous. He directed Mary to take no action against Elizabeth, to prevent any further inquiry into her conduct and to state publicly her own opinion that Elizabeth's servants were involved in the plot without her knowledge and authority.

Once again, Philip appeared to weigh his preference for a Catholic successor to Mary against the extreme danger to Spain and the Empire should pro-French Mary Stuart become that successor. Philip's determination to protect Habsburg interests seemed to prevail over the interests of the Pope. Reluctantly, Mary obeyed Philip's command.

Once again, Elizabeth was in the clear. But she was to be watched. While she was once again under a form of "house arrest," her situation was not unpleasant. She was allowed to remain at Hatfield and was entrusted to the care of Sir Thomas Pope, who was far more intelligent and permissive than her stiff-necked former warden. She continued her studies with Ascham, and was, in every respect, comfortable and even honored. Pope's custodianship lasted for about six months, after which Elizabeth was "free."

Her relationship with Mary became, if not friendly, at least civil. This was probably also due to the continued influence of Philip, whose wishes remained paramount to Mary. Philip realized now that Mary was probably barren. He could see that Elizabeth might well be the key to the future, and he probably let Mary know that he not only wanted her sister spared arrest, imprisonment or worse, he wanted her well treated. And Mary complied.

Mary even visited Elizabeth at Hatfield. Probably, she continued to have feelings of resentment toward her younger, prettier sister. Probably, she remained convinced of Elizabeth's implication in the most recent plot and was loath to think of her succeeding to the throne. Outwardly, however, she seemed reconciled to that result.

Philip's influence had an impact on the nation in other ways as well. He pressured Mary into sending English forces to fight on his side against the French, even threatening that he would not return to England until she complied. Their marriage treaty had specified that English troops would not be required to fight Philip's wars. But, in June of 1557, unable to resist her husband's pressure, Mary declared war on France.

At first, the nation was filled with a martial, anti-French spirit. But, soon enough, England was losing lives and money defending Philip's interests on the Continent, and public enthusiasm waned. The public, already upset with Mary's burning of Protestants, grew seriously disenchanted with her pro-Spanish war policy. In early 1558, public resentment became outrage when the French took Calais. This was England's last foothold on the Continent, a place considered an inseparable part of England and vital to its commercial interests. The English had held Calais for over 200 years, and it was thought to be impregnable. It did not prove so. Its fall was seen as a national disaster, and Mary was blamed.

The remaining three Dudley brothers, sons of the attainted and executed Duke of Northumberland, fought for Philip in France. Robert Dudley distinguished himself in combat, probably establishing a good relationship with Philip that he would seek to use later in life. His brother, Henry, was killed in the campaign, as were many other Englishmen.

In 1558, Mary Stuart married the French Dauphin to whom she had been betrothed. This strengthened her already significant ties to France and vastly increased Philip's concern at the prospect of her becoming Queen of England, creating a single Anglo-French nation, a potential disaster for Spain and the Empire.

It is probable that, in this period, Philip directed his royal wife to recognize Elizabeth as her successor. She was not the only claimant. Aside from Mary Stuart, there were Jane Grey's sisters, Frances Brandon's niece and others. But it was apparent that Elizabeth was the public's favorite. She had been designated next in line by Henry VIII and, since the most likely alternative was Mary Stuart, Philip could see that the interests of Spain and the Empire lay with Elizabeth.

But the succession became uncertain one more time. Once again, Mary became convinced she was pregnant; and, once again, the months passed until it was obvious she was not. By October of 1558, it became clear that Mary was suffering from an aggressive and life-threatening disease. It has been described as ovarian cancer but also as a non-cancerous tumor of the pituitary gland. At this point, it is impossible to know. But, whichever it was, it had reached the terminal stage. Undoubtedly with mixed feelings, Mary finally announced that her younger sister would succeed her. She implored Elizabeth to maintain Catholicism as the established national religion — and also her own. Elizabeth said she would do both. Undoubtedly, she intended to do neither.

Now that Elizabeth was the announced heir to the throne and was about to begin her reign, a "shadow court" formed at Hatfield with distinguished and not so distinguished visitors coming to seek the favor of the young woman who would soon be queen.

Finally, on November 17, 1558, Elizabeth received word at Hatfield that Mary had died and that she was now Queen of England. She was twenty-five. Elizabeth's reported response was her well known comment, "This is the Lord's doing, and it is marvelous in our eyes." Of course, being Elizabeth, she made the comment in Latin.

The bells of every London church rang out, and the people crowded the streets, cheering. The long nightmare of Mary's reign was finally over.

On her coronation day, amid the ringing of bells and the joyous celebration of her people, Elizabeth gave a most appropriate prayer.

O Lord, almighty and everlasting God, I give Thee most hearty thanks that Thou hast been so merciful unto me as to spare me to behold this joyful day. And I acknowledge that Thou has dealt as wonderfully and as mercifully with me as Thou didst with Thy true and faithful servant Daniel, Thy prophet, whom Thou deliveredst out of the den from the cruelty of the greedy and raging lions.

Elizabeth's prayers were never empty cant. She knew how close she had come to death at the hands of "the greedy and raging lions."

* * * * *

In order to better understand the events of Elizabeth's reign, I'll pause here to consider the two major problems that dominated the era.

The first problem was religious reformation and the conflict between Catholics and Protestants. The second was the need to protect the realm by maintaining a balance of power in Europe, fending off the dangerous might of Spain and the Empire and that of their powerful arch-rival France, and dealing with the dangerous actions of those European powers with respect to the Netherlands, Scotland, Ireland and, of course, England itself.

I'll begin with religion. In the 15th century, most European countries, including England, France, Spain and the Holy Roman Empire, were Catholic. Europe was, to a great extent, controlled or at least significantly influenced by Rome, depending on the relative strengths, weaknesses and proclivities of individual Popes and individual rulers.

Over the centuries, the Church had become venal and corrupt in many ways. In 1517, Martin Luther, a professor of theology at the University of Wittenberg, posted 95 "theses" on the door of the Castle Church in Wittenberg. Luther's attack was primarily directed at the Church's selling "indulgences," a sort of "get out of jail free" card, by which a sinner could be absolved of even the most grievous sins by purchasing an "indulgence" from the Church. These sales were a significant source of revenue for the Church, and Rome was determined to see the lucrative practice continued.

At the time, Luther still considered himself a pious Catholic, but that did not deter him from making a slashing attack on this corrupt practice, particularly on the concept that indulgences could be granted retroactively to wipe out the sins of those already dead and in purgatory. He also argued that the Bible, rather than the Pope, was the true authority for Christian beliefs. And, he published pamphlets attacking clerical celibacy, the worship of saints and the Catholic sacraments and advocating that church services be conducted in the vernacular, rather than in Latin. Subsequently, he translated the Bible into German, so that it could be read and understood at least by those German speakers who were literate.

Luther's campaign of reform spread rapidly throughout the Germanic states, into Scandinavia and then into other European countries with populations already disillusioned by Church practices. Others spoke out against those practices and demanded reform. Among them were Ulrich Zwingli in Zurich and the Frenchman, Jean Calvin, in Geneva.

The reformers argued that neither priests nor even the Pope could or should stand between man and God and that, if God decided that a man's sins should or should not be forgiven, no priest or Pope could change that decision. They also believed that man achieved salvation through faith in God, rather than by doing good works. Later attacks were made on many Catholic concepts and practices, including the doctrine of transubstantiation, the celibacy of the clergy, the worship of saints and relics, the use of rosary beads and the Church's insistence that the Bible be in Latin and be read only by the priesthood.

Some leaders of the reform movement were at least as repressive as the most ferociously dedicated Pope. Calvin was one. In Geneva, he presided as a virtual dictator over a regime that regulated almost every aspect of its citizens' beliefs and behavior. Its laws were rigorously and cruelly enforced.

Some monarchs, observing the weakening of the Popes' hold on their subjects, cynically used the reform movement as an opportunity to withhold payments to Rome and even to confiscate valuable Church property.

The reform movement made little headway in Italy and Spain and was slow in coming to England. Although there were anti-clerical stirrings, England was staunchly Catholic when Henry VIII took the throne.

William Tyndale translated the New Testament into English, striking at the heart of English Catholicism. Fearing for his life, Tyndale fled to Brussels. He was captured there by Henry's agents, who killed him by garroting, after which his dead body was burned at the stake.

During Thomas More's term as Chancellor from 1529 to 1532, Protestant booksellers were imprisoned, and "heretical" (i.e., Protestant) books were burned, sometimes along with the heretical booksellers. Certainly Henry VIII knew this was occurring.

Erasmus was a Dutch scholar residing in England at the invitation of the young Henry VIII. From a time shortly before Luther posted his "theses" on the door of the church in Wittenberg, Erasmus attacked the papacy and the clergy. But he did this far more subtly than Luther, through the use of satire.

Erasmus even made fun of Pope Julius II, the "soldier pope" who was something of a Catholic hero for his successful military adventures. Erasmus conjured up an imaginary conversation between the Pope and Saint Peter concerning Julius' possible admission into heaven. When St. Peter's questioning put Julius at a disadvantage, the angry pontiff threatened to excommunicate St. Peter and proclaimed "The invincible Julius ought not answer to a beggarly Jewish fisherman." Then, when it appeared that Julius would still be denied entry into heaven, he threatened to gather his armies and "take the place by storm."

How did Erasmus get away with this when other men were slaughtered for expressing even milder anti-Catholic views? First, it was plainly satire. It was funny. And, Erasmus wrote in Latin, so that his works could only be read by the educated and high born. Thus, they were considered less dangerous than views expressed in English, which could be read by many of the common people.

Moreover, Erasmus had been a friend of Henry VIII since the king's boyhood. He had visited with the young

Henry during trips to England and had even served as a guide for Henry and his brother Arthur on a visit to Venice. And Erasmus was highly respected by other powerful Englishmen, including Sir Thomas More. Still, even Erasmus took a risk, but it was not comparable to the risks taken by men like Tyndale and Luther.

When it was said that Erasmus "laid the egg that Luther hatched," Erasmus replied that, if so, "what Luther hatched was a gamecock," meaning it was no mere chick, but something fierce and potent. Luther, no humorist, was far more outspoken and uncompromising in his attacks on the papacy, the Church and Catholic theology than Erasmus ever was.

As Luther's views proliferated, many reformers took on his name as the name of their movement. They were Lutherans. Luther himself became increasingly vituperative and unguarded in his attacks. He called Rome an "empurpled Babylon." The Curia was the "synagogue of Satan" and the Pope the "Devil incarnate." Ultimately, he even called for putting the Pope and the Cardinals to death. "Why," he asked, "do we not . . . attack in arms these masters of perdition, these Cardinals, these Popes and all their sink of Roman Sodom, which has, without end, corrupted the Church of God, and wash our hands in their blood."

In 1529, an edict was issued in Speyer rescinding all tolerance for Lutherans. The Lutherans protested vigorously, and their protest was heard throughout Europe.

From that point forward, the generic term for those who sought reform of the Church became "Protestants."

The "English Reformation" is somewhat of a misnomer for the changes effected by Henry VIII in order to shed his wife and marry Anne Boleyn. As we have seen, Henry did not abolish most Catholic practices. What he did was to replace the Pope as the Supreme Head of the English Church. Once that was done, instead of submitting the validity of his marriage to a decision by Rome, it was declared invalid by Thomas Cranmer, his own newly appointed Archbishop of Canterbury. Thus, Henry's marriage to Anne Boleyn could become valid . . . for a time.

Cranmer's decision was based on interpretation of the Bible, rather than papal dictate, a process in harmony with Luther's view that the Bible, not the Pope, established the rules by which men should live. But Henry did not believe he was adopting the precepts of Luther, whom he probably continued to view as a heretic. Henry still considered himself a faithful Catholic. Of course, he did seize the opportunity to appropriate monastic and other Church lands and to halt all payments to Rome. But those decisions were motivated by financial and political considerations, not religious zeal.

Generally protected by Thomas Cromwell and with the support of Anne Boleyn, most Protestant booksellers were free to sell their "heretical" works; and Protestant scholars and clerics began to write and speak out. The view of the king generally remained that he was a Catholic and

England was a Catholic realm. But, as we have seen, he certainly knew that his son and heir to the throne, as well as his younger daughter, were being raised and educated as dedicated Protestants.

It was only during the reign of Henry's son, Edward VI, who, like Elizabeth, had been taught by Protestant scholars and raised as a Protestant, that the full panoply of reformist principles was adopted by the Church of England. It was in Edward's reign that Cranmer's *Book of Common Prayer*, written in English for Englishmen, became the religious manual for the realm.

In many European countries, England among them, the majority of the population remained Catholic, at least privately. In the latter part of the 16th century, Catholics began the "Counter-reformation." Highly motivated priests, trained in Rome or in the Netherlands at Douai, spread throughout England and other countries, urging a return to the "True Church" and even the overthrow of Protestant monarchs, such as Elizabeth, who were labeled "heretics." Spain and the Empire remained staunchly Catholic. In France, Catholics and Protestants engaged in decades of sometimes ferocious warfare that sapped much of that country's power.

Historically, the religion of the monarch became the established religion of the state, rather than being the individual choice of the citizenry. In England, as we have seen, the ascendancy of Catholics or Protestants varied with the monarch's own beliefs. From the time of Henry

VIII, however, these two religions contended with each other in every reign. They continued that struggle in the reign of Elizabeth.

But the religious conflict was by no means the only problem Elizabeth faced. England was an island in the midst of a dangerous world. On taking the throne, Elizabeth found the Crown deeply in debt. There was no effective army, and few military leaders. The navy had been allowed to decline. Throughout the realm, city walls and castles were crumbling and becoming indefensible. Surrounded by potential enemies, Elizabeth was unready for a war and convinced she could not afford one. As the Spanish Ambassador put it, the English were "Without money, men, armour, fortresses, practice in war or good captains." When Elizabeth took the throne, it appeared that England would have dire need of all those things.

Spain had traditionally been an ally of England in its centuries-old struggles with France. That began to change as England severed its ties to Rome. During the reign of Elizabeth, Catholic Spain became and remained a serious threat. Although its financial situation varied considerably, Spain was generally able to support its extensive military campaigns through the riches of the West Indies and the wealth and industry of its colonies in the Netherlands.

The danger presented by Spain, with its wealth and military power, was enhanced by its familial ties to the Holy Roman Empire. The Empire was created on Christmas Day 800 A.D., when Charlemagne was crowned as the theoretical successor to the Roman Emperor in the West. Over the centuries, the Empire was ruled by a series of Germanic Emperors chosen by "electors." According to Voltaire, it was "neither holy, nor Roman nor an empire." But in the 16th century, it still had significant power.

After 1438, all of the Emperors were from the Austrian Habsburg family. Philip's Austrian great-grandfather, the Habsburg Emperor Maximilian I, skillfully expanded the Empire, through marriage. By his own marriage, Maximilian acquired the rich and strategic Duchy of Burgundy, which included most of the Netherlands. Then, by marrying his son, Philip the Fair, to the Spanish Infanta, he acquired the riches of Spain. The phrase "Tu, felix Austria, nube" became famous, meaning that, while others fight wars to gain territory, "you, happy Austria, marry."

On Maximilian's death, his grandson, Charles V, became Holy Roman Emperor and King of Spain. Charles was the son of Philip the Fair and "Mad Juana," the insane older sister of Catherine of Aragon, Henry VIII's first queen. Thus, the Emperor was Catherine's nephew. But Charles was perfectly sane; and he ruled for almost 40 years over a vast panoply of European lands.

In 1556, however, Charles abdicated, and, in effect, divided the Empire. The Germanic electors found his son, Philip, unacceptable as Emperor. Already acting as Regent in Spain, Philip was simply "too Spanish." So Charles carved out Spain, Sicily and the low countries (today's Belgium, Holland and Luxembourg) for Philip.

The balance of the Empire (essentially, today's Germany, Austria, Northern Italy and Hungary) went to Charles' brother, Ferdinand, who, being acceptable, was "elected" Holy Roman Emperor. Charles retired to a monastery, where he died three years later. Despite the territorial division, ties of blood and religion between Spain and the Empire created a continuing and powerful alliance that threatened the interests of both France and England.

Throughout Elizabeth's reign, the Spanish were militarily strong; and, when Mary's husband, Philip, already King of Spain, made himself King of Portugal, the addition of the powerful and competently led Portuguese fleet established Spain as a threatening naval power as well.

Fortunately for England, much of Philip's concern was with his arch-rival, France. Spain and the Empire were engaged in fierce competition with France for European domination. This led to shifting alliances, frequent wars and numerous, often meaningless treaties. At one point, the French king, seeking to get the better of his rivals, even forged an alliance with the Islamic Ottoman Empire, whose forces periodically threatened Hungary, Austria and other ports of Europe. This constant state of European tension was to play a critical part in Elizabeth's strategic thinking and even her approach to marriage.

The French always posed a serious threat. They had far greater wealth than England and many times the number of men available to fight. Those forces were led by able and experienced commanders. In addition, an underlying enmity had existed for centuries between the English and French. The English had humiliated the French at Crecy, Poitiers, Honfleur and Agincourt. The French had turned the tables at Orléans and Calais.

During Elizabeth's reign, however, much of France's strength was sapped by vicious and destructive religious wars. From the 1550s on, the Protestant Huguenots were persecuted, and a fierce rivalry ensued between the ferociously Catholic Guise family and the Protestant Princes of Condé and Navarre, who were allied with the Protestant Admiral Gaspard de Coligny. Nevertheless, France continued to be a serious concern to the English, particularly through strong French influence in Scotland.

Scotland had long had a close relationship with France. French advisors and, from time to time, even French troops were there, just north of the English border, where they could mount an invasion that could be difficult to resist. French influence in Scotland was particularly threatening because of Mary Stuart and her mother.

Mary Stuart was born on December 8, 1542. Her father was King James V of Scotland, the son of Henry VIII's sister Margaret. Her mother was Mary of Guise, a sister of the Duke of Guise, whose militant Catholic family held vast power in France. Just six days after Mary's birth, the Scottish King died suddenly, and his newborn daughter became Queen of Scotland. The nation, of course, was ruled by a Regent. Ultimately, the Regent was Mary of Guise, with her close ties to France and the Guise family.

Mary Stuart was raised as a Catholic. When only five, she was sent to the French court, betrothed to the Dauphin, the heir to the French throne. Later, she married this weak young man, who was briefly King of France as François II. On his early death, Mary returned to Scotland, where she was a continuing source of trouble.

Being legitimate and the grandchild of Henry VIII's sister, the Scottish Queen was a direct descendant of both Henry VII and Edward IV, giving her a colorable claim to the English throne. She openly asserted that claim, even gracing her dinner plates with a coat of arms showing her as Queen of England.

French diplomats sought to pressure the Pope to declare Elizabeth illegitimate and Mary Stuart the true Queen of England. This threatening move was blocked by Philip of Spain, who exercised his significant influence with the Pope to keep pro-French Mary Stuart off the English throne. But Philip's position could change at any time; and the dangers posed by the Scots and their queen continued.

And, there was always the problem of Ireland. During Elizabeth's reign, the troublesome Irish, who had never embraced the Church of England, were turning from their ancient, "pagan" beliefs to Catholicism. Much of this was brought about by the efforts of dedicated missionary priests sent to Ireland from Spain and Rome.

A brilliant Irish military leader would arise during Elizabeth's reign. This was Hugh O'Neill, the Earl of Tyrone. For a time Tyrone would seem invincible, defeating one English general after another.

The danger of Spain striking at England through Ireland, rather than from the Channel, was always there, much like the danger of the French striking through Scotland. Toward the end of Elizabeth's reign, the Spanish actually landed thousands of troops in Ireland, seeking to join with the Irish in an attack on England.

Finally, there was the continuing problem of the Netherlands, an area critically important to English commerce. England had sheep in abundance. The Netherlands did not. The English exported wool to the Netherlands, where it was made into cloth that was exported back to England, where it was made into finished goods. The process was profitable to both regions.

In 1551, the seventeen provinces of the Netherlands, long a part of Burgundy, came under Spanish rule. For administrative convenience, Philip's father, Charles II, molded these disparate provinces into a single unit. It was a serious error.

Discontent arose in the newly-formed entity, primarily based on the desire for religious reform, but also because Spain imposed a highly unpopular sales tax. The ringleaders of the unified provinces who petitioned the Spanish king for relief were ridiculed as "beggars," a jibe that came back to haunt the Spanish. Totally unwilling to grant the requested reforms, Philip began a campaign of severe repression, led by the Spanish Duke of Alba. Two of the three ringleaders were publicly beheaded, after which Alba proudly shipped their heads to Philip in Spain.

The third of the "beggars," William of Orange, survived. Under his leadership, the people rebelled against Spanish rule. The provinces in the south, as well as the north, erupted in violence. Highly skilled Dutch seamen, joined by enterprising English sailors, called themselves the "Sea Beggars" and successfully attacked Spanish ships. The Spanish vengeance was ferocious.

The ten southern provinces of the Netherlands were always more inclined to Catholicism, although even many Catholics opposed Spanish repression. Ultimately, the southern provinces made peace with Spain. The seven northern provinces were primarily Protestant, although it was the Calvinist form of Protestantism, rather than the form that prevailed in England. The northern provinces continued the fight against Spanish domination, sometimes with the assistance of the French and sometimes the English. But it was not until 1648, decades after Elizabeth's death, that the Dutch finally won their independence and went on to maritime, financial and, generally, political success.

* * * * *

But all of this lay in the future. The fantastic reign of Elizabeth was just beginning. Characteristically, she began it with a prayer of thanksgiving, one that, repeated in full, gives us insight into the thoughts and feelings of the new young queen. It also shows us that she could be somewhat immodest and quite loquacious, even in addressing God.

Eternal God, creator and Accomplisher of all things, and the same most merciful Father to those who are faithful to Thee, when I think how of late I was altogether nothing — without body, without soul, without life, without sense or any understanding — and when I think that at this point I was as clay in the hands of the potter, so that by Thy will Thou mightst make me a vessel of honor or of disgrace, Thou hast willed me to be not some wretched girl from the meanest rank of the common people, who would pass her life miserably in poverty and squalor, but to a kingdom Thou has destined me, born of royal parents and nurtured and educated at court. When I was surrounded and thrown about by various snares of enemies, Thou has preserved me with Thy constant protection from prison and the most extreme danger; and though I was free only at the very last moment, Thou hast entrusted me on earth with royal sovereignty and majesty.

Beyond this, indeed, when I consider how many — not only from among the common people but also from nobility as well as royal blood, by Thy hidden but just judgment — some are miserably deformed in body, other (more miserably by far) disordered in their mind and reason, and finally how many were and are, even today, insane and raging. Indeed, I am unimpaired in body, with a good form, a healthy and substantial wit, prudence even beyond other women, and beyond this, distinguished and superior in the knowledge and use of literature and languages, which is highly esteemed because unusual in my sex. Finally I have been endowed with all royal qualities and with gifts worthy of a kingdom, and have been given these freely by Thee. I perceive how much I owe to Thy goodness, most merciful Father, for other things that are from Thee, even though of these other things I have not at all been deserving beforehand.

At least in London, the public quickly embraced the new young queen. As one observer wrote, "If ever any person had either the gift or the style to win the hearts of people, it was this Queen . . . All her faculties were in motion, and every motion seemed a well-guided action: her eye was set upon one, her ear listened to another, her judgment ran upon a third, to a fourth she addressed her speech; her spirit seemed to be everywhere, and yet so entire in herself as it seemed to be nowhere else."

But winning hearts was one thing. Managing a complex and troubled nation was another. Elizabeth quickly set about the business of governing. It has been said that she ruled as her father had. It was really not so. Elizabeth may have idolized her father, but she styled herself after no one. From the outset, she intended to be an absolute monarch. Philip's envoy reported that, "She is determined to be governed by no one." But she had considerably more humanity and subtlety than Henry and was far less vindictive. She was, from beginning to end, her own unique person. She adopted as her motto "Semper Eadem", "Always the same." This does not mean she never changed her mind. She did, and often. I will explore in a later chapter whether that was capriciousness, deliberate policy or a little of each. But, whatever the cause, even her changes of mind were distinctively Elizabeth, not an imitation of anyone.

At this time, the monarch governed through the Privy Council, although, constitutionally, she was not bound by its decisions or recommendations. The Council advised the monarch on foreign and domestic policy and was the principal administrative body charged with promulgating the royal policies and decrees throughout the realm and seeing that those policies and decrees were carried out.

When Elizabeth took the throne she faced what may have seemed insurmountable problems. The treasury was empty, the coinage was debased and generally unacceptable. The morale of the nation was low, Calais had been lost to the French, and England faced potential enemies everywhere – France, Spain, the Empire, Scotland, even Ireland. There was no standing army, no experienced commanders and only a pitiful navy. The threat of religious strife clouded every decision. And the Queen was young – and unmarried.

But she was Elizabeth. Within 48 hours of her accession, Elizabeth designated her new Councilors. She reduced the size of the Council from the more than the thirty who served Mary to twenty. As she put it, "a multitude doth make rather disorder and confusion than good council." She had seen that proven in the case of Mary's fractious advisors. She did not reappoint nineteen of Mary's councilors who were unbending Catholics. There were, however, Catholics among the eleven members who were reappointed and among the nine who were newly appointed. Still, the majority were now Protestant. Later, still seeking a more efficient and less contentious body, Elizabeth reduced the number of councilors to twelve.

One of the new Council members was Sir Francis Knollys. He was married to Mary Boleyn's daughter, Catherine, who, on Elizabeth's accession, had returned from her voluntary exile on the Continent. Even before her coronation, Elizabeth ennobled Catherine's brother, Henry Carey, making him Lord Hunsdon. She then appointed him Governor of Berwick and granted him valuable manors and lands. Later, he was made a Knight of the Garter. As we have seen, both Catherine Knollys and the new Lord Hunsdon were probably the children of Henry VIII and thus half siblings of Elizabeth, who probably knew it.

At Elizabeth's direction, her Council was to meet daily to consider the issues of the day. But the new queen made it clear from the start that it was she who ruled the realm, not they. As Philip's envoy expressed it, she "gave her orders and had her way absolutely as her father did," and she was "incomparably more feared" than her sister Mary.

In the sense of "fear" generated by her quick temper and changeability, that may have been true. But she was hardly the kind of "off with his head" monarch her father had been. She almost surely read Machiavelli's *The Prince* in which he asks whether it is better for a ruler to be feared than loved. Perhaps Elizabeth believed the ruler should be both, although Machiavelli concluded that, if the ruler must choose, it was "safer" to be feared.

Certainly, however, in dealing with her Council, Elizabeth tended to use manipulation more than fear. She would listen to their advice — then decide for herself or, as often occurred, postpone the decision, particularly if it was a complex and difficult matter involving serious risks. One tactic she used to delay and retain control was to end a session with a long, ambiguous pronouncement, leaving her Councilors uncertain as to what she really intended and dependent on her future decision. She also tried to avoid situations in which her Council might be unanimously against her by skillfully playing these ambitious, prideful men against each other.

Immediately upon her accession, Elizabeth appointed her advisor, Sir William Cecil, to the key post of Principal Secretary. Prior to the reign of Henry VIII, that position was not particularly important. The Principal Secretary drafted the monarch's correspondence, but had little function beyond that. Henry's brilliant and aggressive Secretary, Thomas Cromwell, changed all that. He expanded the office in many areas to include wide reaching involvement in both foreign and domestic affairs, including reorganization of the English Church.

During Elizabeth's reign, the Principal Secretary was not only effective head of the Privy Council, he played an active role in many diverse areas of governance, including foreign policy and economic issues, as well as the security of the queen and the realm.

While Cecil is often described as having formerly been the steward of Elizabeth's properties, he was hardly some bucolic farm manager. Cecil attended Cambridge, where he was a contemporary of Roger Ascham and a pupil of John Cheke, both tutors of Elizabeth. Cecil studied law at Gray's Inn and began a career at the bar. Later, he developed valuable experience in government, serving as secretary to the Duke of Somerset, Edward VI's Protector. He showed sufficient skill in that office to be appointed Secretary of State. Even when Somerset was removed, and Northumberland ruled in the name of the boy-king, Cecil continued to serve.

On Edward's death, Cecil appeared at first to support Jane Grey's claim to the throne. Always a pragmatist, however, he switched his allegiance to Mary in time to be on the winning side. Although he purported to conform to Mary's religious views, she was evidently not convinced and did not reappoint him Secretary. Despite his suspect views on religion, however, Mary did recognize Cecil's abilities, and selected him for important diplomatic missions. During her reign, he also served as a member of Parliament.

By the time of Elizabeth's accession, Cecil had an excellent working knowledge of every aspect of the English government. He had managed Elizabeth's properties, but it was strictly a part-time occupation. It is likely that both of them had been focused on the future, and that weeks or even months before Mary's death, they had engaged in planning the governance that would soon be theirs.

With Elizabeth on the throne, Cecil could be open about his true religious beliefs. He was a staunch Protestant, married to a Puritan. His fundamentally anti-Catholic views strongly influenced his decisions.

Like Thomas Cromwell before him, Cecil faced the problem of his common birth. The peers on the Council considered him beneath them and tended to resent his power. Later, Elizabeth tried to remedy this by ennobling him as Lord Burghley and making him a Knight of the Garter. Still, some peers continued to think of him as a parvenu. Despite this impediment, he served Elizabeth faithfully and skillfully for many years, first as Principal Secretary, then as Lord Treasurer, which was considered an office of even greater importance.

Cecil's choice of wives sheds further light on this extraordinary man. His first wife was the sister of the noted scholar, John Cheke. His second wife was described by Roger Ascham as England's most learned woman.

The Queen's judgment on Cecil is summarized by her words on first appointing him Principal Secretary. "This judgment I have of you, that you will not be corrupted with any manner of gift, and that you will be favorable to the state and that, with respect of my private will, you will give me that counsel that you think best." A good case can be made that, over many years, he always did just that.

There were many positions to be filled besides that of Principal Secretary; and Elizabeth moved quickly to fill them. Working with Cecil, she filled almost every important post within four days of her accession.

The other part of English government was, of course, Parliament. It already consisted of the House of Commons and the House of Lords. Theoretically, it was the voice of the people, but it was not the functioning legislative body we think of today. It was not until the later reign of Charles I that Parliament began to exercise truly effective political power.

With respect to the Commons, Elizabeth somewhat departed from tradition. In previous reigns, the monarch had generally exerted pressure through local officials to control the candidates elected to the Commons. Elizabeth varied from that policy, generally resulting in a Commons more reflective of the views of their constituents — at least those constituents whose position or wealth qualified them to participate in selecting members of Parliament. This gave the queen something of a window into the views of her subjects. She had no legal obligation to keep the public happy, but she certainly recognized the importance of doing so.

Keeping the public happy required the deft handling of religious issues. Would Elizabeth bring the nation back to the Protestantism of her brother? Mary was given a traditional Catholic funeral, but that seemed only fitting. As was the custom, the officers of Mary's government broke their ceremonial batons of office and threw the pieces into Mary's grave. The dramatic gesture signified an end and a new beginning. Would the change extend to the nation's religion?

Elizabeth immediately put a halt to the burning of Protestants. She released the Protestants who had been imprisoned awaiting that fate. She did not immediately alter the nation's established religion from Catholicism, but she gradually moved in that direction. Establishing Protestantism at once as the official religion of the realm would have been too radical and sudden a change. It could have caused the Pope to call for her overthrow in favor of Mary Stuart, which, in turn, could have caused the French king to invade in support of Mary's claim. It could also have jeopardized Elizabeth's relationship with Philip; and it would certainly have antagonized the multitude of her own subjects who considered themselves Catholic.

The royal chapel did return to the English litany, and the English Bible. But, at the beginning, the rites were not fundamentally changed. In initially listing her titles, Elizabeth did not include, as her father had, "Supreme Head of the Church." The world was watching, and the last thing the new queen wanted was war with the Catholic powers or an uprising of her many Catholic subjects. Her intention was to re-establish the Protestant religion, but to do it gradually, remaining tolerant of Catholics so long as they remained loyal and practiced their religion in private.

For a time, Elizabeth continued saying mass. But, only weeks after Mary's death, Bishop Oglethorpe, conducting mass in the Royal Chapel, held the holy wafer or Host on high in the traditional Catholic manner, signifying Christ's "Real Presence." The doctrine of "transubstantiation" was one about which Elizabeth felt strongly. She, like most Protestants, believed that the concept defied logic and that the bread and wine were merely symbolic.

To Catholics, when Oglethorpe raised the "Host" and held it on high, Christ was there in the room to be worshipped. Elizabeth could not abide that idea. She spoke out, interrupting the service and ordering the Bishop to lower the Host. When he continued to hold it on high, the queen rose and, with obvious disapproval, left the Chapel.

And it was not only the "Real Presence" that Elizabeth opposed. Other symbols of the old religion could give her displeasure as well. Entering Westminster Abbey before the opening of her first Parliament, Elizabeth was greeted by the Abbot and a traditional procession of Benedictine monks carrying lighted candles. The new queen shouted "Away with those torches! We can see well enough."

Gradually, Elizabeth adopted the practices of the reformed Anglican Church. By May of 1559, services in the Royal Chapel were conducted in English, rather than Latin. A month later, Parliament decreed that England was no longer subject to the Pope, repealed Mary's draconian heresy laws and, by the Act of Supremacy, designated Elizabeth "Supreme Governor" of the English Church.

"Supreme Head" was deemed too much for a woman to claim.

By the Act of Uniformity, a somewhat revised Protestant *Book of Common Prayer* became a legal requirement throughout the realm. This substituted the Protestant communion service for the Catholic mass, while deleting the language abusing the Pope that had been part of that service during young Edward's reign. Relics and rosary beads were gone, as were the images of saints and martyrs. The Holy Chalice was no longer reserved for the priest.

Still, Elizabeth retained candlesticks and a crucifix on the altar of the Royal Chapel. And the clergy continued to wear the copes and surplices of a Catholic past. This reflected Elizabeth's "middle way" in religious matters. She favored Protestantism, but chose the form of Protestantism closest to Catholic practice. And she could be touchy on the subject. During a sermon before a large congregation, the Protestant Dean of St. Paul's spoke out against Catholic idolatry. Apparently believing this was a reference to her personal crucifix, Elizabeth interrupted the sermon, calling out loudly, "Do not talk about that . . . leave that out!"

Still, she was quite different from her father or her sister on the issue of punishing those who disagreed with her. When Parliament passed a bill imposing the death penalty on anyone who refused more than once to take the Oath of Supremacy, Elizabeth simply directed that no one should be asked a second time.

Once Elizabeth took the throne, the question of reestablishing her legitimacy arose. She decided against calling attention to the issue. As Nicholas Bacon, her Lord Keeper, put it, the "Crowne, once worne, taketh away all defects whatsoever." He was right, and Elizabeth agreed.

Elizabeth's proficiency in languages gave her a distinct advantage over many of her predecessors. Very few foreign ambassadors spoke English. Often they had to be dealt with by intermediaries, who could speak with them in a common language. But Elizabeth could deal with them directly, employing her fluent Latin, Greek, French and Italian.

One serious and continuing problem was that, despite her coronation, Elizabeth was not the only claimant to the throne. As we have seen, her cousin, Mary Stuart, openly claimed to be the rightful Queen of England, on the ground that Elizabeth was illegitimate. Mary and her young French husband had even adopted the title "Francis and Mary, by the Grace of God, King and Queen of Scotland, England and Ireland."

While the English Queen Mary lay dying, there had been negotiations with the French over the fallen city of Calais. After her death, documents vitally important to the English representatives were somehow missing. In a bizarre episode, the undertakers had used the long rolls of parchment to wrap her corpse.

The momentum of the negotiations slowed, but Elizabeth finally concluded a peace treaty with the French in April 1559. It did not give Calais back to England, but the French promised to give it back in eight years or to pay the English 500,000 crowns compensation. While containing a theoretical return of Calais, the treaty was, in reality, a sale of the city to France for half a million crowns. In the end, even that was not paid. Mary Stuart and her French husband refused to sign the treaty; and they were now King and Queen of France. In 1559, when Henri II, an energetic and effective ruler, died of a horrible head wound incurred in a joust, Mary's fifteen-year-old husband became King François II. Now, Mary's claim to the English throne seemed particularly ominous.

With the French still holding Calais and Mary Stuart on the French throne, there seemed a realistic threat of a French invasion. The Scots had long been allied with the French, and, once again, French troops were stationed in Scotland. Mary Stuart's mother, Mary of Guise, a militant Catholic, ruled as Regent of Scotland in her daughter's absence. She relied heavily on French advisors and was protected by the French soldiers. Indeed, it would not be an exaggeration to describe Mary of Guise as a proxy for her powerful family then dominant in France.

There were Scottish Protestant rebels called "The Congregation"; but they seemed unable to prevail against the French troops protecting the Regent. Worse still, the French appeared ready to land thousands of additional troops in Scotland. That army was likely to crush The Congregation, and then to pour over the border into the north of England, where Catholic sentiment was strongest.

Gathering strength there, it could push on to London and put Mary Stuart on the English throne.

The new Queen of England had a card to play, but a dangerous one. She could call upon the Spanish to stand in the way of French designs. Philip, still friendly to Elizabeth and staunchly opposed to French hegemony, might have been ready to help. To Philip, putting Mary Stuart on the English throne would effectively unite France, England and Scotland, creating a powerful and perhaps unbeatable alliance. This would vastly increase French power at the expense of Spain. Just supplying his colonies in the Netherlands would require Philip to sail up the Channel between two hostile shores and two hostile navies.

But, if Philip was ready to intervene on Elizabeth's side, there would have been a price. It would probably have included Philip's continued influence in England, the return of Catholicism as the established religion, as well as money and men to aid Philip's military adventures, including those in the Netherlands, where English commercial interests favored Dutch independence, not Spanish or French domination.

The handling of this early crisis was an example of Elizabeth's extraordinary skill in balancing the power of France against that of Spain, deciding whether and where to send English troops into foreign wars and, at all times, successfully dissembling.

Elizabeth was almost always opposed to foreign military adventures, and this was no exception. She was reluctant to send English troops openly across the Scottish border. That could start a disastrous, full-scale war with the French. Instead, she quietly sent money and even some men to aid the Scottish Congregation, vehemently denying that this was with her knowledge or approval. The men were "volunteers," she claimed, not sent by her; and, as to the money, who knew its source? Money could come from anywhere. She claimed she had neither written to The Congregation nor given them anything.

If that charade was to be successful, secrecy was essential. Cecil wrote his letters to the Lords of The Congregation by hand, avoiding even dictation to clerks. The truth was even kept from the more conservative members of the Council. Elizabeth steadfastly maintained the fiction that English aid to The Congregation was the work of independent, uncontrollable hotheads. The Scottish Ambassador who, at first, had accepted Elizabeth's protestations, soon concluded that she was creating a clever fiction. "There is more dissimulation in her than honesty and good will," he reported. "She is the best hand at the game."

Ultimately, Elizabeth solved the immediate Scottish problem without having to call on Spanish aid. First, she sent a young Admiral, William Winter, to lead an English fleet into the Firth of Forth. Winter sank a large number of French ships carrying men and supplies to the French troops supporting the Regent. Then, he successfully established a blockade that prevented re-supplying the French troops, or at least made it far more difficult and dangerous.

Of course, Elizabeth told the French that even Winter acted on his own. And Winter corroborated her claim. The French did not believe this. Neither did the Regent, Mary of Guise. She wrote, "The disguise is too transparent — as if a simple subject and officer should have the inclination, and still more the power, to make war without the will and express orders of the Queen." But as long as Elizabeth kept up the charade, at least there was no patent *casus belli* that forced the French to declare war as a matter of honor.

Finally, however, Elizabeth agreed to send an English army openly across the border. War fever spread through the realm. Every day, Elizabeth could be seen mounted, riding among the London recruits, shouting encouragement as they trained for combat.

Ultimately, the English and their Scottish allies forced the French out of Scotland. In part, this was due to the death of the Regent, Mary Stuart's mother. An implacable foe, she had been stubbornly holding out in Leith Castle. Just when the English seemed about to abandon their attempts to conquer the castle, the Regent unexpectedly died, possibly the victim of poisoning — but by whom? An anti-French Scot? An English spy? We do not know.

In 1560, with Mary of Guise dead, and the Lords of The Congregation in control, the Scots and the English signed the Treaty of Edinburgh. This called for the ouster of almost all French troops from Scotland, the recognition of Elizabeth's right to the English throne and the pledge that Mary Stuart would relinquish her claim to that throne. In France and married to the French king, Mary refused to accept that pledge.

Despite Mary's refusal, Elizabeth had achieved a major success. It was her first in the world of international politics, but it was impressive; and her reputation abroad began to grow.

Now, the Scottish Parliament, firmly in the hands of The Congregation, ended the authority of the Pope in Scotland, adopted the Protestant communion service and forbad the saying of Catholic mass.

In December 1560, only months after the Treaty of Edinburgh, Mary Stuart's husband, the young French king, died. He was succeeded by a minor, Charles IX, whose mother, Catherine de Medici, replaced the Guise family as the power behind the throne. After twelve years in France, the newly widowed Mary Stuart, still young and still dangerous, returned to Scotland.

Mary asked Elizabeth for a guarantee of safe conduct in passing through England on her way. Elizabeth conditioned the grant on Mary's ratifying the Treaty of Edinburgh, renouncing her claim to the English throne. Mary angrily refused. Ultimately, Elizabeth relented and prepared to guarantee Mary's safe conduct without condition. But, a determined Mary had already sailed for Scotland, where her dramatic and troublesome life would continue.

* * * * *

At this point, I'll pause to view the routine of Elizabeth's personal life now that she was queen. Her days began in the early morning when her Ladies of the Bedchamber drew back the heavy curtains that surrounded the royal bed.

These ladies and the Ladies of the Privy Chamber were typically members of the leading English families and close friends of the queen. They were supervised by the Queen's Mistress of the Robes. Elizabeth was also "aided" by six young and generally attractive girls of good lineage. These were her "Maids of Honor." They were of some help, but, basically, they were decoration. They were frequently a source of trouble, particularly when they found themselves unable to resist the advances of sexually aggressive male courtiers.

These, of course, were a small part of the positions at the queen's disposal. Out of some fifteen hundred people that made up the royal household, over 100 significant posts were assigned by the queen to persons of aristocratic or gentle birth. Most of these positions went to men. Some were, of course, far more important than others; and there was fierce competition for the prestigious appointments. During much of the year, the holders of the principal offices resided at court. The lesser office holders typically dined there, but resided elsewhere. The salaries that historically went with household and governmental positions were low; but they could be supplemented by rich perquisites and gifts from the Crown and, all too often, by receiving bribes or incurring debts.

Typically, when Elizabeth was in the Capitol, she resided in the Whitehall or St. James' Palaces. Often, however, she stayed at the palaces her father had fancied at Greenwich or Richmond. Occasionally, she spent time at Nonesuch Palace or Hampton Court.

In the summer months, the Queen went on progress. These were extended visits to various parts of the realm that allowed her subjects to see and interact with her. She was accompanied on these trips by an army of courtiers and servants, as well as hundreds of heavily laden carts.

On these massive, slow moving excursions, Elizabeth stayed at the homes of peers, who were expected to supply food, drink and entertainment for the entire company at enormous personal expense. In addition, they were expected to provide an extravagant gift for the queen.

Elizabeth and her most important courtiers would reside at the host's estate. Accommodations for countless others had to be found at local inns and other suitable homes. This, in itself, was an enormous and difficult job. Neither the hosts, nor the courtiers accompanying the queen enjoyed this expensive and exhausting process. But Elizabeth considered it essential; and, in one sense, it was a vacation for her. While on progress, she refused to receive the representatives of suitors or the countless petitioners who otherwise took so much of her time advancing a marriage proposal or seeking a royal favor.

Cecil (later Lord Burghley) and Robin Dudley (later Lord Leicester), each of whom ultimately owned vast and luxurious country estates, rivaled each other in entertaining the queen with extraordinary spectacles and lavish hospitality. If Burghley provided something to amaze and delight the queen at Theobolds, his estate, Leicester would strive to outdo him at Kenilworth, his own massive and splendid estate.

Wherever she was residing, once Elizabeth rose, she embarked on the elaborate routine of her personal toilette. She washed her hair, using a lye compound and cleaned her teeth by rubbing them thoroughly with a tooth cloth. She then applied her makeup, which was a mixture of egg white, borax, alum and poppy seed, prepared with ground alabaster.

After rinsing with a pungent mouthwash and sparingly applying a marjoram-based perfume, she was ready for her undergarments, petticoats, gowns and jewels. Fully dressed and perfumed, Elizabeth breakfasted on beef and ale, after which she began the transaction of state business.

When at one of her royal palaces, Elizabeth handled most business in her Privy Chamber. Here, she received letters and messages, dictated replies, signed orders and made decisions on scores of varied issues. Meetings of the Council were held in the Council Chamber, except, of course, on progress. The Queen would hold court and greet foreign emissaries and others with formal business in the large Presence Chamber. Any gentleman could attend the Presence Chamber; but admission to the Privy Chamber was limited to a chosen few.

After the morning's business, if the weather was good, Elizabeth would often join in the hunt, an activity she adored. She would typically be accompanied by her Master of the Horse, who would ride beside or behind her. She enjoyed exercise; and, when she was unable to hunt, she would walk in the gardens or, if the weather was inclement, in the long galleries of the Palace.

Later in the day, the Queen would usually indulge her passion for reading, devouring books not only in English, but frequently in Latin, Greek, French or Italian. Sometimes, her old tutor, Roger Ascham, would read Latin or Greek with her, once reporting that she read more Greek in a day than an educated priest would read Latin in a week.

Dinner was usually served around three in the afternoon. Supper was around six. Elizabeth would rarely eat publicly in the Presence Chamber, preferring to dine in private with friends in the Privy Chamber, followed by music, cards or just conversation.

When the Queen tired, she would signal to her guests that they should leave. She would then retire to her bedchamber accompanied by her ladies. All the additions of the morning would be removed. She would retire to the royal bed, and the heavy curtains would once again be drawn around her.

* * * * *

As we have seen, Elizabeth carried out her plan gradually to re-establish the Protestant Church of England. She stopped all pretense of being Catholic. But she did this slowly. She sought to avoid antagonizing her numerous Catholic subjects, as well as the Catholic powers in Europe before she was ready to defend her realm and her crown. Even after she changed the established religion, she generally followed a policy of tolerance toward Catholics who secretly practiced their religion, so long as they faithfully attended Protestant services and gave the outward appearance of adherence to the English Church. As she put it, she had no intention of creating "a window into men's souls."

But Cecil feared that Catholics would not view Elizabeth as moderate and that, between Catholic activists and foreign agents, Elizabeth was in danger. One such danger was perceived to be poison in her food or even in her clothing. In 1561, just three years after Elizabeth's accession, Cecil wrote her that "Your majesty's apparel, and especially all manner of things that shall touch any part of your majesty's body bare, be circumspectly looked into and that no person be permitted to come near it but shall have the trust and charge thereof . . . that no foreign meat or dishes being dressed out of your majesty's court be brought to your food without assured knowledge from whom the same cometh." Elizabeth paid little attention.

Later, in 1570, Elizabeth was excommunicated and theoretically "deposed" by the Pope. The papal bull not only freed Catholics to kill Elizabeth without committing a sin, it could be construed as obligating them to do so. Most English Catholics, however, were uncomfortable with any such obligation and tried to reach a different conclusion as to the bull's meaning. Nevertheless, given that potentially lethal command from the Pope and other threatening developments, Elizabeth's attitudes hardened.

What were those other developments? Dedicated English priests, trained in Douai or Rome, returned to England and secretly spread out across the country seeking to rally the religious fervor of closet Catholics and to convert others to the "True Church." They hid in Catholic homes and were fiercely hunted by the government, since their conduct was now against English law.

The seminary at Douai was run by and trained Englishmen. That seminary alone sent one hundred priests into England. Many others came from the seminary in Rome. And they were successful. They created a resurgence of Catholicism throughout the realm. Some of the militant priests were caught, tortured and executed, principally at the direction of Francis Walsingham, a dedicated Protestant in charge of Elizabeth's security. This was the fate of Edmund Campion, a brave and scholarly priest, who was respected by Elizabeth, although, as discussed in a later chapter, her respect did not save his life. Centuries later, Campion, like Thomas More, was made a saint.

Although Elizabeth tended to deplore extremism in religious matters, she could and did authorize the imposition of harsh measures in dealing with radical Catholics who schemed to replace her with Mary Stuart. Generally, however, despite the resurgence of English Catholicism, the Pope's excommunication and the horrors of the religious wars in France, Elizabeth was reluctant to take draconian measures in dealing with her Catholic subjects.

But Catholics were not the only religious extremists in the land. Early in Elizabeth's reign, there were Protestants who railed loudly against every aspect of Catholicism. They wanted the Church to be "pure," free from every aspect, every hint of the old religion they despised. They were "Puritans."

Throughout her reign, Elizabeth faced a powerful Puritan movement. Its leaders were determined to eliminate all vestiges of Catholicism, such as the Bishops and clerical vestments that remained a part of the Anglican Church. They preached the need for regular study of the Bible, a constant search for "godliness" and the elimination or shunning of many pleasurable activities. Most important to Elizabeth, they wanted a Church governed by committee, not by the monarch. That was something the queen could never accept.

Elizabeth opposed extremism in both the Puritan and Catholic camps. But, where possible, she preferred to use moderation in dealing with both. It was not always easy. It was not always possible.

The Queen was notoriously reluctant to spend money and typically sought to avoid costly and dangerous foreign conflicts. Generally, her policy was to avoid war and seek peace. She sent troops to fight in Scotland, Ireland, the Netherlands and France, as well as naval forces to conduct raids in Spain and expeditionary forces to Portugal. But she did so reluctantly and only under the most pressing circumstances, often seeming to change her mind as to the proper course of action.

She encouraged English raiders to prey on the rich Spanish galleons carrying gold and jewels from the New World. This was a way to deter Spanish military adventures by denying Spain the funds it needed for those adventures. It also increased badly needed English capital. To Elizabeth, this was preferable to wasting that capital in costly military campaigns.

This policy created a risk of pushing the Spanish to the point at which they might attack. But Cecil and Elizabeth weighed that risk and considered it likely that, as long as the French remained the major threat to Spanish interests, Philip's finances remained shaky and pro-French Mary Stuart remained Elizabeth's likely successor, Spain would probably try to avoid a war against England.

When Sir Francis Drake returned from circumnavigating the globe, his ship was laden with silver and gems taken from the Spanish. His investors, including the queen herself, reaped an enormous profit.

Elizabeth's reign was not all conflict and crisis. Her court was enlivened with music, drama and dance. The Queen loved and wrote poetry, but was especially fond of plays, a taste shared by her subjects. The public theatre began its meteoric rise in her reign. James Burbage obtained a license to operate the first public theatre. In 1576, he cleared land in Shoreditch outside the walls of London and built "The Theatre." It proved so popular that an imitation, "The Curtain" was soon built nearby. Nine years later, "The Rose" was built on Bankside opposite St. Paul's. Later, came "The Swan" nearby, as well as the now famous "Globe" and Henslowe and Alleyn's "The Fortune." Although theatres were considered disreputable and actors generally considered rogues, legend has it that Elizabeth disguised herself and attended the public theatre. Possibly, but she had no need to. The plays of Shakespeare and other dramatists were frequently presented at court.

Elizabeth could be formal and strict. Yet she had a wry wit. Even at her coronation, when she was about to be anointed with the holy oil, she called the process a "great superstition" but added that it would be "very good for salads." When the Earl of Oxford loudly broke wind while kneeling before the queen, he was so mortified that he left the country for a long stay on the Continent. When he finally returned and nervously knelt before Elizabeth, she told him not to be hesitant, adding, with a grin, "I've completely forgotten the fart."

In her relationships with those who were close — or as close as one could be to the queen, she was inclined to be teasingly informal. She had nicknames for them. Robin Dudley was "Eyes." Christopher Hatton was "Mutton." Dark complected Walsingham was the "Moor." Burghley was "Spirit," and his son, Robert Cecil, the hunchback genius she deeply respected, was (perhaps insensitively) called "Pigmy." Lady Norris was "Crow," Lady Hertford was "Francke" and the Queen's favorite cleric, Bishop Whitgift, was affectionately dubbed her "black husband."

Elizabeth could be a nurturing friend. She wrote moving letters to Lady Norris when her sons were killed in battle and to Lady Hertford urging her not to fear needlessly when her husband was imprisoned in the Tower. And, when the Earl of Huntingdon suddenly died, she ordered his death kept secret until Elizabeth herself could break the news to his widow and comfort her.

The Queen was always concerned about disruptive personal issues affecting the lives of her courtiers. She sought to keep herself fully informed about such matters, even when they were of a private nature. For example, when she learned that Edward Stanley, the Earl of Derby, was unhappy with his aristocratic third wife, Elizabeth let him know her feelings at characteristic length:

> We greet you well. Hearing sundry wise of some unkindness or strangeness of late of your part towards your wife, whereof for both your parts we were sorry, and being informed that no matter can be understood by her friends and kinfolks of her desert, but that upon some misliking conceived against her by your children, you should by them be occasioned to deal strangely with her and in other sort than you were accustomed or than is convenient, we, being very sorry to hear of this alteration (considering we know how well you esteemed her and we

ourselves having always had very good estimation of her, both for her good parentage and for her own discreet behavior), cannot, for the favor and goodwill we have to you both, but require you either to restore her to such favor as heretofore you did bear her, without inclining to credit such as of evil will and without just cause shall be disposed to maintain variation betwixt you; or if you shall think her otherwise to have defied, that we or some of our Council may be duly and particularly thereof advertised, to the end her friends may understand how to deal for the answering thereof. Who justly think her to be rather by evil will of others than by yourself touched in her fame, and the fault in them by slandering her to you with obscure speeches and not in her at all by any kind of deserving. And hereof we require you to give us a letter.

Not only was Stanley a powerful northern Lord and a Privy Council member, his family had played a great part in putting Elizabeth's grandfather, Henry VII, on the throne. In 1485, at the Battle of Bosworth Field, they had thrown the Stanley forces into the battle on the Tudor side at the decisive point in the fighting. In doing so, the Stanleys had betrayed Richard III, the reigning king, so that Henry Tudor could take his crown. But, after seventy-five years of Tudor rule and Tudor histories (including Shakespeare's *Richard III*), these facts did not deter Elizabeth from giving Lord Stanley a piece of her mind.

Throughout most of Elizabeth's reign, the most significant issue for the Council, Parliament and the people was the need for Elizabeth to marry and produce an heir or, at least, to name a successor. Should the Queen die without an heir, the probable result would be years of controversy, even civil war. Henry VIII, who was diligent in the matter of naming his successor, told Parliament, "If our true heir be not known at the time of our death, see what mischief and trouble shall succeed to you and your children." Elizabeth's Council was well aware of this danger and continually pressed Elizabeth to marry and produce an heir and, in the interim, to name a successor. The people were also aware of the potential problem and clamored for a royal marriage and royal heir.

Elizabeth told Parliament that she would deal with the question of a successor "in convenient time." In fact, she was probably determined from the start never to name her successor. All of her experience told her of the peril inherent in doing so. She certainly was aware, from the reign of her sister Mary, that the living presence of a designated heir — in that case, Elizabeth herself — was a focal point for rebellion and a constant danger to the reigning monarch.

This can be seen from the experience of other rulers. The King of Sweden was overthrown by his brother who was his heir. Henry III of France imprisoned his brother, the heir, for scheming against him. Mary Stuart was ultimately removed from the Scottish throne and replaced by her infant son. And even the powerful Philip of Spain faced what he believed was a treasonous plot by his son and heir. The power of the throne was often a dangerous temptation to the person next in line to enjoy that power.

Besides, Elizabeth faced a situation in which there were a number of potential claimants to the succession. All of their claims had arguable points and arguable defects. There was, of course, Mary Stuart. But there were also other living descendants of Henry VIII's sisters, Margaret and Mary. There was Henry Hastings, a descendant of Edward III, and there were still others who could mount a potential claim.

To select one of these would not only create the danger of rebellious subjects rallying around the designated successor, but also of earning the enmity of the disappointed candidates, who also had powerful supporters. According to the Scottish Ambassador, Elizabeth herself said, "If it were certainly known in the world who should succeed her, she would never think herself in sufficient surety."

The need for an heir became a more critical issue in 1562, when Elizabeth contracted smallpox, then a serious and life-threatening disease for which physicians had no cure. Even when their patients survived, they were often hideously scarred. Typically, the disease began with a high fever. If the victim survived, the fever abated in a few days. Then, red spots appeared, and these would be replaced by deep pitted scars.

Elizabeth's illness did not follow this typical pattern. Her fever continued to rise and no spots appeared. She was extremely weak and sometimes barely conscious. The physicians and her Council began to fear that she would not survive. Apparently, Elizabeth shared their view. Naturally, discussions turned to potential heirs. Since there was no clear choice, religion was a prime concern. As some of the likely successors were staunch Catholics, the fear of conflict grew.

Finally, however, Elizabeth's fever broke, the red spots appeared and it was plain she would survive. She would have some pockmarks, but none of the disfiguring scars that often followed the disease. Still, the illness had dramatically emphasized the need for an heir. Yet, Elizabeth continued to avoid designating her successor.

Marriage was another matter. Suitors were plentiful, including Philip of Spain and the Habsburg Archduke Charles. Either match would have promoted an English alliance with Spain and the Empire, giving protection against France. Later, the French Duke of Alençon became a likely husband, bringing with him a valuable tie to France to offset the power of Spain and the Empire. There were also Englishmen who considered themselves potential husbands. Notable in this group was Robert Dudley, son of the attainted and executed Duke of Northumberland, who had plotted to put Jane Grey on the throne, having married her to Robert's younger brother, Guilford.

Elizabeth had known Robert Dudley, her "dear Robin", since they were young children. They were born in the same year and were fond of each other from the beginning. As he attained maturity, Dudley became an extremely handsome man, always attractive to women. The queen was no exception. His dark, "dangerous" looks led to his being called "Gypsy," although, to the queen, he remained "Robin" or "Eyes."

Dudley had married Amy Robsart, a minor provincial heiress. Their marriage may not have been a particularly loving one, but, often, upper class marriages of the period were not. Normally, the pair were apart, with Dudley at court and Amy in the country with friends. That was also quite common. Elizabeth discouraged the presence of wives at court. Overcrowding was always a problem, and probably the queen preferred to have the male courtiers to herself — especially the handsome ones.

Robin's marriage to Amy did, however, save his life. When his father, Northumberland, schemed to have one of his sons marry Jane Grey and to place the couple on the throne, Robin was already married. The role of royal bridegroom went to Robin's brother, Guilford, who married Jane, became king for a few days and was then executed. Robin was also imprisoned at the time, along with his three other brothers. Except for Guilford, however, the brothers were released without punishment.

When she became queen, Elizabeth appointed Robin Dudley her Master of the Horse, and he quickly rose to prominence and favor. She made him a Knight of the Garter and gave him at least one very large gift of money. The two were openly affectionate with each other and probably were in love for years. Much of Europe thought they were lovers, as did many of the English. Some writers still think so.

There were persistent rumors that the two would marry, a result viewed with horror by Dudley's numerous enemies. Such talk grew into a major scandal in 1560, just two years into Elizabeth's reign. In September of that year, Robin's wife, Amy, was found dead at the foot of a staircase in a country home. Her neck was broken, and the circumstances were highly suspicious. Dudley was widely suspected of murder, and Elizabeth was rumored to have been complicit in the crime. A local inquest cleared Dudley, but the suspicion and scandal continued, and he remained a highly controversial figure.

For years after his wife's death, Dudley continued scheming to marry Elizabeth. But the suspicion and enmity that surrounded him seriously decreased his chances — if he ever really had any. Nevertheless, Elizabeth continued to treat him with open affection and to shower him with favors. It is doubtful, however, that she ever intended to marry him.

Part Two of this book will analyze whether Elizabeth had a sexual relationship with Robin Dudley, or anyone else, as well as whether his wife was murdered, and, if so, by whom and why.

Christopher Hatton, the handsome captain of the queen's personal bodyguard, wrote her passionate love letters in the fervid, dramatic style of the time. "I love you. I cannot lack you . . . Bear with me most dear sweet lady.

Passion overcometh me. I can write no more. Love me for I love you." Hatton may really have been in love with her; but he swore that he had never been her lover. Although he received many favors from the queen and ultimately was even made Lord Chancellor, Hatton rendered loyal service in all of the positions to which he was assigned. But he was never considered a suitable husband.

Sir Walter Raleigh also became a favorite of the queen. He was handsome and highly intelligent, and Elizabeth enjoyed his company. Like Leicester and Hatton, however, he was probably not considered material for a royal marriage.

Philip of Spain and Archduke Charles were, of course, serious and formidable candidates. Nevertheless, Elizabeth deftly and politely fended off both matches at the appropriate time and in a manner calculated to avoid giving offense.

The Duke of Alençon was another matter. A small, rather ugly, but charming man, he seemed to delight the queen. He became her "Froggy," and their courtship tended to suggest the likelihood of an Anglo-French alliance against Spain. At times, that was just the picture Elizabeth hoped to create. At times, it was not. The idea of an Alençon match seemed to wane.

As Elizabeth continued her diplomatic "dance" with one suitor after another, Mary Stuart's re-marriage became a heated topic of discussion in European courts. With the death of her first husband, the young French king, Mary was a splendid catch, second only to Elizabeth. She was considered quite attractive, with auburn hair and lovely hazel eyes. The fact that she was almost six feet tall — taller than most men and far taller than virtually all women — was not mentioned.

Elizabeth was concerned about an alliance between Scotland and France, or any foreign power brought about by Mary Stuart's marrying a European ruler or prince. For example, she learned, to her dismay, that a match between Mary and Philip's mentally troubled son, Don Carlos, was being discussed. That match, creating the possibility of a Spanish-Scottish alliance, would have been a disaster for England. It would also have been a bad choice personally for Mary, and, certainly, it would have been strongly opposed by the French. In any event, it never came to pass. Still, it made Elizabeth more aware of the threat.

Soon, she had a solution. Since Elizabeth had apparently concluded that she was never going to marry Robin Dudley herself, she proposed Dudley as a husband for Mary, putting Scotland in what she considered safe and reliable English hands. When Mary and her advisors reacted to the proposal with disdain, pointing out that Dudley had no title and that his father had been executed as a traitor, Elizabeth made him the Earl of Leicester, hoping that this might remedy the problem.

It did not. Dudley (I'll now call him "Leicester") was not anxious to wed Mary; and, ultimately, she fell in love with Lord Darnley, a softly handsome but cruel and arrogant young man. She married Darnley, who, like Mary herself, was descended from Henry VIII's sister Margaret and, thus, was a grandson of Henry VII, with his own claim to the English throne. Now, with two potential claimants united by marriage, Elizabeth had even greater reason to fear Scotland. And, since Mary still had powerful French ties, a Franco-Scottish alliance was a dangerous possibility.

But Mary soon realized that Darnley was a stupid and vicious scoundrel, and their relationship deteriorated. A woman often dominated by impulse and passion, Mary became the close confidant and possibly the lover of her secretary, David Riccio.

Riccio had been a close friend of Darnley. It has been suggested that they were even more than that. But Riccio's close relationship with Mary drove the unstable Darnley to seek revenge.

One evening, in March 1566, when Mary was dining privately with Riccio, Darnley burst into the room, accompanied by his friend, Patrick Ruthven, in full armor and brandishing a sword. By this time, Darnley cared nothing for Mary, but, enraged at the wound to his pride, he had Riccio butchered with 56 strokes of Ruthven's sword. Mary was pregnant at the time, but survived the shock. In June 1566, she gave birth to the future James VI of Scotland, who later became James I of England.

While James is generally considered Darnley's son, there were many who believed that his father was actually David Riccio. Henri IV of France remarked years later that James was "the modern Solomon," since he was "the son of David."

Having lost a possible lover and given birth to a royal son, Mary continued to be ruled by passion and emotion. She now loathed Darnley, but may have hidden those feelings. In any event, she turned to the bold and brutal Earl of Bothwell. Apparently, Bothwell showed his interest in the Scottish Queen by raping her. If so, this did not alienate Mary, and the two became lovers.

But, how to be rid of the degenerate Darnley? Ever a man of action, Bothwell and his accomplices planted explosives in the house in which Darnley was staying. Possibly, Mary, pretending to be concerned for his welfare, had led Darnley to stay there. But events did not go quite as planned. Hearing men below in the garden and assuming they were up to no good, Darnley had himself lowered from a window. Unluckily, he landed amid the conspirators. They quickly strangled him and then blew up the house. This is why Darnley's body was found "mysteriously" outside the house, in one piece and unburned. It was rumored that his murder was an act of revenge, done at Mary's urging. It may well have been.

Having killed Darnley, Bothwell promptly divorced his wife and married the Scottish Queen. But Bothwell was extremely unpopular with the powerful lords of Scotland. They had despised Darnley, and were glad to see him dead; but they had no intention of allowing Bothwell to replace him as a King of Scotland or to exercise power over their queen. And, Mary, herself, was hardly in their good graces. To them, she was an adulteress and an accessory to the murder of her husband.

Ultimately, the Scottish Lords crushed Bothwell's forces, and he escaped to exile in Denmark. Mary was held captive by his conquerors and was forced to abdicate in favor of her infant son, James. She pleaded with her captors to let her join Bothwell in exile, but they were unwilling to go along with that romantic idea. Their probable intention was to kill her.

Evidently, Mary expected the French to free her. She was after all of Guise blood and a former Queen of France. But the French king, seeing an opportunity to foster a relationship with the victorious Scottish nobles, made it plain that he would take no action.

Even English Catholics were dubious about Mary. They considered her complicit in the murder of her husband and an adulteress in her relationship with Bothwell. Moreover, she seemed to cause nothing but trouble and strife.

Elizabeth too deplored what she considered Mary's immoral and possibly criminal behavior. Nevertheless, she was always reluctant to see a reigning monarch killed or overthrown by her subjects. She expressed that opinion and was prepared to step in to prevent further harm to Mary.

But English intervention proved unnecessary. In May 1568, a Scottish nobleman, enamored of the captive queen, helped her to escape. Once free, she was able to raise some troops; but they were soundly defeated by her former captors. Mary fled across Scotland and crossed into England. Once there, she was placed by Elizabeth in comfortable, but guarded confinement. There was no reconciliation with Bothwell, who ultimately died in a Danish prison.

Elizabeth created the impression that she hoped to restore Mary as the Scottish Queen, if only Mary would ratify the Treaty of Edinburgh, giving up her claim to the throne of England. That may or may not have been Elizabeth's true intention. Cecil proposed that the evidence against Mary be brought to England and that, if she was found innocent, Elizabeth should restore her to the Scottish throne, but, if she was found guilty, she should be turned over to the Scots lords or kept in some place where she could cause no trouble.

Elizabeth agreed with Cecil's plan, retaining the condition that Mary ratify the Treaty of Edinburgh. At the same time, she suggested quietly to Mary's representative that, even if the decision was against Mary, Elizabeth would still try to reach a just settlement with the Scottish lords. Apparently, Mary agreed to this plan.

The Scots arrived in England ready for the proceedings. They were armed with the famous "casket letters," a "little coffer of silver and gilt" containing what appeared to be incriminating correspondence between Mary and Bothwell, showing her to be both an adulteress and complicit in Darnley's murder. Mary claimed the letters were forgeries, and possibly they were. Real or not, they were not made public at this point, since there still was the possibility that Elizabeth would seek to restore Mary to the Scottish throne.

Theoretically, "the inquiry" began in October 1568. But it produced no result. There was disagreement over Mary's request to present her case directly to Elizabeth, rather than to royal Commissioners and also over Mary's fate if the decision went against her. There were unsuccessful attempts at a settlement; but no decision was reached as to Mary's guilt or innocence. She remained in English custody, creating a troublesome and dangerous situation that would continue for the next nineteen years.

In December 1568, Spanish ships carrying a mass of gold bullion toward Antwerp entered an English port to escape pirates. Elizabeth seized the gold and refused to return it. Ostensibly, her stand was based on "the law of the sea." In reality, Elizabeth realized that the money was to be used by the Duke of Alba to pay Spanish troops in the Netherlands, a use she was determined to prevent.

Technically, the gold was not even Philip's property, but that of his Genovese bankers. It was to be loaned to Philip on its arrival in Antwerp. Until then, the bankers retained ownership. Since the landing in Antwerp had never occurred, title to the gold never passed to the Spanish. There is some indication that Elizabeth quietly made her own arrangement with the bankers to keep the gold by assuming the debt that was to have been Philip's.

Under the circumstances, such an arrangement may not have been unlawful.

But the Spanish didn't see it that way. Philip had changed ambassadors to England, replacing Guzman de Silva, a likeable and prudent representative, with Don Guerau de Espés, a stupid, arrogant and bellicose man, who did significant damage to relations between the two countries. Espés was, of course, enraged over Elizabeth's refusal to return the "Spanish" gold. For a time, the possibility of war with Spain seemed quite real.

It didn't come to that. To Philip, fighting the English as well as the Dutch rebels seemed expensive and impractical. Besides, victory might lead to pro-French Mary Stuart attaining the English throne, an outcome the Spanish king seemed generally disinclined to promote.

The Spanish seized some English ships and goods and closed Dutch ports to English ships. Elizabeth responded by halting all English trade with the Netherlands, and the English merchants moved their business to Hamburg, putting an end to cloth manufacturing in the colonies and creating economic havoc there.

However, to Mary Stuart, "imprisoned" in an English castle, a Spanish invasion of England seemed a real possibility and something for which she prayed. She sent word to the Spanish Ambassador that, "if his master [Philip] will help me, I shall be Queen of England in three months and mass shall be said all over the Country."

This was not the first such message. Mary had previously written the Queen of Spain asserting her right to the English throne and promising that, if she could hope for help from abroad, she would overthrow heresy in England or die trying.

From Mary's point of view, seeking Spanish intervention was not a foolish idea. Since the power of her Guise relatives had lessened, and the French had refused to come to her rescue in Scotland, Philip's concern over her French ties might have receded. Perhaps now, he might be prepared to see her on the English throne, rather than the difficult and heretical Elizabeth.

Of course, at this point, Elizabeth was unaware of Mary's communications with the Spanish. She continued at least to pretend that she sought a way to restore Mary to the Scottish throne, if it could be made consistent with Elizabeth's own security.

Late in 1568, a Catholic plot had been formed to marry Mary Stuart to the Duke of Norfolk, then the only remaining English Duke and the grandson of the Duke of Norfolk, who had been saved from execution by the death of Henry VIII. Although Catholic, this Norfolk was a wealthy and powerful peer, since his family's massive holdings had been restored. The rationale of the plotters was to marry the unpredictable, somewhat unstable Mary to a reliable and respected English nobleman and to have her recognized as Elizabeth's successor, ultimately restoring Catholicism. Oddly, no one seems to have mentioned that the lady was already married to Bothwell, who, while rotting away in a Danish prison, was still very much alive.

Moreover, Norfolk, while "respected," may not have been quite so "reliable." Angry with Cecil, he had asked the Spanish Ambassador to encourage Philip to attack an English merchant fleet about to sail for Hamburg, so that the commercial loss would be blamed on Cecil. This, of course, was unknown to Elizabeth and probably to Norfolk's supporters.

Whether or not Leicester knew of Norfolk's perfidious suggestion to the Spanish, he supported the match between Mary Stuart and the Duke. Perhaps this was for a different reason. Leicester may have been convinced that, with Mary wedded to a responsible Englishman and assured of peacefully succeeding Elizabeth on the throne, there would be less pressure on Elizabeth to make a French or Imperial marriage. If so, Leicester, himself, might finally be considered the right bridegroom.

Leicester apparently had a good relationship with Philip, having fought for him in his Lowlands Campaign, when Mary, then queen, provided her husband with English military support. And Leicester had also developed friendships with Spanish noblemen who might persuade Philip to look favorably on a match between Leicester and Elizabeth.

It appears that, to gain Spanish support for such a match, Leicester may even have been prepared to see England restored to Catholicism. First through his brother-in-law, Henry Sidney, and later through Leicester himself, the Spanish Ambassador was told that, if Philip would support his plan to marry Elizabeth, Leicester would rigorously support Spanish policy and would personally attend the Council of Trent to be reconvened by the Pope. This has been construed — perhaps unfairly — as an implied promise to see England returned to the True Church and the Pope. Somehow, Cecil learned of Leicester's promises and made sure that it was widely spread that Leicester was promising to make England Catholic. Already unpopular with much of the aristocracy, Leicester was now reviled, and the chances of his marrying the queen were even further diminished.

Soon enough, Elizabeth came to suspect the existence of the Norfolk marriage scheme. She confronted Norfolk, but he flatly denied it. He embroidered his denial with an outrageous lie. "What? Should I seek to marry her, being so wicked a woman, such a notorious adulteress and murderer? I love to sleep upon a safe pillow."

But the plot continued. Mary and Norfolk wrote fond letters to each other and exchanged tokens of affection. The queen confronted Norfolk again. This time, the Duke equivocated.

Elizabeth was growing angry and impatient. Leicester was shrewd enough to read the signs of danger to his own position as a supporter of the Norfolk marriage scheme. Feigning illness, he called for the queen to come to his bedside. He confessed the existence of the scheme and even of his own support for it. He insisted, however, that his motive was not to put Mary on the English throne or even to make her Elizabeth's successor, but was simply to control Mary with a trusted and reliable English husband.

Elizabeth, however, no longer considered Norfolk "trusted" or "reliable." If the match went forward, with Norfolk becoming King of Scotland, she believed that, within months, she would be in the Tower or dead, while Norfolk and Mary occupied the English throne. Although determined to prevent the match, Elizabeth forgave Leicester for his participation in the plot.

Now, even Norfolk realized his peril. He left the court, but was commanded by Elizabeth to return. Defying the queen's order, the Duke fled to his northern estates and tried to get word to Mary's Spanish contacts. Failing in that attempt, he was commanded by Elizabeth to return to court "on his allegiance." This meant he was committing treason if he refused.

Norfolk realized that Elizabeth was aware of his double dealing. He discussed the possibility of rebellion with his brother-in-law, Charles Neville, the Earl of Westmoreland and with Henry Percy, the Earl of Northumberland. Both men, like Norfolk, were fiercely against Cecil and longed for the days when the Percys and Nevilles ruled the north of England like kings. They resented the "parvenus" who they felt were controlling the queen and destroying the fabric of the nation.

Northumberland was also sympathetic to the cause of Mary Stuart. He had secretly converted to Catholicism and had even suggested to the Spanish Ambassador that the widowed Philip should marry the Scottish Queen, creating an obvious threat to Elizabeth's rule.

The two northern Earls assured Norfolk that they were ready for rebellion. Although Norfolk held the title of Earl Marshall, he was not a particularly brave man. After agonizing over the decision, he concluded that his best course of action was not rebellion, but to return to court and throw himself on the mercy of the queen.

On his journey back, however, Norfolk was arrested and sent to the Tower. His arrest lit the spark of what became the "Northern Rebellion." Led by Northumberland and Westmoreland, and joined by the forces of other northern, Catholic lords, the rebels intended to free Mary Stuart and place her on the English throne. To accomplish these goals, the rebels had about a thousand poorly armed foot soldiers and a somewhat larger force of cavalry that was well armed and effective. Summoned by Elizabeth to court, the two rebel leaders refused to come. The Northern Rebellion began.

On November 14, 1569, led by Northumberland and Westmoreland, the rebels broke into Durham Cathedral, destroyed the Bibles and prayer books in English, smashed the Protestant communion table and restored the Catholic altars and the Catholic mass. The rebel army then moved southward saying a daily mass and cheered by provincial

Catholics. They headed for Tutbury, where Mary had been held. Unknown to them, however, she had been hurriedly moved to Coventry, where the defenses were extremely strong.

Elizabeth wisely issued a proclamation that the rebels only pretended to act in the name of religion, while their true aim was to turn the country over to foreign rule. This discouraged even Catholics from swelling the ranks of the rebel army, as did the rebel's widespread seizure of cattle and crops to feed themselves as they moved southward. Other northern Lords, on whom the rebel leaders had counted, saw the wisdom of refraining from what could be a dangerous and probably losing fight.

Soon, it became apparent that the south and the Midlands were standing firmly for Elizabeth. Word spread among the rebels that a large royal army under the Earl of Sussex was moving northward to confront them. The rebel troops began to melt away, Sussex and his army arrived and killed many more. Recognizing that the game was up, the leaders of the rebellion fled to Scotland in December of 1569.

One rebel leader, Leonard Dacres, held out. Dacres was a member of another powerful northern family and he still commanded a large rebel force. His troops encountered a contingent of royal forces led by Mary Boleyn's son, Lord Hunsdon. In a remarkable feat of arms, Hunsdon's men totally obliterated a rebel force that outnumbered his loyal troops two to one. Hunsdon's men had marched all night, only to find themselves backed by Dacres' much larger force against the edge of a high cliff overlooking a swiftly flowing river. But Hunsdon withstood the charge of Dacres' mounted northerners and sent his cavalry sweeping around Dacres' flank. The rebels broke and fled.

The Northern Rebellion was over; and Elizabeth was thrilled at the outcome. She wrote a letter of gratitude to Hunsdon, whom she probably believed was her half-brother. In a postscript she said, "I doubt much, my Harry, whether that the victory was given me more joyed me, or that you were by God appointed the instrument of my glory, and I assure you that for my country's good, the first might suffice, but for my heart's contentation, the second more pleased me." She went on to tell Hunsdon, with affectionate understatement, that she gratefully intended "somewhat to increase your livelihood."

The Earl of Northumberland was seized by the Scots, who turned him over to Elizabeth. He was promptly executed. Westmoreland and Dacres fled to the Continent and faded into obscurity. Their unfortunate followers were harshly punished. More than five hundred rebels were publicly hanged. The wealthier rebels were spared, but their property was forfeited. Elizabeth would have preferred executing the rich as well, but was prevailed upon to follow the more "practical" course of simply taking their lands.

Pius V had been elected Pope in 1566. He was extreme in his anti-Protestant views and urged rigorous enforcement of the Inquisition. In February of 1570, anxious to overthrow England's "heretical" queen, Pius issued his bull *Regnans in Excelsis* excommunicating Elizabeth, depriving her of her "pretended" title to the Crown, freeing Catholics from all obligations to her, calling on them to overthrow her and even authorizing them to kill her.

Evidently, the Pope issued his bull based on the out-of-date "intelligence" report that an enormous uprising of northern Catholics was about to begin and would likely be successful. In fact, the Northern uprising had already been defeated before the bull was published.

In any event, the Pope had no effective way of enforcing his bull. The majority of English Catholics were not prepared to rebel; and, if he expected his command to be enforced by the armies of France, Spain or the Empire, he was disappointed. Ironically, both Philip and the Emperor resented the papal bull. The French king even refused to publish it. Probably, they deplored the idea that the Pope could order the overthrow and death of a reigning monarch. After all, if the Pope could use that weapon against Elizabeth, it could be deployed against any of them should they incur the Pontiff's displeasure. They may also have seen correctly that the radical nature of the Pope's act would be counter-productive and likely to harm the cause of English Catholics, rather than strengthen it. Indeed, the Pope's draconian order hardened Elizabeth's attitude toward militant Catholics, and particularly toward the European-trained priests who were being smuggled into England.

In 1571, another plot against Elizabeth originated with Roberto di Ridolfi, an Italian banker living in England. Ridolfi dabbled ineffectively in espionage. Acting as an agent of the Pope, he had brought into England copies of the bull excommunicating Elizabeth. He had even played a minor role in the planning of the Northern Rebellion.

Ridolfi had been placed under surveillance, because of his frequent contacts with Mary Stuart's ambassador and his bringing large sums of money into England, apparently to support the Catholic cause. In late 1569, he was taken into custody by Francis Walsingham, who had been gathering intelligence to protect the queen since 1568. "Detained" for months at Walsingham's London home, Ridolfi was questioned in detail, and even threatened with torture, but was released in 1570. At that point, he was mysteriously granted an audience with the queen. He promised to serve her loyally and was permitted to travel on "private business." After this, Elizabeth personally signed his passport; and he left for Rome.

It is possible that Ridolfi was released and allowed to travel to Rome because he had agreed to serve as one of Walsingham's undercover "plants." If so, he would appear to plot against Elizabeth and would urge Englishmen and Scots to join in his plot. He would then report these "plotters" to Walsingham. The use of such "plants" was characteristic of his methods of counter-espionage. For example, he and Cecil employed William Herle to pose as a treasonous plotter in order to ensnare others tempted to join in Herle's apparent schemes.

In Ridolfi's case, however, the plan may have simply been to release him so that he could be watched and his contacts noted. We do not know. But, whether known to Walsingham or not, Ridolfi's "private business" on the Continent turned out to be a plot to overthrow the queen. His "plan" called for an invasion of England by thousands of Spanish troops under command of the Duke of Alba, after which Elizabeth would be replaced by Mary Stuart, who would marry the Duke of Norfolk. With Spanish support, the newlyweds would then rule as King and Queen of both England and Scotland.

Having withdrawn from the Northern Rebellion before it began, Norfolk had been released from the Tower. He was foolish enough, however, to become involved in Ridolfi's plot. Mary Stuart knew of the plot as well. Norfolk had given Elizabeth a written commitment on his allegiance never to deal in the cause of the marriage of the Queen of Scots or in any cause regarding her. But the Duke had no intention of keeping his word. He even submitted his written commitment to Mary for her approval, continued to send her letters and gifts and discussed plans for her escape. Mary heartily approved of his duplicity, writing "You have promised to be mine and I yours." She then wrote Norfolk that Ridolfi would inform Philip that numerous English nobleman would rally to her side if only "said King of Spain will sustain and embrace my causes."

The Pope was an enthusiastic supporter of Ridolfi's scheme. Apparently, Philip was ambivalent. He asked the

Duke of Alba to meet with Ridolfi to discuss his plan. Alba was a practical man of considerable intelligence. He considered Ridolfi a loose-lipped fool. He flatly advised Philip against sending a Spanish army to England, unless a sizeable army of English rebels had already launched an attack on the queen and was able to sustain that attack for at least forty days.

But Philip never had to make that decision. Walsingham and Cecil (having now been made Lord Burghley) intercepted letters between the plotters, uncovered the plot and stopped it before it began. They discovered that Ridolfi's plan was supported by a powerful English nobleman referred to in encoded letters as "40." But they did not know "40's" identity. This might indicate that Ridolfi was not a "plant" of Walsingham and Cecil, or at least not a successful "plant," since Ridolfi would seemingly have known who "40" was and, if a "plant," would have informed them.

At this point, they suspected the Duke of Norfolk. Under torture, the Duke's servants had implicated him in the plot; but, they could not identify him as "40." Given Norfolk's high noble standing, the evidence against him was still considered insufficient.

Burghley (as I will now call him) was sure that Mary Stuart's ambassador, the Bishop of Ross, knew the identity of "40." When questioned, Ross claimed diplomatic immunity. But Burghley was not a man to leave any stone unturned when Elizabeth's security was at stake.

He obtained the opinion of a panel of judges that an ambassador who supported rebellion forfeited his right to diplomatic immunity. Threatened with the rack, Ross confessed not only the plot and Mary's involvement, but also that "40" was Norfolk.

Espés, the stupid and arrogant Spanish Ambassador, had been up to his ears in Ridolfi's plot. He was declared *persona non grata* and instructed to leave the realm at once.

In January 1572, Norfolk was tried, found guilty of treason and sentenced to death. He had clearly been guilty of treasonous conduct that threatened Elizabeth's crown and life. Yet, she was reluctant to see him executed. He was related to her, was England's only remaining Duke, and, despite his duplicitous conduct, he remained popular.

Time after time, the queen signed Norfolk's death warrant, only to countermand it before it could be carried out. On one occasion, Burghley was awakened at 2:00 a.m. by a message from the queen. She had changed her mind again. The death warrant she had signed earlier that day was countermanded. At last, in June 1572, she permitted Norfolk's execution to take place.

Also in June 1572, Burghley was appointed Lord Treasurer, an important and prestigious office. He was replaced as Principal Secretary by two men, Walsingham and Sir Thomas Smith. But Burghley remained the queen's closest advisor.

Perhaps reflecting on his difficulties in convincing Elizabeth to execute Norfolk, Burghley wrote, for his own eyes only, a list of her faults as a monarch. There were four. First was her stubbornness about marriage. Next, was her overly generous treatment of Catholic noblemen, who, all too often, were secretly in favor of Mary Stuart's claim to the throne. He contrasted this with the queen's failure to bestow greater favor upon those who loyally supported the Protestant cause. Third was Elizabeth's reluctance to aid the "King's party" that governed Scotland in the name of James VI, Mary's young son and staunchly opposed Mary's claim to the throne. Finally, Burghley's memo focused on Elizabeth's reluctance to follow the practices of her father and other kings in creating new nobles, who would have a vested interest in supporting and protecting her.

Burghley's candor in this memo is surprising. But he often wrote memos that only he was to see; and there is no evidence that anyone else ever saw this one, or that he was ever so brutally frank in speaking directly to the queen.

Before the Ridolfi Plot, Elizabeth had been unaware of Mary Stuart's scheming communications. She had at least pretended a continued willingness to restore Mary to the Scottish throne, if adequate controls could be established over her reckless behavior and if she would recognize Protestantism as the established religion in Scotland and relinquish her claim to the English throne.

Mary's restoration was strongly opposed by Elizabeth's advisors and, of course, by the King's party in Scotland. But the decision never had to be made. After the Ridolfi Plot, Elizabeth abandoned any thought of restoring Mary to the Scottish throne or even setting her free. Angered at Mary's complicity in the plot, she even permitted Burghley to arrange publication of a tract revealing the "casket letters" that depicted Mary's adultery and involvement in her husband's murder.

Still, Elizabeth would not agree to Parliament's desire to charge Mary with treason; and the problems presented by Mary would not go away. Over and over again, new Catholic plots were formed to depose Elizabeth and put Mary on the English throne. Some of those plots involved Spain. Although Philip was generally unwilling to undertake a war to make Mary queen, there were moments when he wavered in that view. Philip was regularly urged by the Pope and his advisors that the heretic Elizabeth must go, even if the price of that was giving the crown to Mary Stuart. Certainly, there were moments when Philip indicated to the Pope and others — perhaps insincerely — that he was prepared to aid Mary's cause. He could hardly tell the Pope to "go pound sand." But, at least while Mary was alive, he seemed generally reluctant to invade England in her behalf. Of course, Elizabeth could not know that.

Although the French had not come to Mary's rescue when she was imprisoned in Scotland, if Philip did invade England with the object of putting her on the English throne, Elizabeth could not count on French aid in resisting that invasion. After all, Mary was a Guise and the widow of a French king. England would be alone, faced with a powerful — perhaps unbeatable enemy. Nevertheless, despite the continuing danger Mary posed and the urging of Parliament and her advisors, Elizabeth remained unwilling to take more rigorous action against her troublesome Scottish cousin.

Meanwhile, France continued to be torn by religious controversy. During the brief reign of François II, Mary Stuart's young husband, the militantly Catholic Guise family had been ascendant. French Protestants, called "Huguenots," had been viciously persecuted, and Protestant leaders were hung from the Château d'Amboise. The name "Huguenots" appears to have been derived, through misspelling and mispronunciation, from the word "Eidgenossen," a name attached to Protestants in Geneva, originally meaning "confederates."

The successor to François II was Charles IX, then a minor. His mother, Catherine de Medici, assumed power as Regent of France. Catherine was a descendant of the once rich and powerful de Medici family of Florence. She was the great-granddaughter of Lorenzo de Medici, called "Lorenzo the Magnificent." Despite the decline in her family's fortunes, she had married into French royalty and was the widow of Henri II. Three of her sons became French kings, François II, the deceased young husband of Mary Stuart, Charles IX, the somewhat unstable brother who succeeded him, and their younger brother, Henri III, who succeeded Charles.

Catherine led a faction called the "politiques" that was more concerned with French nationalism than religious issues. She played the two religious factions against each other, shifting from side to side and exercising powerful influence over her sons.

Catherine had tended to show more tolerance than the Guise family toward the Huguenots. In 1572, however, that changed. Admiral Gaspar de Coligny, a key Huguenot leader, was pressing aggressively for a French war against Spain to "liberate" the Netherlands. Catherine's impressionable son, Charles IX, seemed to be strongly influenced by Coligny and appeared to support the Admiral's bellicose policy toward Spain. Moreover, the Huguenot cause, under Coligny's effective leadership, appeared to be gaining considerable strength throughout France. This particularly enraged the Duke of Guise, who believed that Coligny had killed his father and was determined to see the Admiral dead and Huguenot power suppressed.

In August 1572, in a display of their influence and power, vast numbers of Huguenots flocked to Paris for the wedding of the French Princess Marguerite to Prince Henri of Navarre. Henri was not only a popular Protestant leader, he was a potential successor to the French throne.

Prior to the arrival of Huguenots for the wedding, there were already at least 15,000 of them in Paris, a significant part of the population. While they had been growing in power over the preceding decade, the more recent presence of Huguenot forces near the capital fostered a climate of suspicion and fear on the part of Catholic Parisians. Now, with the massive influx of Huguenots for the wedding, those fears were exacerbated.

Meanwhile, Catherine worried that Coligny was pushing France toward a costly and destructive war with Spain. Possibly she feared that such a war could bring conflict with England as well, that Elizabeth would expect English commercial interests to suffer more from French domination of the Netherlands than Spanish. Yet, Coligny seemed determine to lead France in that direction. Catherine feared that such a war would necessarily weaken France, and, worse, that the French were likely to lose. Apparently she also felt that the Huguenots were becoming much too powerful throughout France and that Coligny was having much too great an influence on her royal, but unreliable son. Possibly, she and Guise even believed that Coligny planned to launch a Huguenot revolution.

Whatever her actual beliefs, Catherine appears to have persuaded her malleable son that she had uncovered a Huguenot plot led by Coligny to overthrow the French monarchy and that they must join with the Guise family in striking a severe and immediate blow against the Admiral and the Huguenots. Evidently, he agreed, and they struck that blow with a ferocity that had lasting international consequences and that remains a black day in French history.

On August 22, 1572, Admiral Coligny was shot and wounded by a Guise agent. He accidently escaped death by bending over to adjust his boot just as the shot was fired. The gun was later found to have been borrowed from the personal collection of Catherine's youngest son, the Duke of Alençon. Coligny was taken to his home, where he was treated by the king's physician. Royal Guards were assigned to protect him. But the royal concern was feigned. Something quite different was planned.

On August 24, St. Bartholomew's Day, a Guise assassin was allowed past the guards at Coligny's home. He ascended to Coligny's bedroom where he stabbed the Admiral to death and hurled his body into the street below. There, the Duke of Guise completed his revenge. He and the King's illegitimate brother ordered the Admiral's head severed and his headless body publicly hung in chains. Guise was heard to cry out, "Let us go on to the others. The King commands it!"

That was the beginning. Perhaps Catherine de Medici agreed only to the murder of Coligny. Even Guise claimed later that he had a list of only 70 Huguenots who were to be killed. Perhaps they intended the killing to stop there. But, it certainly did not. The vast majority of Parisians were staunch Catholics. They resented their Princess marrying a Protestant and the presence in Paris of so many seemingly affluent Protestants. Whipped into a frenzy by Guise agents, rampaging Catholic mobs ran through the streets marking the doors of Protestant homes with a white cross. Then, others, enraged and filled with blood lust, smashed their way in to strangle, slit throats, impale bodies or bash skulls. And, since the militia included numerous radical Catholics, many other Protestants were methodically killed by brigades of soldiers moving through the city. As the bells rang out all over Paris, thousands of Huguenots — men, women and children — were slaughtered. Only the bridegroom, Henri of Navarre, and a few other Protestants were spared. The young King, Charles IX, was quoted as saying "Kill them all, so that none shall reproach me for it."

Walsingham, then the English Ambassador to France, offered refuge in his home to terrified Englishmen visiting or residing in Paris. The French king, anxious to avoid war with England, dispatched another Royal Guard, this time with real instructions to protect the Ambassador's home. Nevertheless, when Walsingham tried to give shelter to a Huguenot general, the Royal Guard forcibly entered the home and dragged the general into the street, where he too was murdered.

And the killing didn't stop with Paris. In the following days, it spread throughout France. Huguenots were massacred in almost every city and town. An estimated 3000 of them were killed in Paris alone; and the estimated number murdered in all of France has varied from 10,000 to 70,000. Whichever number is closer to the truth, the slaughter was enormous.

Having sent his wife and daughter back to England, Walsingham met with Catherine de Medici. Perhaps she had really believed that Coligny was planning a Huguenot revolution. But, even if she had not planned or even wanted the extensive killing, she was no longer the voice of tolerance. From now on, the Queen Mother announced, Catholicism would be the only religion in France.

The new Pope, Gregory XIII, was overjoyed at what appeared to be the triumph of the True Church over the forces of heresy. A special mass was celebrated and a medal struck to commemorate the slaughter of Protestants. Philip of Spain was similarly pleased, laughing and dancing happily at the news.

The reaction in England was quite different. The massacre of St. Bartholomew's Day was viewed with horror and disgust. The Protestant members of the Council, and the Protestant population as a whole, tended to believe that a similar fate would be in store for them if another Catholic took the English throne. There were rumors that Mary Stuart was overjoyed at the massacre. This may not have been true; but, fueled by the rumors, many Englishmen cried out for her immediate execution.

Elizabeth was personally appalled at the slaughter in France, particularly since, only two years earlier, the Pope had issued his bull excommunicating her and authorizing Catholics to kill her. Still, she wanted conflict with neither France nor Spain; and she did not let her personal feelings jeopardize what she saw as England's best interests. Even with this extreme provocation, she was not prepared to terminate diplomatic relations with France, which she continued to see as a deterrent to Spanish military adventures.

The French Ambassador was granted an audience with the queen. He was greeted by courtiers clad in black and ominously silent. Elizabeth listened to his claim of a Huguenot plot to murder the French royal family. She pressed him to explain the horrible extent of the slaughter.

Although hardly satisfied with his explanation, when he assured her of France's desire to remain a friend and ally of England, she at least pretended to accept his words.

At the same time, however, she sought friendlier relations with Spain. Persuaded by Alba, Philip agreed to end the Spanish trade embargo that had prevented English trade with the Netherlands, causing the English to use Hamburg as the port of entry for their goods. This was not really a display of Spanish goodwill. Alba had realized that the embargo was severely hurting the Netherlands — still a Spanish colony — and was doing the English little harm.

The reactions of Burghley and Walsingham to the French massacre were much stronger than that of the queen. Although a committed Protestant, Burghley had tended to steer a pragmatic middle course on religion, as on most subjects. Walsingham had generally been less ready to compromise. Now, Walsingham's militant Protestant opinions were hardened and strengthened by the horror he had personally witnessed in Paris. And even Burghley became far more concerned about the threat posed by English Catholics and the Catholic powers. We can only speculate on the impact of the French massacre on their subsequent conduct. Probably it was significant, particularly in the case of Walsingham. As a Principal Secretary, Privy Council member, Elizabeth's spy master and head of security, his zeal to root out Catholic conspiracies and to protect the Queen became the dominant force in his life.

Walsingham's protective zeal was needed. The times were dangerous. In 1574, Charles IX died, succeeded by his brother, the Duke of Anjou, who took the French throne as Henri III. Anjou had also been considered a potential husband for Elizabeth; but his unyielding Catholicism precluded the match, as did his proclivity for wearing female attire. With Henri on the throne, France remained a serious threat, particularly if the fervently anti-Protestant Guise faction regained control. In the 1570s, thousands of French Huguenots emigrated to England, strengthening the Protestant Church and even the Puritan movement.

Meanwhile, despite the ending of the Spanish embargo on English trade with the Netherlands, Spain continued to pose a serious threat, and Spanish power seemed to be increasing. The problems caused by the Spanish did not all flow from Philip or his advisors. In the "Spanish Fury" of 1576, marauding hordes of mutinous Spanish troops sacked Antwerp. They massacred thousands of innocent citizens — mostly Protestants, and they burned almost a thousand homes to the ground.

But, Philip himself continued to represent a serious threat. His illegitimate half-brother, Don John, had defeated the Turks at the Battle of Lepanto. In 1576, Philip appointed Don John Governor of the Netherlands. He suggested that Don John make peace with the Dutch rebels, allowing the Spanish army to withdraw from the low countries. The Spanish troops would then feign an intent to return to Spain, but instead would invade England.

Don John would marry Mary Stuart, and Spanish troops would put her and Don John on the English throne. Philip apparently believed that Don John could control any pro-French tendencies his queen might still retain.

Proceeding with this plan, Don John announced the withdrawal of the Spanish army from the lowlands and wrote to Elizabeth asking her permission for the withdrawing Spanish troops to stay temporarily in England, if driven there "by storms" on their way back to Spain.

From a trusted agent in the low countries, Walsingham learned of the deceitful Spanish scheme and that, because it would put Mary Stuart on the throne, it had the support of the Guise family. He also learned that Don John was enlisting the support of English Catholic exiles, that his marriage to Mary Stuart was already arranged and that Elizabeth was to be poisoned when the invasion began.

Warned by Walsingham, Elizabeth mustered 10,000 English troops, deliberately letting Don John know of this armed preparation. It became obvious to him and to Philip that their plan had been discovered. Evidently, Philip reconsidered its wisdom. In 1577, the Spanish troops departed from the Netherlands; but they sailed back to Spain without "seeking shelter" in England.

When Don John died, Philip sent a new Spanish army into the Netherlands, commanded by the very able Duke of Parma. Parma's powerful force began to succeed in separating and defeating the rebels, creating the renewed threat of a Spanish invasion of England.

This threat led Elizabeth to turn again to France. It had been feared that Henri III would be controlled by the Guise family and would further terrorize the Huguenots. Instead, he proved rather moderate in that regard. Evidently, these factors led Elizabeth to rekindle talks of marriage to the French Duke of Alençon. Those talks had seemed to start and then evaporate. At the time of the St. Bartholomew's Day massacre, opposition to a French marriage by the English public had been widespread and strident. Elizabeth had been well aware of it. Six years later, in 1578, public anger had dissipated; and, although a French marriage would never be popular, Elizabeth began again to consider an Alençon match — or at least to discuss it.

Alençon had been active in combating the Spanish in the Netherlands, even receiving the lengthy title "Defender of the Liberties of the Low Countries Against Spanish Tyranny." Elizabeth was by no means pleased at the idea of French success in the lowlands. She continued to believe that French control of that critical region would be even more damaging to English commercial interests than continued domination by Spain.

Also, militant priests, trained on the Continent, were now stirring up Catholic feelings in England. Many were reminding English Catholics that the Pope's bull of excommunication directed Elizabeth's overthrow and even permitted her assassination.

Evidently, Elizabeth felt she could best deal with all of these problems by reviving the possibility of a French marriage — a marriage to Alençon. That could divert the Duke's attention from the Netherlands and possibly lessen French support for training priests to be smuggled into England. At the same time, it could create a serious deterrent to Spanish thoughts of an invasion. If Elizabeth knew it was Alençon's gun that had wounded Admiral Coligny, she gave no sign of it, and it did not deter her rekindling their "romance."

Discussions of the Alençon match began again. In 1579, the Duke sent his close friend and Master of the Wardrobe, Jean de Simier, to plead his case. Simier was a charming man with a shady reputation. He had murdered his own brother for having an affair with Simier's wife. Whether or not Elizabeth was aware of this, she seemed delighted with the suave and witty Frenchman. In a play on his name, she quickly dubbed him her "Monkey." She sent affectionate letters to Alençon, praising Simier's courtly skills and giving the hopeful Duke reason to believe that the queen was finally ready to commit.

She gave the same indication to those around her. When one of her ladies spoke in favor of the queen marrying Leicester, rather than Alençon, Elizabeth responded with anger, "Dost you think me so unlike myself and unmindful of my royal majesty that I would prefer my servant whom I myself have raised, before the greatest prince of Christendom, in the honor of a husband?"

Alençon was encouraged to make a personal visit to pursue the match. Simier began to prepare the way.

He presented marriage terms. They were extravagant, including a coronation for Alençon as King of England, an allowance of £60,000 per year, the right to make certain appointments and the grant to France of an English port to be guarded by French soldiers. These terms were so extreme, arrogant and one-sided that Elizabeth might have been expected to fly into a rage and terminate the discussions. She did not. To her Council's surprise, she seemed inclined to agree to the French demands. Was this mere pretense? Almost certainly.

Marriage to Alençon, like any French match, remained unpopular with the English and was opposed by the Council. But Elizabeth, with her usual focus on the international situation, sought to keep the French friendly and the Spanish off balance. She reassured Simier that she would marry Alençon, even if her Council opposed it. Almost surely, the Spanish were aware of this. Certainly Elizabeth hoped they were.

Meanwhile, Elizabeth was obviously enjoying Simier's sophistication and daring *double entendre*. Soon, the two were observed romping and laughing in each other's bed chambers early in the morning. Of course, rumors began — Simier was using love potions on the Queen; he was teaching her the skilled French way of making love; she was smitten with him, instead of his master. None of this was true. Simier was sincerely doing his best to advance the match with Alençon, while using his charm and humor to entertain the queen.

Still, public opposition grew. A shot was fired at Simier, evidently an attempt on his life. This was followed by what seemed another such attempt. When it appeared that Elizabeth might turn away from the proposed marriage because of its growing unpopularity, Simier played his most cynical card. Having developed excellent sources of information in England, he had discovered that Leicester had secretly married the beautiful Lettice Knollys and that she was pregnant with his child.

Lettice, short for Leticia, was said to resemble Elizabeth; and, on more than one occasion, she had caused royal anger by trying to outshine the queen. There was good reason for the resemblance. Lettice was the daughter of Katherine Knollys, Mary Boleyn's child, who was born during Mary's liaison with Henry VIII and was probably Elizabeth's half-sister. Thus, Lettice was not only Elizabeth's cousin, she was probably a grandchild of Elizabeth's father.

Now Simier arranged for Elizabeth to learn of her rival's marriage to Leicester. As he anticipated, the Queen was deeply hurt and enraged. But there was another reaction, the one on which Simier had counted. Elizabeth appeared to turn more positively than ever toward marrying Alençon. Perhaps now, she was personally and emotionally motivated to marry, rather than simply making sly moves in a game of geopolitical chess. Perhaps. But probably not.

When Alençon arrived, he appeared to charm Elizabeth quickly and completely. Soon they were spending considerable time together, often alone. When his visit was over, they sent each other love letters and exchanged tokens of affection. He gave her a golden frog pin and a handsome diamond ring. She proudly wore both and announced somewhat ambiguously that "she would not prevent his being her husband."

But the public was always anti-French and continued to oppose the marriage. When John Stubbs, an outspoken Puritan, published a diatribe against Alençon and the French marriage, Elizabeth, in a rage, ordered his right hand cut off. When the harsh sentence was carried out, Stubbs removed his hat with his left hand, cried out "God save the Queen" and fainted.

Had Leicester's "betrayal" with Lettice Knollys really pushed Elizabeth into agreeing to the marriage or had her "frog's" apparent charm had that effect, or was she simply carrying out a politically motivated charade? We cannot know for sure. Certainly, she tried to create the impression that she had genuine affection for the Duke and was about to marry him. Probably this was pretense.

Philip of Spain certainly believed it was pretense; but, perhaps, that's what he wanted to believe. Philip wrote his ambassador, "I have always looked upon the idea of a marriage between the Queen and Alençon as a mere invention. I nevertheless believe they will continue to discuss it, and even may become reconciled for the purpose, but I believe that she herself is the person who will refuse." Certainly Philip hoped that was so. The last thing he wanted was an Anglo-French alliance.

In any event, Elizabeth appeared ready to proceed with the match. Simier left for France carrying the marriage treaty in final form. The Council was divided on the question, with the majority opposed to the marriage. This vote brought on a remarkably angry and emotional response from Elizabeth. Evidently, her outburst shocked the Council. Seeing what appeared to be the queen's fierce determination to marry Alençon, the council finally, and reluctantly, decreed their approval "if it shall please her" — hardly a ringing endorsement.

Now, characteristically, Elizabeth slowed things down. She wrote Alençon of her growing concern about his Catholicism. She asked for a delay in finalizing the marriage treaty in order, she said, to allow popular support for the marriage to develop. The matter seemed indefinitely on hold.

But, once again, the political situation intervened. The young King of Portugal had been killed in battle. His great uncle, a dying old man, had succeeded to the Portuguese throne. But Philip of Spain had a claim to succeed the dying king, and Philip was not one to wait or to leave such matters to the Portuguese. In July 1580, the arrival in Portugal of the Duke of Alba with 50,000 Spanish soldiers quickly softened any Portuguese resistance; and, in April 1581, Philip was crowned King of Portugal. This added to Spanish wealth and power vast Portuguese colonies and a powerful fleet of Portuguese galleons, well manned and commanded by experienced captains. The newly more powerful Spain had to be deterred from attacking England, and a French marriage seemed the most effective deterrent.

Moreover, there were reports that Alençon's brother, the French King Henri III, was ill and might soon die. Alençon was next in line to the throne. France was still a Catholic nation. If Alençon became king, he might consider marriage to a Protestant impossible, even if she was Queen of England. Certainly, as King of France, Alençon would become a great match for Catholic princesses throughout Europe. Well aware of these potential dangers, Elizabeth seemed receptive to rekindling her French "romance."

Simier wrote expressing Alençon's continuing love for her; and she began, once again, to give the appearance of wanting to marry him. This time, the Spanish Ambassador was convinced. Naturally concerned about a French-English alliance, he wrote that "Signs seem to indicate a real intention to effect the marriage."

The French quickly sent commissioners to England, once again seeking to conclude a marriage treaty. They were accompanied by a huge contingent of French courtiers. Elizabeth saw that they were lavishly entertained. There were lengthy discussions of the marriage terms, but Elizabeth held back certain matters she said must still be worked out between Alençon and herself. Nevertheless, she continued to encourage the Duke, sending him £30,000 to help finance his campaign against the Spanish in the Netherlands.

Finally, in 1581, Alençon came to England once again, determined to press the match to a successful conclusion. Elizabeth received him cordially. Evidently, she sensed that he was seeking money as well as marriage. She promised to provide further financing for Alençon's Netherlands campaign in return for his promise to aid the moderate anti-Guise cause in France. Theoretically at least, this gave her some of the benefits of a French alliance without the need of an actual marriage or even a formal treaty. Marriage may have been implied, but it was not an express part of their pact.

Nevertheless, Elizabeth acted as if she intended to proceed with the match. When Alençon accompanied her to Protestant services in St. Paul's Cathedral, she kissed him in public. Then, an extraordinary act by Elizabeth furthered the impression that the marriage was on. In the presence of others, she told the French Ambassador that "the Duke of Alençon shall be my husband." Turning to Alençon, she kissed him on the mouth and, taking a ring from her finger, slipped it on his. The Duke responded to this symbolic act with a ring from his own finger.

By ancient tradition, developed when priests were not always on hand, this form of pledge and exchange of rings was thought to make a couple husband and wife. Alençon wrote at once to his brother that he and Elizabeth were now wed. The significance of the impromptu ceremony was not lost on either the French or English observers. Nor was it overlooked by the Spanish, for whose benefit the dramatic scene may have been staged.

But Elizabeth was rarely predictable. The very next day, she sent for Alençon. She had been unable to sleep, she said tenderly. She was torn between her strong desire to marry him and the unmistakable feelings of her people. She had come to a painful decision. Although she would always love him, she had decided that she must sacrifice her own happiness in order to better serve her subjects.

Even so, she seemed unready to put a definite end to the diplomatically useful possibility of a French marriage. When the disappointed Alençon asked leave to return at once to the Netherlands, Elizabeth asked him to stay – she would marry him. Just not now. What?

Alençon, undoubtedly confused, but still hopeful, stayed on in England for months. He continued to be lavishly entertained, but foolishly patronized a number of London whores. That conduct – reported to the queen – must have confirmed the decision she had probably already made that the marriage would never take place.

Elizabeth assured intimates that she had never committed unconditionally to the marriage, an assertion probably reported to Alençon. Finally realizing that the game was at an end, the Duke became angry and threatening. Perhaps his true character was now revealed. He demanded cash as the price of leaving, and Elizabeth was willing to pay. Alençon was paid £10,000 and promised £50,000 more when he was aboard the ship conveying him to the Netherlands.

Now, the Queen played out a dramatic scene, probably for the consumption of both the French and Spanish.

She accompanied Alençon part way to the coast, weeping and telling him she would be miserably unhappy until he returned. Leicester and other notables were to accompany the Duke all the way, since her "frog" was "the person she loved best in the world." Despite the tears and expressions of love, her true thoughts are apparent from the orders she gave privately. Leicester's instructions were that Alençon was to be prevented from returning to England – ever!

Of course, political needs continued. When Alençon died the following year, Elizabeth wrote his mother, Catherine de Medici, that she hoped soon to rejoin him in death. For a time, she wore only black and even referred to herself as his widow. But, as the French Ambassador cynically remarked, "She is a Princess who can act any part she pleases."

Her status as a "widow" notwithstanding, Elizabeth began to turn her attention to the tall, handsome and highly intelligent Sir Walter Raleigh. This may have been the result of her bitterness at Leicester's marriage to Lettice Knollys or simply that she found Raleigh attractive and stimulating company. In any event, the Queen showered him with honors and estates and kept him by her side as much as possible, despite his proclivity to seek distant voyages and adventures.

Raleigh had attended Oxford, was widely traveled and was fluent in three European languages. He apparently was the leader of the "School of Night," a clandestine gathering of open-minded, intellectually curious men, including Christopher Marlowe, Thomas Herriot, George Chapman and Henry Percy, 9th Earl of Northumberland, known as the "Wizard Earl."

But Raleigh's was not just a life of the mind. He fought on land and at sea and sought to establish English colonies in what is now Virginia and North Carolina. Of course, the Virginia Colony was named after Elizabeth, who rewarded Raleigh with a knighthood and appointed him Governor of the colony. Undoubtedly, the Queen was drawn to Raleigh. Were they lovers? Probably not.

Meanwhile the problem of Mary Stuart continued, as did the dangers posed by both France and Spain. Englishmen still remembered the St. Bartholomew's Day massacre and the "Spanish Fury." Parliament and the Council were well aware of the increased might of Spain and the possibility of a Franco-Spanish Catholic alliance.

In 1579, the English College in Rome was taken over by the Jesuits, an organization founded in 1534 by Ignatius Loyola, a Spanish ex-soldier and priest. Loyola brought military order and discipline to the priesthood; and, by his death in 1556, he had created an army of more than 1000 well trained and highly disciplined priests. Many Jesuits made their way into England, where they urged Catholicism on the English and were at least perceived as encouraging the overthrow of Elizabeth. To most of the English, it appeared that, at the center of every Catholic, French or Spanish plot, poised like a spider in her web, was the former Scottish Queen. And they were not wrong.

Mary was pretending friendship and loyalty for Elizabeth, while secretly beseeching the Pope, Philip, the French and anyone else she could think of to free her, bring down Elizabeth, put Mary on the English throne and restore England to the True Church.

A messenger employed by the Spanish Ambassador sought to cross the Scottish border disguised as a dentist. After being searched, he was allowed to cross. But, apparently, in gathering up his belongings after the search, he left behind a mirror. Hidden behind the glass were letters referring to the "Enterprise."

Of course, Walsingham was anxious to learn what the "Enterprise" was and who was involved in it. He began to suspect Francis Throckmorton, a well-known Catholic. A search of Throckmorton's home revealed papers describing desirable landing sites for invading foreign troops and listing Catholic notables who might support them once they landed.

On the rack, Throckmorton confessed to being a principal organizer of the "Enterprise," which was apparently intended to have Spanish forces free Mary, place her on the English throne and restore Catholicism as the national religion. And Throckmorton had corresponded with Mary about the plan.

The "Enterprise," was subsequently called the "Throckmorton Plot." It was stopped, but the threat posed by Mary Stuart continued. The public was enraged, as were Parliament and the Council. They wanted action.

Burghley stoked the fires of anti-Mary feeling by causing books and pamphlets to be published and widely circulated attacking her, attesting to the truth of the casket letters and repeating the stories of Mary's complicity in the murder of her husband and of her adulterous relationship with his murderer.

But, despite public outrage and the pleas of Parliament and her Council, Elizabeth remained unwilling to take punitive action against her Scottish cousin. On the contrary, she at least pretended to seek an arrangement by which Mary could share the Scottish crown with her son James, if sufficient guarantees of her behavior could be obtained and she would finally accept Elizabeth's other conditions. If accomplished, this could conceivably lessen the threat posed by Mary. And, someday, if James became Elizabeth's successor, it could serve to unite England and Scotland.

In reality, however, the shared Scottish throne was never going to happen. James was hardly a filial son. He had not seen his mother since his infancy; and he and his supporters were not about to have his crown shared with this difficult and troublesome woman. Moreover, James had been raised a Protestant, while Mary was, of course, a Guise and a Catholic.

Meanwhile, Englishmen became more and more outspoken about the danger they saw in Mary and their determination to protect their queen. Even many English Catholics had become leery of Mary, believing her complicit in her husband's murder and an outrageous adulteress based on her relationship with Bothwell.

In 1584, the "Bond of Association" was drawn up by the Council and circulated among the public. The Bond called upon Englishmen not only to exact "the ultimate revenge" upon anyone who plotted to harm their queen, but to exclude from the succession "any person" whom the plotters intended to crown in her place, and even the heirs of such person. "Any person" was generally understood to mean Mary Stuart, and the Bond would have excluded Mary from the throne. It was widely and enthusiastically signed by many thousands of ordinary citizens. Elizabeth, however, was against the concept of citizens taking the law into their own hands and was concerned that the Bond would also exclude Mary's son, James, a step she was not prepared to take.

In 1585, Parliament passed the Act For the Queen's Security. This was a more temperate version of the Bond of Association. It provided for the exclusion from the throne of any "pretended successor" for whose benefit the queen's death was to be procured, but not the heirs of that person, unless they had participated in the plot. Thus, it would exclude Mary, but not her son James. Moreover, Parliament's Act provided for the trial of persons accused of plotting the queen's death, rather than the vigilante justice to be exacted under the Bond of Association.

In 1586, Mary fell into a trap set by Walsingham by giving her written approval to a plot to assassinate

Elizabeth. Gilbert Gifford, a lapsed Catholic deacon, had served as Mary's agent on the Continent. On arriving in England, however, Gifford had been arrested and "persuaded" to work as one of Walsingham's undercover "plants." Gifford arranged to meet Mary and suggested she employ a "secret" method of corresponding with her agent in Paris, with the French Ambassador in London and with others who supported her cause.

Gifford's secret method was tested. It appeared to work. Now, Mary put her trust in Gifford and urged the French Ambassador to trust him and to adopt his secret method of communicating with her.

The "secret" method was to place the letters in waterproof containers inserted in the bung hole of beer kegs delivered to and picked up from Chartley, the estate where Mary was now confined. The letters to Mary were to be retrieved by her servant from the beer kegs delivered to Chartley. The letters from Mary were to be removed from the beer kegs picked up from Chartley by a "trusted aide" and delivered to the French Ambassador or other intended recipients.

In fact, the "trusted aide" was another of Walsingham's agents. All the letters to and from Mary were opened and deciphered by Walsingham's key agent, Thomas Phelippes, and delivered to Walsingham. They were then copied and undetectably resealed by Arthur Gregory, Walsingham's expert in that arcane process. The original letters from Mary were then passed on to the intended recipient.

Original letters to Mary were passed by the "trusted agent" to Walsingham, who read them, had them copied and then inserted the originals in the beer kegs delivered to Chartley, where they would go to Mary.

Anthony Babington was a wealthy young Catholic who had known Mary Stuart as a boy and apparently worshipped her. Babington became the architect of a plot to kill Elizabeth and to replace her with Mary. During July 1586, he exchanged letters with Mary, using Gifford's "secret" method of communication. His letters to and from Mary were, of course, read by Walsingham. They clearly showed Mary acquiescing not only in the plot to rescue her, but also in Elizabeth's assassination and even giving advice on how the plot might best be carried out.

According to Babington's letter to Mary, six accomplices were in readiness to murder the queen, after which Mary would be rescued and a foreign army would invade England, presumably to put Mary on the throne. Mary replied carefully, dictating her response to two secretaries, rather than writing it herself. After giving advice on steps that should be taken to obtain the foreign assistance and to release her, Mary added "then shall it be time to set the six gentlemen to work." This, of course, referred to the six men that Babington wrote were to kill Elizabeth. Their "work," acquiesced in by Mary, was to murder the queen.

Walsingham had his key agent, Thomas Phelippes, add a paragraph to Mary's reply asking the names of the six men. Phelippes was no ordinary spy. Highly intelligent, he had a Cambridge degree in mathematics and was fluent in five languages. Among other skills, he was an excellent forger. Phelippes had rendered successful services for Walsingham in the past; but adding a bogus paragraph to Mary's letter was a dangerous gamble. It could lead to identifying the six potential assassins. But it also created the risk that, when he received the letter, Babington would spot the forgery and realize the game was up. It created the additional risk that, if Mary was ultimately tried, she or her secretaries would point out the forged paragraph and discredit the entire document.

Babington was arrested, along with a fellow conspirator, who provided Walsingham with the names of the six intended killers. Babington had destroyed Mary's letter on receiving it, but, under questioning, he described it as seeking the names of the assassins. This was the forged inquiry added to Mary's letter by Phelippes. Obviously, Babington had not realized that this part of the letter was a forgery.

Before his arrest, Babington had commissioned portraits of himself and the six killers, evidently intending them to become a proud part of English history. Instead, he and his co-conspirators were hung, drawn and quartered. As historian William Camden described their end, they "were all cut down their privities cut off, bowelled alive and quartered."

But what of Mary? At this point, Elizabeth had no choice. Mary was charged with high treason and served with formal notice that she would be on trial for her life.

There was concern among English jurists as to whether an English court had jurisdiction to try a foreign queen. They concluded that jurisdiction existed, since Mary's crimes had been committed in England, not Scotland, and, in any event, having abdicated, she was no longer a queen.

There was another problem. A person who was not an English subject owed no duty of loyalty to the English queen. Could such a person be guilty of treason? But Parliament had made it unnecessary to rely on the common law definition of "treason." It had passed the Statute of 1585, making it a capital crime for anyone to participate in planning "the hurt of her Majesty's most royal person" if the accused "shall or may pretend any title to the crown of this realm after her Majesty's decease." Parliament had set a legal trap, and Mary had stepped into it.

The trial was carefully planned. Burghley personally drew the plans for altering the Great Hall at Fotheringhay to accommodate the proceedings. The large room was redecorated to simulate a courtroom with tables for the lawyers, benches for the Commissioners who were to determine Mary's guilt or innocence and a "bar," behind which spectators would sit.

The walls were hung with black velvet, and one wall bore the English Coat of Arms. There was an upholstered armchair for Mary, and a raised throne for Elizabeth, should she decide to attend.

At first, Mary refused to appear at the trial. She was a queen, she argued, not Elizabeth's subject, so there was no jurisdiction to try her. The Commissioners made every effort to convince her, but could make no headway. Christopher Hatton, considered persuasive, was called upon to assist. He argued that, if Mary did not appear and present her case, her voice would never be heard, and she would be universally perceived as guilty. Still she refused.

Finally, on the night before the trial, Mary received a personal letter from Elizabeth suggesting (but carefully not promising) that, if Mary appeared at the trial "you may receive greater favour from us." The key word was "may," rather than "will."

The next morning, October 13, 1586, Mary met with the Commissioners and agreed to appear and defend herself against the charge of plotting Elizabeth's murder. As to a second charge of dealing with foreign rulers, however, she insisted that such dealings were her absolute right as a monarch. To that charge, she would remain silent.

Later that morning, the trial began. The 36 Commissioners filed in and took their places along the benches set aside for them. In the "well" of the court sat seven judges who were to advise the Commissioners on the law and to rule on evidentiary questions. They were joined by other "experts" in such matters, as well as the prosecutors and court clerks.

Mary entered dramatically, wearing a black velvet gown, and accompanied by her physician and other attendants. She mistakenly moved to the throne intended for Elizabeth, but was quickly guided to her armchair. When she was seated, the court formally opened, and she registered her objections to the proceedings. Then, the chief prosecutor, Thomas Gowdy, stood and, gathering his robes around him, forcefully accused Mary of participation in the Babington Plot and corresponding with Babington and others in a conspiracy to murder the queen.

Mary interrupted Gowdy, vigorously denying that she even knew Babington and demanding that he produce any letter to or from Babington. Mary, of course, had no idea that the letters had all gone to Walsingham. The prosecutor replied with a note of triumph that indeed there were such letters, as the Commissioners would soon see.

But Mary remained aggressive in her attitude, even if somewhat less so than before. She demanded again that the letters be produced, adding emphatically that she never wrote any such letters.

At this point copies of the letters were read, and Mary realized that Walsingham might have outwitted her. But the prosecutor had only the copies made by Walsingham's man, Phelippes. Babington had burned the originals after reading them. We do not know if, on hearing the letter containing the forged final paragraph, Mary recognized that it was not something she had dictated. She could hardly make that point, however, without admitting that the rest of the letter was hers.

Instead, Mary continued to deny writing or receiving any such letters, and scoffed at the supposed "proof." "What have you in my handwriting?" she demanded. Of course, there was nothing. They had Babington's admission that he had received the letters; but Mary attacked the reliability of anything Babington said on the ground that it was obtained through torture, which was undoubtedly the case.

As the trial was about to adjourn for lunch, the prosecutor announced confidently that Mary's denials would all be disproved in the afternoon.

When the trial resumed, Mary was stunned to hear the evidence of men to whom Babington had shown the original of Mary's reply acquiescing in the "work" to be performed by the six assassins. Even worse was the written testimony of her two secretaries, Nau and Curle, that they had written that incriminating reply just as she had dictated it.

Mary responded that "the majesty and safety of all princes falleth to the ground if they depend upon the writing and testimony of secretaries." It was a thin argument, and it availed her not at all.

Losing confidence, Mary shifted her ground. She sought to generate sympathy, arguing that her long confinement had destroyed her health and taken her youth. Plainly that tactic also failed. Next, she bitterly attacked Walsingham as the devious agent of her destruction. This too was unavailing.

More evidence was produced, but the outcome was no longer in doubt — if it ever was. Elizabeth, still troubled by the proceedings and concerned with how the trial and verdict would be perceived abroad, directed the Commissioners to return to London before reaching their verdict. More evidence was taken there. On October 25, 1586, sitting in London's Court of the Star Chamber, the Commissioners reviewed the evidence, and Mary's two secretaries repeated in person the testimony they had previously given in writing. Curle added that he had even urged Mary not to become involved in the plot and not to respond to Babington's letter. The Commissioners unanimously found Mary guilty of conspiracy to murder the Queen.

Still, Elizabeth was not quite ready to see her cousin executed. Despite the urging of her Council and the Commons, she delayed taking the essential action to bring about Mary's death — signing her death warrant. Perhaps this was reluctance to kill an anointed monarch, although Mary had abdicated in favor of her son, James. Perhaps it was concern about the reaction of other rulers to executing a woman who had at least been such a monarch, and was Elizabeth's cousin as well. "What will they now say," she remarked, "when it shall be spread that for the safety of her life, a maiden queen could be content to spill the blood even of her own kinswoman?"

And perhaps it was the possibility that Philip of Spain had held off invading England, because he was reluctant to see the pro-French Mary Stuart on the English throne.

With the threat of Mary removed, would Philip act more aggressively? Would he try to seize the English throne himself, returning the realm to Catholicism, ending English aid to the Dutch and vastly increasing the power, wealth and influence of Spain? It would be surprising if this was not a factor in creating Elizabeth's reluctance to have Mary executed.

Finally, on February 1, 1587, after a delay of three months, Elizabeth signed the death warrant. She gave the signed warrant to her Second Secretary, William Davison, instructing him to have the Lord Chancellor affix the great seal of England. Davison, who had been in office only four months, carried out this order. He then gave the sealed warrant to Burghley, who called an emergency meeting of the Council. The councilors voted unanimously to send the warrant to Fotheringhay at once, in order to bring about Mary's prompt execution. A trusted courier left immediately to deliver the signed and sealed warrant to Fotheringhay. Evidently, no one told the Queen.

A week later, at 7:00 a.m. on February 8, 1587, almost 300 spectators filed into the great hall at Fotheringhay to witness Mary's death. A platform three feet high had been hastily constructed and shrouded in black. It was the stage on which this drama was to be enacted. Soon, Mary approached and mounted the platform. She wore a black gown with her rosary beads hanging from its belt and a crucifix in her hand. Gone was the glamorous seductress of the past. After almost twenty years of confinement, she had aged badly and grown fat. A pronounced double chin showed between her gown and her now rotund face.

Mary was accompanied to the scaffold by her physician and her female servants. At first, the officials refused to allow anyone to accompany her. But, when it appeared that an undesirable scene would ensue, she was allowed to select a handful of personal servants to witness her death.

She greeted the headsman and his assistant courteously and gave them the customary forgiveness for what they had to do. They began to remove her outer garments, revealing a petticoat of bright crimson, the color of Catholic martyrdom.

As they fitted a blindfold over her eyes, a cleric began to intone Protestant prayers for her soul. At once, Mary and her servants recited Catholic prayers with sufficient volume to drown out the reform cleric.

Next, Mary knelt, placing her head on the block, still reciting her Catholic prayers. Finally, she uttered "In Manus Tuas, Domine," "In your hands, God," and stretched out her hands to show she was ready. The headsman raised his axe and struck. There was a gasp as the axe caught the blindfold and inflicted a deep wound in Mary's neck without killing her. Mary uttered a small sound, but remained with her head on the block. The headsman swung again, this time severing her head except for a bit of gristle, which he quickly cut away.

Then, as was the custom, he lifted Mary's severed head by its hair to display it to the spectators. Shockingly, her head fell from his grasp and bounced across the scaffold floor, leaving the headsman holding her red hair aloft.

She had been wearing a wig. The hair on her severed head was gray and extremely sparse. Her lips were said to have continued moving, as if still praying.

As Mary's body was being removed, her tiny Skye terrier crept out from beneath her petticoats where it had been hiding throughout the proceedings.

There was exultation in the streets of London at the news of Mary's death. Bells were rung and a general celebration ensued. In European capitals and in Scotland, however, the news was received with anger and dismay.

Elizabeth learned of Mary's execution, and of the drama and horror of it, only after it occurred. She went into a towering rage, primarily at Davison, but also at Cecil, claiming furiously that they had deceived her and violated her orders.

The Spanish Ambassador reported that Elizabeth had instructed Davison not to release the death warrant to anyone until she gave further instructions. Probably that was the story she "leaked." Probably it was untrue.

Davison was confined in the Tower. He was tried and convicted by the Court of Star Chamber of disobeying the queen's order to hold the signed death warrant. He was sentenced to confinement in the Tower "at the Queen's pleasure" and subjected to a fine. However, he was later released, and the fine was never collected. Although he was deprived of the title "Second Secretary" and no longer carried out the duties of that office, he continued to receive its salary and perquisites. If Davison had really been given a direct order by the queen not to release the death warrant and had deliberately disobeyed that critically important order, he would surely have been cruelly executed, rather than suffering these relatively mild and seemingly cosmetic penalties. Indeed, Henry VIII would have executed Davison whether or not he had disobeyed a royal order.

Without question, the Council members could be accused of keeping the immediacy of Mary's execution a secret from Elizabeth, hoping to avoid another last minute change of heart. But, there were other reasons for secrecy and, putting it cynically, it gave Elizabeth "plausible deniability" — the ability to claim she didn't know the execution was about to happen. But, Elizabeth had signed the death warrant on February 1st. Assuming she hadn't really told Davison to hold the warrant, she had to have expected the execution to take place relatively soon.

In fact, there was a full week between her signing the death warrant on February 1st and the execution on February 8th. If, as Davison claimed, he had been free to deliver the warrant, and if Elizabeth was concerned as to when an execution was scheduled, she certainly could have inquired. And, if she found out and wanted to stop it, there was time to dispatch a fast rider to Fotheringhay with such an order. The fact is she never asked. Probably, she didn't want to know.

The preponderance of evidence points to the conclusion that Elizabeth acquiesced in Mary's execution, but, concerned with the likely outrage in Spain, France, the Empire and Scotland, she strove mightily to create the impression that she had not known, that it was the fault of others — Davison, Burghley and the Council.

Nevertheless, while making sure her anger was seen, Elizabeth was fair enough not to exact any harsh punishment for this "miserable accident," as she described it in a letter to Mary's son, James VI of Scotland. That description supported the impression she hoped to create through Europe. She probably had little concern about what James himself believed. She was paying him a "pension" of £4000 per year; and she certainly realized that he had no intention of taking any hostile action that would jeopardize his chances of succeeding Elizabeth on the English throne.

James did write before the execution that "my honor constrains me to insist for [his mother's] life." But his letter also said that he would be "inconstant" if he "should prefer my mother to the title" and that his religion (i.e., Protestant) "ever moved me to hate her course." There had never been a personal relationship between them; and the Scottish king believed that she had killed Darnley, his father. At an earlier time, when there was talk of returning Mary to Scotland, James' envoy wrote that such a request "should neither be granted nor spoke of hereafter." A Scottish Privy Councilor summed up James' feelings before the execution. "In so far as his mother may be burdened . . . I find his majesty in no way minds that rigors shall be used against her."

Any lingering feelings of regret James may have had about his mother's execution were undoubtedly destroyed by seeing her letter purporting to disinherit him, which was found among her papers. Characteristically, as soon as Mary's letter was discovered, Elizabeth sent it to James.

Whatever remorse James may or may not have felt, there was strong resentment in Scotland over Mary's execution. The Scots, who had previously screamed for her head as an adulteress and murderer, were now enraged at the English for executing her. When Lord Hunsdon's son, James Carey, crossed the border to deliver Elizabeth's "miserable accident" letter to James, the Scottish king warned Carey to remain at the English border town of Berwick lest he be murdered by angry Scots.

Meanwhile, relations with Spain had been growing steadily worse. Hawkins and Drake had openly attacked Spanish shipping and Spanish colonies in the New World. This was obviously done with Elizabeth's acquiescence. She had even been a personal investor in their "ventures." The Spanish now controlled the southern provinces of the lowlands, jeopardizing the rebels in the north, and creating continued pressure on Elizabeth to support the Dutch fight for independence. Always leery of military adventurers, she reluctantly agreed to permit an English army to fight in the lowlands in 1585 and 1586. They were to be under Leicester's command.

Hoping for continuing English support, the Dutch were even willing to give Elizabeth sovereignty over their provinces. She rejected the idea. She had no desire for such personal aggrandizement; and her exercising English sovereignty over a people rebelling against Spanish rule would almost surely force Philip to attack England. Perhaps, sending English troops to aid the rebels would not have that result. But, even that was a risk.

While it did not start a war with Spain, the English expeditionary force in the lowlands achieved little success. It led to a rare period of conflict between Elizabeth and Leicester, even rivaling in intensity her anger over his clandestine marriage to Lettice Knollys. This time, her "sweet Robin" had spent a fortune on the lowlands campaign, had accomplished next to nothing, had disobeyed her explicit orders and frustrated her decision to refuse any form of sovereignty by accepting the title "Governor General" of the Dutch provinces.

Elizabeth was extremely angry. But her anger turned to rage when she learned that Lettice Knollys, now Lady Leicester, was about to join her husband in the lowlands, accompanied by a vast group of friends. It seemed as if the beautiful Lettice intended to establish a rival court in what Leicester had seemingly turned into his personal fiefdom.

The Queen ordered Leicester to announce publicly that he surrendered his title. She was persuaded to relent by Burghley, who, surprisingly, threatened to resign if she forced Leicester to suffer that public humiliation. Probably Burghley believed that the embarrassment to England would be greater than to Leicester. In any event, Elizabeth ultimately cooled down. Reluctantly, she permitted Leicester to retain his title. After a time, Raleigh wrote Leicester that "The Queen is on very good terms with you, and thanks be to God, well pacified and you are again her 'Sweet Robin.'" Evidently, this feeling of goodwill did not extend to Lady Leicester, whose "rival court" in the lowlands never came to pass.

Meanwhile, Philip could hardly ignore the fact that English troops were fighting his own men in the Netherlands. Nor could he ignore Leicester's title of Governor General, implying English sovereignty over the rebel provinces. Almost as annoying was the damage done by Elizabeth's "privateers," who were still raiding his treasure-laden galleons.

For a considerable time, Philip had borne such insults, seeking to avoid an open war with England — especially since it could have led to an English-French alliance against him and the unpleasant possibility of pro-French Mary Stuart succeeding to or taking the English throne. If someone other than Spain had to control England, Philip seemed generally inclined to prefer English heretics to French Catholics.

Now, however, the situation was significantly changed. Elizabeth was fighting Spain in the lowlands, and, thanks to Leicester, was asserting a form of sovereignty over what Philip still considered a Spanish colony. She was also reputed to be torturing and executing priests and imprisoning Catholic subjects. Not only that, she was encouraging English "privateers" to capture Spanish treasure ships, which was costing Philip a lot of money.

Philip's position *vis-à-vis* France was also quite different. With Mary Stuart's execution in 1587, Philip no longer had to be concerned about the possibility of her replacing or succeeding Elizabeth on the throne, essentially placing England under French control. An invasion of England to support a new candidate, instead of pro-French Mary, was a far more appealing prospect.

Besides, Henri of Navarre, a committed Protestant, was next in line to the French throne. The militantly Catholic Guise faction needed Philip's help to avoid that result, which could be disastrous from their point of view. This left France unlikely to oppose any attack that Philip might launch against England, even though Philip's candidate for the throne would no longer be pro-French. If Philip invaded England now and did away with its heretical queen, he could put a reliable English Catholic on the throne or possibly even take it himself, as he had done in Portugal. That would hardly be a good thing for France; but, if it was the price of Philip's help against the Huguenots, the Guise would live with it.

Despite the raids of the English privateers, Philip had far greater sources of revenue than Elizabeth. The queen's annual income was less than ten percent of what Philip received each year just from the West Indies. Still, carrying out an invasion of England would require an enormous expenditure, and the continuing campaign in the Netherlands was already consuming vast amounts of Spanish wealth. Philip was expecting financial aid from Italian bankers. Walsingham did his best to cut off that funding. But there was no way to prevent all of the treasure ships from getting through, and those that did brought funding enough.

Given the political situation and Philip's wealth, it now became clear to Walsingham and his spy network that the Spanish king was preparing a mighty armada to effect an invasion of England. In a daring and devastating raid on Cádiz in the Spring of 1587, Drake caught much of the Spanish fleet off guard and destroyed twenty fighting ships without the loss of a single English vessel. Drake's raid forced postponement of the attack on England for a year.

Philip was enraged and determined to rebuild the armada and carry out the invasion. About this time, he and Elizabeth, who had been brother and sister-in-law (and, at one time, potentially even husband and wife), exchanged rather "edgy" verses. The originals were in Latin. They are translated here. Philip's message was plainly an ultimatum.

1. *I bid you make no armed defense of the Belgians.*

2. *See that you restore Drake's plundered treasures.*

3. *Rebuild the (monastic) cells your father emptied.*

4. *Restore perfectly the religion of the Pope.*

Elizabeth's reply was brief and characteristic.

When Greeks measure months by the moon,

Then, Spanish Philip, thy will shall be done.

Since the Greeks were known for *never* measuring months by the moon, Elizabeth was telling Philip "Never, Spanish Philip, never!"

Philip ordered his nephew, the Duke of Parma, to negotiate with the English, to pretend he was seeking a peaceful accommodation, but never to close a deal. Parma was to keep extending the negotiations, constantly lulling the English into complacency and buying time for the Spanish to prepare for their invasion of England.

The English were not deceived. Through a spy in Rome, Walsingham was able to obtain a copy of the Spanish invasion plan Philip had sent to the Pope. Walsingham also received reports on the Spanish Armada from French sources and from his spies on the coast of Spain. He knew the munitions, soldiers, sailors and provisions, as well as the ships that would form the Armada, including their strengths, weaknesses and planned strategy.

But espionage was not a one-way street. Philip had his own spy. The English didn't know it at the time, but the spy was Sir Edward Stafford, Elizabeth's Ambassador to France. He was supplying the Spanish with detailed information on Elizabeth's plans to defend England against the Armada. Walsingham suspected Stafford, but could find no proof.

In May 1588, the Armada was ready to sail one hundred thirty-five ships, fifty of them towering Spanish and Portuguese galleons. The magnificent fleet was under the command of the Don Alonzo Perez de Guzman el Bueno, the Seventh Duke of Medina Sidonia. Medina Sidonia was descended from a long line of heroic warriors. But he was not one of them. An intelligent man, he had no military or naval experience. His pleasure was riding around the vast farms and orchards surrounding his ancestral castle near San Lucar de Barrameda, inland from Cádiz.

Philip's first choice to command the Armada had been Don Álvaro de Bazán, Marquis of Santa Cruz, an able and experienced naval commander. Santa Cruz participated in planning the Armada's strategy. But he died before the great fleet was to sail. On Santa Cruz's death, the King turned to Medina Sidonia, feeling he needed a respected aristocrat in command to control his hot tempered officers and prevent their fighting among themselves. This was not something Medina Sidonia wanted; but he had a deep sense of duty. Reluctantly, he accepted the command.

The Armada carried soldiers as well as a full complement of seamen. But the primary goal of the massive fleet was not to land a military force in England. The main invasion force was to be provided by the Duke of Parma, who had been fighting in the Netherlands. Parma intended the Armada to destroy or neutralize the English fleet and then to rendezvous with him on the Channel Coast. With the English fleet defeated or forced out of the battle, Parma planned to ferry 30,000 seasoned Spanish troops plus hundreds of horses across the Channel on flat-bottomed barges and rafts. This principal force would subsequently be joined by 18,000 additional troops aboard the Armada, who would land and form a reserve.

There was a religious component to the Armada as well. Most of the ships had a priest aboard; and Medina Sidonia's flagship flew an enormous banner blessed by the Pope, depicting Christ on the cross with the Virgin Mary below him on one side and Mary Magdalena on the other. Psalms were recited, and the ship's boys sang *Ave Maria* at sunset.

Many of the largest warships in the Armada were Portuguese. Some Portuguese officers undoubtedly resented the Spanish domination of their country and may have been less enthusiastic than the Spanish about the combined attack. Still, the English were heretics, and, when the battle was joined, the Portuguese would undoubtedly fight.

The Armada sailed from Lisbon in May, encountering heavy weather that made it difficult to keep the ships together and to make headway toward the Channel. Also, the high-sided ships of the Armada were unable to move against the wind, even by tacking. Each tack simply drove them backwards. They would have to wait.

That June, the weather was no better, and severe problems with provisions were becoming evident. In his raid on Cádiz, Drake had burned many thousands of seasoned barrel staves intended for the Armada's use. Medina Sidonia had been forced to store much of the fleet's provisions in barrels of green, unseasoned wood, which quickly allowed the meat to rot, the wine to sour and water to become foul.

In July 1588, the Armada finally sailed and reached the Channel. Meanwhile, the English had taken defensive measures. Troops had been raised from all the counties. Signal fires were readied along the entire coast and, from there, inland from hilltop to hilltop, to be lit at the first sighting of the Armada. In the coastal areas, cattle had been moved inland and crops destroyed, to keep anything of value from the invaders. A barrier of ships' masts, linked together by heavy chains, had been stretched across the Thames, to prevent an upriver passage of the Spanish fleet.

Most effective of all, the English navy had been readied to fight, the crews fully prepared and the ships fitted out and ready to sail. In a very real sense, Henry VIII had created the English navy that was now to defend the realm. Henry had improved the design of the ships and the skills of the crews and had installed the guns positioned to unleash devastating broadsides at the enemy. The condition of the navy had been allowed to deteriorate during the reigns of Edward VI and Mary. But it had been significantly improved under Elizabeth. The English ships were again properly fitted, armed and maintained; and the caliber of the English commanders, many of whom had acquired their skills as privateers, was generally excellent.

Until Philip acquired the Portuguese navy, his maritime force was a mighty fleet of high-sided galleys designed for the calm waters of the Mediterranean. He had virtually no ships intended for warfare on the open ocean or the choppy waters of the Channel. His crews were trained to fight by grappling with the enemy's ships, boarding them and fighting hand to hand, not by firing cannons at enemy ships maneuvering in heavy seas. The addition of the Portuguese vessels improved the situation somewhat, but did not solve the basic problems facing the fleet as a whole.

Through his spies, Walsingham had been made aware of these deficiencies, and the English were poised to take advantage of them. Hawkins had redesigned the fleet, replacing the huge, slow, cumbersome vessels with ships that were smaller, faster, more maneuverable and better suited to fighting in the Channel. Their upper decks were significantly lower than those of the Spanish, making it more difficult for the Spanish to use their boarding tactics. The English ships had longer range guns, mounted on tracks that allowed them to slide backwards after firing. In that position, they could be quickly reloaded and slid forward ready to fire again. In addition, their crews were well trained in gunnery, as well as seamanship. The English commanders were experienced seamen. Most of the Spanish ships were commanded by military officers, since their battles at sea were primarily matters of boarding the enemies' ships and defeating them in hand-to-hand combat.

On the 19th of July, word was received that the Armada had been sighted off the "Lizard," the narrow peninsula at the tip of Cornwall. Charles Howard, the Lord Admiral, and a few of his senior officers, including Francis Drake, were having an afternoon bowling match. According to legend, Drake remarked coolly that there was ample time to finish the game and then beat the Spaniards.

Probably, Drake did make that famous remark. The game was in the mid-afternoon, the Armada was moving very slowly and, in any event, the tide would not permit the English fleet to move out to sea until evening. Though they may have adopted a cool and jocular attitude, the fate of the nation depended on these men, and they faced the very real possibility of defeat and death in the next few days.

The beacon fires were lit, and the alarm was spread from town to town all the way to the Scottish border. Those fires near the coast could even be seen from the Spanish ships. England prepared to defend itself. But Elizabeth and her advisors were well aware that, if tens of thousands of battle-tested Spanish troops were able to effect a landing, it would probably be impossible for England's newly recruited and relatively untrained militia to stop them. It seemed clear that, if the nation was to be saved, it would have to be by the English fleet and such men as Drake, Hawkins and Howard.

The Spanish plan was to take advantage of the design of their ships and the training of their crews. They intended to fight, as was their custom, not by exchanging gunfire but by placing their high-sided galleys next to the English ships, grappling, boarding and defeating their crews in hand-to-hand fighting. Warned of this strategy by Walsingham's intelligence reports, the English ships avoided moving close enough for the Spanish to grapple and board.

At first, the English fired at the massive Spanish galleons from a distance, scoring some hits but not doing serious damage. The English found it difficult to penetrate Medina Sidonia's powerful crescent formation that defied customary forms of naval attack. Despite the English cannon fire, the massive Armada stayed together and continued its menacing voyage up the Channel toward a rendezvous with Parma.

Soon, both fleets were running low on ammunition. The English obtained replacement supplies and ammunition from English coastal towns. The Spanish could not. Philip had ordered Medina Sidonia to sail up the English side of the Channel, but, under no circumstances, to halt his progress in order to capture an English port. This was a serious error. Had the Armada sailed up the French side of the Channel or had it been allowed to capture an English port, even temporarily, it could have obtained critically needed supplies.

Nor was ammunition the only problem. Cask after cask was opened to reveal spoiled meat, sour wine and foul water. If they did not rendezvous with Parma soon, the Armada could not continue its role in the invasion.

As often happens in warfare conducted on a large, international scale, communications to and from the Armada were extremely poor. Philip's generals in the Netherlands had always suffered from poor communications with Spain; and this situation was no better. Philip, sitting in his monastic room in the Escorial Palace northwest of Madrid, communicated with his commanders only by written letters. Even aside from the delay this caused, Philip's orders were sometimes confusing and inconsistent. This hardly made for swift and flexible tactics or even coherent strategy.

And worse, once he was at sea, Medina Sidonia received no commands at all. Lacking any communication from either the king or Parma, the Spanish Admiral expected to meet Parma at Calais or Dunkirk. Apparently, he believed that, as soon as the Armada arrived, Parma would embark his army and cross the Channel, relying on the Armada to protect him against attack by the English fleet.

Parma, on the other hand, planned to have his troops cross the Channel in flat-bottomed barges, with his horses on rafts. English gunnery could easily sink them; and Parma had no intention of embarking his troops and their mounts in such extremely vulnerable craft until the Armada had already destroyed the English fleet or had at least forced it out of the action.

Philip was aware of that sensible plan and had ordered Parma to follow it. Medina Sidonia, however, either misunderstood Philip's instructions or was simply kept in the dark. He dispatched urgent messages to Parma, seeking to know when and from what port Parma's men would embark. Strangely, Parma didn't reply. Either he failed to receive the messages, or he was willing to communicate only with his uncle, the king, and not with some untested, newly made Admiral. In any event, Parma wasn't ready. Even if he had been willing to embark with the English fleet still able to attack his flat-bottomed barges, it would have taken another week before his forces could be assembled and ready to board.

Awaiting word from Parma, and with severe shortages of ammunition and provisions, Medina Sidonia anchored the Armada off Calais. The English followed suit, and the two fleets continued firing at each other.

That night, July 28, 1588, the English sent fire ships among the large and clumsy galleons anchored closely together. These were small vessels filled with pitch, oil and wood and then set afire to create havoc and panic among the enemy ships. When the Spanish tried to avoid the fire ships by fighting free of their anchorage, there were collisions, and, once free of those dangers, the Spanish faced fierce attacks by the smaller, more maneuverable English vessels.

Somehow, Medina Sidonia managed to keep much of the Spanish fleet together. But he could not reestablish the powerful crescent formation that had previously protected his ships. The next day, English gunnery sank a number of them. This was the Battle of Gravelines. The English had realized, by then, that they had to get close enough to create serious damage, but not so close that they could be boarded. They had also learned to attack in line, delivering one damaging broadside after another.

After firing, the retractable English guns slid backward on their rails, where they could be quickly reloaded, firing round after round with devastating effect. The Spanish guns – mostly field artillery pieces – were fixed in place to prevent their careening wildly about the decks, creating chaos and serious injury. Loading required access to the mouths of the guns, which protruded from the gun ports. Once they were fired, they did not retract like the English guns, so that manhandling and reloading a hot and heavy gun in the midst of a battle was extremely difficult and dangerous. Many of the Spanish guns fired only once during the entire battle.

And the English guns were of cast iron, with superior rifling that made for greater distance and accuracy. The Spanish guns were bronze, given to becoming dangerously hot, sometimes even to explode. The quality of the English shot was also superior. It penetrated the Spanish hulls, while most of the Spanish balls broke up on striking the heavy oak of the English hulls.

Drake sent word to Walsingham that "the Duke of Sidonia" would soon "wish himself back at Saint Mary

Port among his orange trees." That was probably just what the Spanish Admiral was wishing.

Fierce winds now threatened to drive the Spanish ships toward the Dutch coast, where treacherous sandbars and the swift, maneuverable boats of the hostile "Sea Beggars" awaited them. At least two galleons were driven aground. Faced with the dangers of the Dutch coastline and the increasing menace of English gunnery, Medina Sidonia moved the rest of the Armada northward, aided by a shift in the wind. In the following days, however, he realized that this direction held even greater peril.

The remaining ships of the Armada were driven into the North Sea, where severe storms did enormous damage. Having no charts of those waters, they were sailing "blind." Many of the ships were forced onto the rocks and cliffs of Scotland and Ireland, leaving thousands of drowned sailors and soldiers washed up on the shore.

Quite a few reached shore alive. Except for those who seemed rich enough to hold for ransom, most were killed. According to legend, however, some were welcomed into Irish seaside homes, where they remained and "fraternized" with the local girls, resulting in dark complected descendants now called "black Irish." The story is probably apocryphal.

The surviving vessels, with their wounded and dying crews, limped home. Nearly two-thirds of the sailors and soldiers who had originally sailed aboard the Armada lost their lives. Only sixty of the one hundred thirty-five original ships made it back to Spain. The rest — seventy-five ships — were either sunk by English gunnery or lost to the heavy seas and rocky coasts of Scotland and Ireland.

Not a single English ship had been lost. Only 68 English sailors were killed in the fighting, although many more died of disease. It was a complete triumph of English seamanship and gunnery. As Lord Admiral Howard said of the English seamen who fought the Armada, "God send us to sea in such a company together again, when need is."

In his report to Philip, Medina Sidonia recognized the successful English strategy and gave credit to the English fleet. The Armada, he said, was "distressed and battered" by the English gunnery, his own "shot had run out" and, on the whole, "the Queen's fleet was superior in this sort of fighting...Your Majesty had the advantage only in small arms and since we could not come to hand stroke, experience has shown that this could avail us little."

Without realizing it, the Spanish Admiral was giving credit to Walsingham's espionage coup. It enabled him to warn the English commanders to fire at a distance, staying away from the larger Spanish ships lest they be grappled, boarded and "come to hand stroke," the fight with "small arms" on which the Spanish had relied.

While unaware of the Armada's northward retreat after the victory at Gravelines, Elizabeth addressed the troops deployed at Tilbury to resist the expected invasion up the Thames estuary. It was perhaps her most dramatic moment.

*Let tyrants fear: I have always so behaved myself that,
under God, I have placed my chiefest strength and safeguard in
the loyal hearts and good-will of my subjects . . . I am come
among you at this time . . . being resolved in the midst and heat
of the battle to live and die amongst you all, to lay down for my
God and for my kingdom and for my people mine honor and my
blood even in the dust. I know I have the body but of a weak and
feeble woman, but I have the heart and stomach of a King — and
a King of England too!*

When the Queen concluded her speech, the assembled troops gave "a mighty shout." Leicester, who was in command of the troops at Tilbury, wrote:

*Our gracious mistress hath been here with me to see her camp
and people, which so inflamed the hearts of her good subjects
as I think the weakest person among them is able to match the
proudest Spaniard that dares land in England.*

They could not and did not land. England was saved, and Elizabeth, as well as the fleet, was seen as its savior.

If the Armada had succeeded, England would have become a Catholic nation ruled by a Catholic monarch, possibly Philip himself. It has been argued that the colonies of North America would have been Spanish, rather than English, that there would have been no American

Revolution and that Spanish would be the language of America even today.

I think not. A Spanish controlled, rigorously Catholic England would, if anything, have hastened and increased the flow of Protestants to the North American colonies, possibly even hastening the American Revolution. My bet is that, even if the Armada had prevailed, most Americans would still be speaking English.

In any event, the triumph over the Armada was followed by events of great sadness for Elizabeth. She was now fifty-five, near her father's age when he died. She remained slim and agile, continuing to ride, hunt and dance as before. And she continued to read voraciously.

However, Leicester, her dear "Robin," had aged badly. His dark good looks had faded, leaving him pale, paunchy and balding. The strain of the Armada defense may have taken too great a toll. After a brief illness, he died in 1588, only a month after the Armada's defeat.

It has been reported that, learning of Leicester's death, Elizabeth shut herself in a room and refused to come out until the door was broken down. Probably this never happened. But, certainly, she was deeply grieved. On the surface, she soldiered on. But the depth of her feeling for her "Robin" could be seen from her treatment of a note he had written her shortly before he died. On her own death, an envelope containing the note was found in a small chest near her bed. Across it she had written "His last letter."

Then, in 1590, came the death of Francis Walsingham, long her trusted spymaster and protector against the numerous plots and schemes that had so often threatened her crown and her life.

Walsingham had become a committed Protestant at Cambridge and remained one for life. When Mary overcame the supporters of Jane Grey and turned the realm back to Catholicism, Walsingham went into self-imposed exile, traveling widely in Europe and teaching law in Padua. On Elizabeth's accession, he returned, taking a seat in Parliament. His European connections allowed him to supply Cecil's government with critical intelligence. Disapproving of the French, he reluctantly served as the English Ambassador in Paris, where he personally observed the horror of the St. Bartholomew's Day Massacre. Later, he was recalled and was made one of the two Principal Secretaries.

Probably, however, Walsingham's most significant contribution was as Elizabeth's head of intelligence and security. Famous for his long hours and fierce determination to protect the queen and the kingdom, he held his demanding positions for many years. His loss was a staggering blow. Burghley took over many of Walsingham's duties, but he too was suffering the disabilities of old age.

In this period, Elizabeth was still comforted by the tall, handsome Raleigh, who remained a favorite, highly attractive to the aging queen. But, as intelligent as he was, Raleigh made a mistake like Leicester's. He fell in love with

Bess Throckmorton, one of Elizabeth's ladies in waiting. By 1591, Bess was pregnant, and they married. Soon, they had a son. When Elizabeth found out, her reaction was predictable — rage. Raleigh and Bess were sent to the Tower. Raleigh was released in five weeks. Bess remained somewhat longer.

Raleigh was never again the favorite he had been; but he continued to serve the queen in many ways. His marriage to Bess endured. After Elizabeth's death, he was falsely accused and convicted of treason. James I commuted his sentence of death but he spent years in the Tower. Ultimately, he was freed so that he could lead an expedition up the Orinoco River seeking gold. When he returned with no gold, having killed numerous Spaniards, James reimposed the death sentence. Shortly before his execution, Raleigh wrote Bess from the Tower, "I chose you and I love you and I loved you in my happiest times." Did he mean that he "chose" Bess over the Queen? Perhaps. It may even have been true.

But I'm getting far ahead of the story. In the 1590's Elizabeth's personal losses continued. In 1591, she came to the bedside of the dying Christopher Hatton, who had suffered a stroke and whose passing saddened her greatly.

Then, in 1596 came the death of Elizabeth's loyal friend and kinsman, Henry Carey, whom she had made Lord Hunsdon. The supposedly parsimonious queen even paid for his elaborate and expensive funeral. As we have seen, Hunsdon was the son of Anne Boleyn's sister Mary, born during her long affair with Henry VIII. Out of respect for Mary's complaisant husband, he was given the name Carey and was publicly known as Elizabeth's "cousin." In fact, he was probably the king's son and Elizabeth's half-brother.

In her letter congratulating Hunsdon on his military victory against the northern rebels, Elizabeth had addressed him as "Right trusty and well beloved cousin" and referred to him as "My Harry." She signed the letter "Your loving kins-woman, Elizabeth R." And, when the Queen thought she was dying of smallpox, she had included in her oral bequests a direction singling out Hunsdon for special recognition and reward. Elizabeth probably knew the truth about his parentage. Whether or not she did, he was a trusted and special friend.

Hunsdon served as a member of Elizabeth's Privy Council, as Captain of the Gentlemen Pensioners and as Lord Chamberlain. He was also a patron of the acting company of which Shakespeare was an actor and co-owner, and he was the longtime lover of the darkly attractive Emilia Lanier, thought by some to have been the "dark lady" of Shakespeare's sonnets. A year after Hunsdon's death, his son George became Lord Chamberlain and a patron of the same acting company. Perhaps because he was thought to be the grandson of Henry VIII, George Carey had once been suggested as a husband for Mary Stuart; but the match never progressed.

Finally, in 1598, Elizabeth lost her trusted old friend Burghley, her "partner" in governing the kingdom for forty years. When Burghley became seriously ill, the Queen came to his bedside and spoon-fed him. Even when he seemed at death's door, he rose from his bed to attend one last meeting of the Council. Exhausted, he returned home and soon died.

It seemed that all of the men who had supported Elizabeth personally and politically for so long were falling away, one at a time, leaving her alone and unprotected. Although there were other members of the Council, much of the important business of government had been conducted by Burghley, Walsingham, Leicester and Hatton. Now all of them were gone. So was her "beloved" Hunsdon and the friends of her youth. Even those two seagoing stalwarts, Drake and Hawkins, died of disease on a fatal treasure hunt to the Indies.

Elizabeth must have had bittersweet memories of them all in the radiant glow of their earlier years. Shakespeare wrote that "Golden lads and girls must, like chimney sweepers, come to dust." Would that express what the queen was feeling? Probably.

But Elizabeth had one last personal relationship – one last "golden lad." Maybe it was just a lengthy and ego-building flirtation for the aging queen. Maybe it was more. Robert Devereux, the young Earl of Essex, was a tall, handsome youth, with curly auburn hair, dark eyes and royal blood. He was a descendant of Edward III, and probably of Henry VIII as well. Essex was the son of Elizabeth's "cousin" and longtime rival, Lettice Knollys, and her deceased first husband. Lettice, Mary Boleyn's granddaughter and the daughter of Katherine Carey

Knollys, was probably also the granddaughter of Henry VIII, which would make Essex a great-grandson of the late king. His stature and appearance would have supported that possibility. He was also Leicester's stepson.

Leicester brought Essex to court in 1584, when he was only 18. Elizabeth, who was 51 at the time, was much taken with the well built, charming young man. Her beauty had long ago faded. She wore a red wig and used heavy cosmetics in a vain attempt to thwart the ravages of time. But she was still a brilliant and fascinating woman. She had abandoned pastels and wore dramatic gowns of silver, white and black.

Possibly, as he grew into a bold and dashing courtier, Essex was attracted to the queen. Despite her age, both Hatton and Raleigh had apparently found her not only fascinating but attractive. Essex, however, was more likely attracted by her being queen and the opportunities this offered for his personal advancement. There was, after all, more than thirty years difference in their ages.

Fairly soon, a special relationship developed between the two. Obviously, the queen enjoyed the ardent attention and lavish complements of the handsome young Earl. He flattered her outrageously, referring often to her incomparable beauty. She appeared ready to believe whatever he said. Understandably, she wanted to believe it.

By the time he was 20, Essex had plainly become the queen's "favorite." He was appointed Master of the Horse, the office previously held by Leicester, and was made a Knight of the Garter. Other lucrative offices and benefits were bestowed on him, including a monopoly of the importation of sweet wine. These "favors" helped him meet his debts and the staggering expenses of his extravagant lifestyle.

Did Elizabeth know that, as Mary Boleyn's great-grandson, Essex was probably also the great-grandson of her own father? It's difficult to believe that she was not aware of that possibility. But her favors to Essex did not seem based on the likelihood of his being a blood relative.

Portraits of Essex in the 1590s show him handsome and arrogant in black and white costumes, the queen's colors. But the young Earl was hardly just a drawing room fop. Brave, adventurous and skilled in arms, he enjoyed considerable success in tournaments and fought in Leicester's lowlands campaign. Later, as he achieved political influence, he consistently advocated an aggressive war policy toward Spain. This brought him into conflict with the more thoughtful, diplomatic approach of Burghley and, later, that of Burghley's brilliant son, Robert Cecil.

Essex was brash, prideful and quick to anger. He fought a duel with Sir Charles Blount over Blount's wearing a gold chess queen given him by Elizabeth for success in jousting. Essex was wounded in the duel, and the queen was concerned and angry at him. Next, the jealous young Earl challenged Sir Walter Raleigh to a duel, but, this time, the queen forbad it. Later, Essex issued challenges to others, including a challenge outside the gates of Lisbon to fight any champion the Portuguese might send out to oppose him, a similar challenge to the Governor of Rouen, and, supposedly, a challenge to the Irish Earl of Tyrone.

Essex was in Portugal as part of an expedition led by Francis Drake to replace Philip on the Portuguese throne with Don Antonio, an illegitimate member of the Portuguese royal line. At the time, Essex was heavily in debt and evidently saw the expedition as an opportunity to acquire riches as well as glory. He stole away at night and rode headlong for Plymouth, where he boarded a ship and sailed for Portugal before the riders sent by Elizabeth could overtake him.

The expedition proved a dismal failure. The Portuguese did not rise up for Don Antonio as had been expected and countless Englishmen died of disease.

The queen was angry — at Drake for the expedition's cost and failure and at Essex for leaving without her permission, a serious transgression for one who held an important royal office. Still, she forgave him and in a short time was basking again in his compliments and company.

Essex's judgment, however, did not improve. Soon he began a secret affair with Walsingham's 22-year-old daughter, Frances Sidney. When she became pregnant, he secretly exchanged vows with her, which was considered a marriage. Possibly this was demanded by Walsingham as the price of silence.

Later, Essex impregnated Elizabeth Southwell, Catherine Knollys' granddaughter. Faced with another difficult situation, Essex bribed Thomas Vavasour to claim that he was the father. Elizabeth imprisoned Vavasour; and, later, when she finally discovered that she had imprisoned an innocent man, she was, once again, enraged at Essex.

Ultimately, the queen even discovered the Earl's secret marriage; but he was able to quiet her initial anger by promising that Frances would live separately from him in her mother's home.

But this was all later. In this period, religious turmoil in France had continued. When Charles IX died two years after the St. Bartholomew's Day Massacre, the effeminate, cross-dressing Henri III became king. During his ineffective, but surprisingly moderate reign, the Guise family and the Catholic League, led by the Duke of Guise, rivaled the power of the king and generally opposed his policies. In 1589, the Duke was assassinated, probably at the direction of Henri III. But vengeance was soon to come. Only nine months later, Henri was fatally stabbed by a Catholic monk to whom he had granted an audience while seated on a close-stool moving his bowels. The monk pulled a long dagger from his sleeve and plunged it into Henri's stomach. He was the third son of Catherine de Medici to die. Catherine herself had died a few months earlier.

As he was dying, Henri had supposedly called upon the Protestant Henri of Navarre to take the throne, urging him, however, to convert to Catholicism. The Protestant leader had the strongest claim to the throne, and his supporters were already referring to him as Henri IV. But he was bitterly opposed by the Catholic League, and the League not only controlled Paris, it had potential Spanish support. This began a long series of battles in which Henri tried to take Paris in order to assert effective rule over France. His first attempt on the capital failed. Attacked by strong Catholic forces, he moved his army to Normandy. Later, he advanced again on Paris and besieged the city, only to have the capital saved again for the Catholic cause by Spanish troops under the Duke of Parma.

In 1591, Elizabeth was faced with the potential arrival in Brittany of a Spanish army that could ally itself with the French Catholic force already arrayed there. Unwilling to see Philip gain a deep water Channel port, which could facilitate his invasion of England, and unaware that Henri's real goal lay in taking Paris, rather than protecting the Channel ports, the Queen authorized a small English expeditionary force to fight in France alongside Henri, but for no more than two months.

Essex pleaded with Elizabeth to let him command this force. Elizabeth refused. Essex continued pleading. Finally, with deep misgivings, she relented. But she wrote to Henri cautioning him that her young commander needed the bridle more than the spur; and she assigned other experienced officers the task of controlling Essex. That proved impossible.

Henri had tempted Elizabeth with the prospect of taking Rouen, a strategic and vulnerable city. Essex's instructions were to aid Henri in his siege of Rouen, which was stubbornly held by French Catholic forces opposed to the would-be Protestant King. When Essex arrived in France, however, Henri was not at the site of the siege, but at Compiègne, one hundred miles away. Rather than carrying out his assigned mission, the young Earl set off on a wild and dangerous ride through enemy territory to visit Henri. When he arrived, there were lavish festivities and exciting contests, but no fighting. Ultimately, Essex had to send for English troops to convey him safely back to Rouen.

As time went on, the majority of the English forces invading Rouen died of disease. Henri did little to aid the siege and disappeared completely when the Duke of Parma appeared before the city with a large Spanish force. It became clear that the siege had failed. The expensive mission had risked much and accomplished nothing. An irritated Elizabeth ordered Essex to return to England.

Before he left France, however, Essex used his position as commander to confer knighthood on twenty-four of his friends and supporters. They had done nothing to earn that honor. This infuriated Elizabeth. Her policy was to knight only on those very few men who exhibited extraordinary bravery or accomplished some outstanding military feat. She believed that Essex's profligate creation of knights cheapened the concept and honor of knighthood and wedded these new and unworthy knights to his personal cause — whatever that might be.

Finally, Henri realized that taking Paris and, indeed, ruling France, would elude him so long as he remained a

Protestant and that, if only he were Catholic, the French, who were fundamentally anti-Spanish, and even the Parisians, would support him against Parma. Not one to stand on religious principle, he converted to Catholicism in 1593, famously remarking "Paris vaut bien une messe" ("Paris is well worth a mass").

Finally accepted by the Catholic League, Henri entered Paris in triumph, the acclaimed ruler of all France. Although now a Catholic, Henri, officially Henri IV, issued the Edict of Nantes, assuring Huguenots of general religious tolerance. The vicious French wars of religion were essentially at an end.

Meanwhile, despite her disgust at the costly and unsuccessful Rouen campaign and her anger at Essex's rash behavior, Elizabeth forgave him, and their relationship continued. If anything, they appeared to grow closer. Elizabeth began to call him her "wild horse."

Essex was also acquiring enormous popularity with the people, who remained generally unaware of his conduct in the Rouen campaign. He developed a circle of enthusiastic friends and supporters, including the brilliant Francis Bacon and his remarkable brother Anthony. Repeatedly, Essex urged Elizabeth to appoint Francis Bacon and Essex's other friends to high office — usually without success. Elizabeth seemed to understand the inadvisability — perhaps even the danger — of packing the government with grateful allies of this ambitious and mercurial young man.

But, the Bacons added significantly to Essex's effectiveness and power. Accurate information as to the actions and intentions of other rulers was critical to Elizabeth. It was one reason she had placed such a high value on Walsingham and why she was so concerned at his loss. Anthony Bacon had spent years on the Continent, and his European contacts allowed him to create an espionage network for Essex approaching the one that had been so successfully operated by Walsingham. To strengthen that network, Essex even retained the somewhat sinister services of Thomas Phelippes (alias Halins, alias Morice), the expert code breaker and forger, who had been a key operative in Walsingham's organization and had played such an important role in trapping Mary Stuart.

The foreign intelligence this network generated was passed on to the queen by Essex, enhancing his value to her, creating dependence upon him and making him a realistic successor to Walsingham in the field of espionage and intelligence. Based primarily on this valuable service, Essex was appointed to the Privy Council. He was now a man of significant political influence.

But Essex had a cruel and vindictive side. Dr. Roderigo Lopez was a Portuguese Jew who had converted to Christianity. Lopez had been the physician to Leicester, had cured Walsingham of kidney stones and later became personal physician to the queen. Elizabeth was fond of the doctor, whom she dubbed her "little ape." It appears that Lopez, who had contacts in many places, may also have been a valuable double agent for Walsingham.

After Walsingham's death, Essex set out to destroy Lopez. Perhaps this was because of the physician's prior association with Walsingham or his unwillingness to serve Essex in spying on Elizabeth, or, more likely, Lopez was now supplying his information directly to the queen, bypassing Essex. It is also possible that Essex acted against Lopez as a means of weakening Burghley, who may have been involved in using Lopez as a double agent.

Whatever the reason, Essex began his attack with the claim that Lopez was spreading malicious stories about him. This was probably untrue. It would have been dangerously foolish of Lopez, and Lopez was no fool. With Walsingham's protection gone and Essex determined to bring him down, Lopez found himself charged and convicted of trying to poison the queen. The "evidence" was equivocal. It consisted primarily of letters probably planned by Walsingham to fool the Spanish into believing the doctor was ready to do their bidding if sufficiently paid. If so, with Walsingham dead, there was no one to explain — except Lopez. Even faced with torture, he insisted that the letters were only a device to extort money from Philip. But who would believe this Jewish foreigner when his accuser was the powerful and popular Lord Essex?

Apparently, Elizabeth did. She was troubled and angry with Essex over the episode. But, Essex's popularity was increasing. He was personally important to Elizabeth, and he did have the confessions of other agents implicating Lopez, albeit given under torture. In the end, the Queen did not prevent Lopez's trial for treason or overturn the verdict of guilty or even the sentence of death. She did, however, order the officer in charge of the Tower not to release Lopez for execution. Probably, she intended to see him imprisoned, but not executed.

But Essex was not to be denied. On a ruse, he succeeded in having Lopez brought out from the Tower. The doctor was seized by Essex's men and rushed to Tyburn, where he was hung, drawn and quartered before an enthusiastic crowd.

It appears that, between Lopez's trial and his execution, Essex fostered anti-Semitic fervor in London by encouraging numerous performances of Marlowe's *The Jew of Malta*, in which Barabas, a Jewish money lender, is portrayed as a villainous, murdering traitor. Perhaps these events moved Shakespeare to give us the towering and multi-faceted Shylock in *The Merchant of Venice*. A later chapter will analyze the bizarre case of Dr. Lopez in greater detail.

Elizabeth was facing other critical problems. Philip of Spain was aging and becoming more conscious of his duties to the True Church. In his spartan quarters above the Escorial, he was planning another armada. He was determined to effect an invasion and conquest of England — and with it, overthrow of the heretical Elizabeth and re-establishment of the old religion. Elizabeth continued her efforts to turn the forces of the Ottoman Sultan against Philip; but the Sultan was occupied elsewhere, battling other European powers and threatening Vienna.

Facing Philip's massive preparations for a renewed assault on England, the Queen permitted Essex to join Lord Admiral Howard in leading a daring naval and military raid on Cádiz. Their hugely successful attack resulted in the destruction of the Spanish fleet and the frustration — at least for a time — of Philip's new plan.

Essex, however, was given to foolish and arrogant behavior that created dangerous enemies. He incurred Howard's enmity by signing a joint report on their Cádiz mission immediately below the text of the report, leaving the proud Lord Admiral no place to sign but below Essex.

During the Cádiz raid, Essex had also increased the queen's suspicions by once again knighting numerous men, a few deserving, most not. Once again, Elizabeth realized that the new knights would become dedicated supporters of Essex; and who knew what the bold and reckless young Earl might do or seek in the future? After all, to the public, Essex was "the victor of Cádiz."

Robert Cecil, Burghley's younger son, was a member of the Privy Council. He was slight in stature and hunchbacked. His had been a troubled life. His youth had been marked by ridicule at his physical appearance. His young wife had died. His daughter had inherited his deformity, and his son was chronically ill. But he was brilliant and courageous. Although young Cecil and Essex had known each other since childhood, Essex treated Cecil not only as a rival, but as an enemy. And Essex insisted that others treat him as an enemy as well. When Lord Grey, a respected military officer, declined to take sides between Essex and Cecil, Essex threatened to prevent Grey's ever attaining promotion — presumably by exercising Essex's personal influence with the queen. As Grey, himself, put it, Essex "hath forced mee to declare myself either his only or friend to [Cecil] and his enimy, protesting that ther could bee noe neutrality."

While Essex was away on the Cádiz raid, Elizabeth made Robert Cecil Principal Secretary. When Essex returned, his resentment of Cecil became even more intense, and the rivalry between the two increased in bitterness. Essex began to display a streak of paranoia to go with his being uncontrollable. He complained that others, notably Cecil and Howard, were exerting an evil influence on the queen and trying to destroy him or at least deprive him of the credit and rewards he deserved.

Despite his complaints that other men were getting too much credit for the Cádiz raid, it was Essex who was becoming enormously popular with the English people. Elizabeth was of two minds about that. Popularity and praise were fine. But adulation of anyone other than the Queen herself could become dangerous, especially if, like Essex, the object of that adulation was arrogant, prideful and could muster a reasonable claim to the throne. Despite this risk, Elizabeth still appeared to enjoy Essex's company and was less cautious than she might otherwise have been.

Finally, in 1597, Philip was able to assemble a mighty new armada designed once again to invade England

and depose Elizabeth. Faced with still another Spanish invasion, Elizabeth addressed Parliament.

It may be thought simplicity in me that all this time of my reign have not sought to advance my territories and enlarged my dominions, for both opportunity hath served me to do it, and my strength was able to have done it. I acknowledge my womanhood and weakness in that respect, but it hath not been fear to obtain or doubt how to keep the things so obtained that hath withholden me from these attempts; only, my mind was never to invade my neighbors, nor to usurp upon any, only contented to reign over my own and to rule as a just prince. Yet the King of Spain doth challenge me to be the beginning of this quarrel and the causer of all the wars — that I have sought to injure him in many actions. But in saying that I have wronged him, that I have caused these wars, he doth me the greatest wrong that may be. For my own conscience cannot accuse my thought wherein I have done him the least injury; but I am persuade in my conscience if he knew what I know, he himself would be sorry for the wrongs he hath done me. I fear not all his threatenings; his great preparations and mighty forts do not scare me. For though he come against me with a greater force than ever was his invincible navy, I doubt not (God assisting me, upon whom I always trust) but I shall be able to defeat him and utterly overthrow him. I have a great advantage of him, for my cause is just.

With the massive Spanish fleet in the harbor at Ferrol, Essex pressed the queen for permission to lead another preemptive strike, like the one at Cádiz. Reluctant, as usual, to take on the expense of such an expedition, she finally relented. This time Essex was unwilling to share credit for the raid. He insisted on sole command of the fleet. The queen agreed. Essex's orders were to destroy the Spanish warships massed in the harbor at Ferrol. Once that powerful force was destroyed, ending the threat of invasion, Essex was authorized to venture out to the Azores in search of Spanish galleons bearing treasure.

Essex set sail with a fleet of 120 ships carrying 6000 men. He led his massive flotilla south toward Ferrol, hoping to add to the glory he had achieved at Cádiz. It was not to be. A sudden and violent storm scattered the English ships and prevented any attack.

Unwilling to return home to Elizabeth with vast sums spent and nothing accomplished, Essex took his fleet out into the Atlantic, making for the Azores, hoping to capture Spanish treasure ships on their way back to Spain. He knew that, after his successful raid on Cádiz, Drake had sailed for the Azores and had captured a treasure laden Spanish ship. But Drake had done this *after* destroying the Spanish fleet. Essex sailed away leaving that fleet intact.

Once in the Atlantic, Essex accomplished nothing. He even failed to intercept a Spanish treasure fleet transporting three and a half million pounds worth of bullion from the Spanish possessions in the New World.

Somehow, the Spanish fleet slipped past him. Had Essex captured or sunk the treasure ships, the lost wealth to Spain would probably have forced Philip to abandon any thought of invasion or war.

But Essex's folly was far more serious. What he had not grasped was that, unlike Drake's sailing to the Azores after destroying the Spanish fleet, his own diversion of the English fleet into the Atlantic left England wholly unprotected against the massive armada that still lay untouched in the harbor at Ferrol. This is why the queen's orders to Essex had been explicit. He was to venture into the Atlantic *only when the Spanish fleet had been destroyed*.

Realizing the magnitude of Essex's error, Philip gave the order for his new armada to sail at once. He was old and had not long to live. Before he died, he would invade England and finally rid the world of this troublesome, heretical woman.

The Spanish Admiral protested vigorously. His ships were not ready. His men were not adequately trained. But Philip would hear none of it. His enemy lay unprotected and open to invasion. The fleet must sail at once. Sail it did. But not to England. Almost as soon as it left port, the new armada was hit with another major storm. Between the devastation caused by the fierce winds and high seas and the Spaniards' lack of seamanship, much of the great fleet was lost or rendered unable to fight. What remained of it limped back to the harbor at Ferrol.

Once again, England was saved. But, Elizabeth realized the grave peril in which Essex had placed her realm

— and herself — through his irresponsible conduct and disobedience of orders. In her anger, she wrote him that, by sailing into the Atlantic without destroying the Spanish fleet, "You have given the enemy leisure and courage to attempt us and left us unprovided to resist them with that provision which is necessary for so important an action."

The public, however, failed to grasp Essex's dangerous error. They continued to idolize the dashing Earl. This left the Queen in a state of conflict. She was beginning to realize how unreliable and even unstable Essex could be. He threw a jealous fit at Admiral Howard's being made an Earl and stormed from court in a rage when the Admiral was made Lord Chamberlain, since that position gave Howard precedence over Essex.

Despite these unseemly episodes, Elizabeth seemed once again to forgive him. She made him Earl Marshall, a position that restored his precedence over Howard. Stupidly, Essex used the opportunity to begin more ill-concealed affairs with ladies of the court, humiliating and angering the aged queen. Yet, he still seemed able to pacify her — until July, 1598, when an extraordinary scene occurred.

Elizabeth was discussing with her advisors the appointment of a new Lord Deputy for Ireland. The queen indicated her intention to appoint Sir William Knollys, Essex' uncle. But Essex hoped to continue his uncle's influence at court and vociferously opposed his being sent so far from the seat of power. He suggested, instead, that an enemy of his, George Carew, be sent off to that distant and thankless post. Elizabeth rejected the suggestion out of hand.

Soon, tempers were flaring. Essex spoke to the queen in an insolent tone. Then, he did worse — much worse. He turned angrily on his heel, showing his back to her. This was a grave insult. One never turned one's back on the monarch. Elizabeth rushed forward and boxed the Earl's ears, crying out "Go to the devil!" Furious, Essex put his hand on his sword. No one knew what he intended. He shouted at her. "This is an outrage that I will not put up with. I would not have borne it from your father's hands."

Before anything further could occur, Lord Admiral Howard placed himself between Essex and the queen, pressing the Earl backward. After a moment, Essex turned and rushed from the room to a collective gasp from those present. He left at once for his country estate.

Now a long separation ensued. Elizabeth was, once again, torn. She could not appear to overlook Essex's gravely insulting conduct. Yet, with all his faults, she missed his company, his lavish compliments, his professions of love. She turned to Francis Bacon for advice. Despite Essex's unstinting efforts to help Bacon in the past, Bacon cautioned the queen against the mercurial Earl. Essex, he said, if free and humiliated, was so popular and so irresponsible as to be dangerous. If the Earl remained free, it would be prudent for the queen to avoid anything he might consider an insult. Bacon did not say so explicitly, but Elizabeth was certainly bright enough to catch the unspoken inference that perhaps Essex should not remain free.

Characteristically, the Queen chose the less drastic alternative. When Essex became ill, she sent him her personal physicians. He wrote thanking her with suitable humility. Soon, a reconciliation followed. She would avoid humiliating him if she could, and she would enjoy his company. But she was alert now to the danger he posed, and their relationship was never the same.

Meanwhile, September 1598 brought the death of Philip, Elizabeth's onetime suitor and longtime enemy. Although England and Spain were technically still at war, it seemed unlikely that his son, the new Spanish king, would soon undertake any renewed attempt at an invasion.

But trouble loomed in Ireland in the form of Hugh O'Neill, the Earl of Tyrone, leader of the Irish rebels. Tyrone had become the local power in Ulster, the least anglicized part of Ireland. Although a Catholic, he had proposed that the queen appoint him to govern Ulster in her name. When his proposal was rejected, Tyrone turned on the English with a vengeance, attacking them repeatedly and successfully. He defeated or outwitted one English commander after another. If the military situation was favorable, he would fight and inflict a costly defeat on his English opponents. If it was not, he would make a truce, which he would violate as soon as the danger passed.

In August 1597, Tyrone destroyed a major English army at the battle of Yellow Ford. Thousands of English settlers were killed or dispossessed. Philip had previously supplied funds to Tyrone and had been considering sending troops as well. With Philip's death, a dangerous Spanish-Irish alliance seemed less likely, but it could not be ruled out.

Although deeply concerned about the cost, Elizabeth discussed with her Council appointing someone capable of leading an English army into Ireland and destroying this troublesome rebel once and for all. She was determined to demonstrate that Ireland was not a place where Spanish interests could be advanced or Englishmen slaughtered. The problem was that no one seemed eager for the risky assignment.

Essex was the nation's most popular military leader and the people's choice for the job. The Earl appeared ready to take it on, although this may have been only pretense. Francis Bacon had long advised Essex that political advancement was more important than military command. This time, Bacon may have advised Essex to feign willingness to lead the Irish expedition, but, under no circumstances, to accept that command. If so, that was sound advice. Tyrone was a skilled commander and could, quite possibly, inflict a humiliating and career-ending loss on whoever undertook the high profile assignment. Even if success was achieved, Elizabeth would, characteristically, resent the cost. And Essex's strategy for creating grateful allies seemed unavailable, since the queen had made it clear that knighthoods were to be conferred only in those few instances where men had shown unique bravery in battle.

If Bacon advised Essex to avoid the Irish command, we can't be sure why he failed to heed that sage advice. Possibly, it was the work of Robert Cecil. Cecil's rivalry with Essex had continued. He considered Essex a serious danger to the queen and the nation. There had been a rivalry between Essex's stepfather, Leicester, and Cecil's father, Burghley. But, over the years, the two had been able to work together when it proved necessary. The rivalry between Essex and Robert Cecil was deeper. It was lethal.

Cecil thoroughly grasped the Irish situation, as well as Essex's pride and lack of judgment. He tended to encourage Essex's military ventures, assuming that, even if successful, their cost alone would irritate the queen, and, if they failed, they could destroy him.

We know that Essex criticized other candidates who were suggested to lead the Irish expedition, pronouncing them inexperienced, incapable or of insufficient stature. Cecil may have intimated that Essex was quick to condemn other candidates, but was afraid to take the command himself. Possibly allowing hubris and his resentment of Cecil to get the better of him, Essex may have announced his readiness to lead the Irish expedition himself. If so, it was a critical mistake. Cecil would have immediately passed Essex's announcement to the Council and the queen, and would have trumpeted it to the public. Essex, always commanded by his ego and obsessed with his reputation, would have found himself irrevocably committed.

Whether or not he was tricked into accepting the Irish command, Essex certainly created the opposite impression, claiming that, in getting the appointment, he had won a significant victory, prevailing over rivals for a prized command.

Once it was announced that the command was his, Essex made unprecedented demands upon Elizabeth for men and arms. He was granted virtually everything he requested — a benefit, but, at the same time, a serious risk. If he failed in Ireland, there would be nothing and no one to blame but himself.

The one thing Elizabeth refused Essex was the right to appoint his inexperienced young friend, the Earl of Southampton, as Commander of the English cavalry. Southampton was probably the "lovely boy" of Shakespeare's sonnets. Contemporary portraits show him as rather feminine in appearance. Nevertheless, he had seduced and married one of the queen's maids of honor. While he may have been bold and brave, he was immature, rash in judgment and completely unfit to lead the English cavalry. But Essex planned to make this foolish appointment anyway — just as soon as he reached Ireland and was out of the queen's reach.

The public was filled with martial spirit, and Essex was hailed as the hero of the day. Even the chorus to Shakespeare's *Henry V* contained a resounding tribute to the swashbuckling Earl.

Were now the general of our gracious Empress,

As in good time he may from Ireland coming,

Bringing rebellion broached on his sword,

How many would the peaceful city quit

To welcome him!

"The general" was, of course, Essex; and subsequent events must have led Shakespeare to regret his tribute.

Essex left for Ireland in March 1599, at the head of a large, well-equipped English army. He had 16,000 foot soldiers and 1400 cavalry, plus artillery and siege equipment. It was the largest English expeditionary force of Elizabeth's reign. It was costly, but it was more than sufficient to deal with Tyrone. Essex was ready to bring "rebellion broached on his sword."

The Earl's explicit orders were to use his formidable army to launch an immediate and devastating attack on Tyrone in Ulster. Both Essex and the Queen had been present at the Council meeting that decided on this strategy. Indeed, Essex had pushed for it, insisting that all prior English commanders had wasted time and effort fighting unimportant battles in other Irish counties, when their proper objective should have been to destroy Tyrone in Ulster.

When he reached Ireland, however, Essex was told that there would be some advantage in postponing the attack on Ulster until June. By that time, the grass would be green and the cattle would be fat, so that it would be easier to feed his men. He learned that Tyrone had minor allies in Leinster and Munster who might support him against the English. Foolishly, and contrary to what he had promised the queen and the Council, Essex decided to ignore his orders and to attack these lesser allies first. Only when they were defeated, would he turn his large, well armed force against Tyrone. By then, he reasoned, finding adequate food for his men would be less difficult.

Even before his campaign started, Essex conferred knighthood on two patently undeserving supporters, an act in clear disobedience of Elizabeth's order to use this power sparingly and only as a reward for extraordinary service. Once in Ireland, he also defied the queen's orders by appointing young Southampton Commander of the cavalry. When Elizabeth learned of the appointment, she again vetoed it. Essex ignored her and proceeded with the appointment. When she insisted that Southampton be dismissed, he refused. Far from London and feeling invulnerable, he was prepared to defy any order he didn't like — even orders from the queen.

The English won some insignificant battles against minor chieftains in Leinster and Munster and took an indefensible castle of no military value. Nothing was accomplished. Worse, valuable time had been lost. Essex was still struggling in Munster in June, when, even on his rationale of waiting for the grass to grow green and the cattle to fatten, he should have been in Ulster attacking

Tyrone. Worse still, a significant number of Essex's men had been killed or wounded, and thousands more were lost to disease. His original force of more than 17,000 had been reduced by almost half.

Finally, in mid-July, Essex returned to Dublin, where he came to the horrifying conclusion that he had insufficient men left to defeat Tyrone's main army. He became utterly distraught at the dilemma he now faced. If he attacked Tyrone and lost, he'd be ruined, if not killed. If he returned to London, having violated his orders, spent a fortune, lost a significant part of his army and accomplished nothing, the Queen would be enraged — especially since he believed his enemies in London were already trying to turn Elizabeth against him. At the very least, he would be a laughing stock. What could he do?

He did nothing — for months. Meanwhile the size and fighting ability of his army continued to deteriorate. The Queen wrote angry letters urging him to attack at once. Ultimately, she ordered him *not* to return to England until Tyrone was beaten.

In her last letter to Essex in Ireland, Elizabeth was scathing in denouncing his delays, excuses and ultimate failure to carry out his orders to attack Tyrone. "If sickness of the army be the reason," she wrote, "why was not the action undertaken when the army was in better state? If winter's approach, why were the summer months of July and August lost? If the spring were too soon, and the summer that followed otherwise spent, if the harvest that succeeded were so neglected as nothing hath been done, then surely we must conclude that none of the four seasons of the year will be in season for you." She pointed out that it could not be want of means, since "You had your asking; you had choice of times, you had power and authority more ample than ever any had, or ever shall have . . . you have taken great pains to prepare for many purposes which perish without undertaking."

Humiliated and enraged, Essex told Southampton and others that he should take his army back to England and force the queen to treat him with respect and rid herself of his enemies. His listeners were not yet prepared to join him in any such radical and dangerous move.

At last, in desperation, Essex led his diminished force out of Dublin, ostensibly to meet Tyrone's army. He had only five thousand men in condition to fight a battle. Probably, he had something else in mind.

First, Essex supposedly challenged Tyrone to a personal duel. Such a challenge may or may not have been issued, but it sounds like Essex. He had done it before at Rouen and Lisbon. He may have reasoned that, if he could kill the rebel leader in man-to-man combat, Elizabeth might forgive him everything. If such a challenge was ever really issued, Tyrone certainly refused it. To risk his cause and his life in unpredictable personal combat would have been foolish, and the cunning Irish leader was neither a fool nor a man ruled by hubris or unthinking pride.

In any event, before their armies met, Essex and Tyrone exchanged messages and agreed to a parley. With the two armies facing each other on the eve of what was to have been a great battle, the two commanders met at the River Lagan. Essex stood on the bank, while Tyrone sat astride his horse in shallow water. The two men were supposed to meet alone. But it would have been prudent for each side to have men secreted nearby to prevent a surprise attack.

In fact, men did claim to have been nearby and to have overheard the conversation. What they claimed to have heard was extraordinary. Tyrone had previously said that, if Essex would only follow his advice, he could make the Earl "the greatest man there ever was in England." Now, in their "secret" parley at the river, it was reported that this suggestion was revived, that Essex revealed a plan to destroy his enemies at court and, perhaps with Tyrone's aid, even seize the throne. In that event, Essex would be king, and Tyrone would govern all of Ireland in his name.

Whether or not these things were really said, Essex and Tyrone did agree to a truce, and Essex agreed to present Tyrone's "peace terms" to the queen. All Irish lands forfeited to the Crown over two centuries were to be restored to their prior Irish owners. Every important office in Ireland was to be filled by an Irishman. And, perhaps worst of all from Elizabeth's point of view, the English were to recognize the Pope as head of the Church in Ireland. This was no compromise. By accepting those terms, the English would essentially have surrendered completely to every Irish demand.

Meanwhile, in defiance of Elizabeth's express order, Essex created a remarkable thirty-eight more knights, another sign that he was seeking to develop supporters for what apparently was a treasonous plan. Half the knights in England now owed their rank to the ceremonial touch of Essex's sword. As the Irish taunted, Essex "never drew sword but to make knights."

Robert Cecil had been quietly communicating with men in Essex's camp and keeping the queen informed. When word of the Earl's conduct reached Elizabeth, she was furious. The vain fool had lost thousands of good men. Contrary to her explicit orders, he had created a plethora of knights for no good reason other than to make them personal supporters. He had squandered a fortune and accomplished nothing, except to make dedicated allies for whatever nefarious plans he had in mind. Probably, she had even heard reports that Essex had spoken boldly of bringing an army back to England, that he had assured Tyrone he would soon seize power there and that their "truce" was, in reality, a mutual aid pact — directed against her crown.

In fact, Cecil and the Queen appear to have taken measures to deal with those very threats. Evidently they did so by employing a clever ruse. Word was widely circulated that the Spanish were preparing still another invasion. Large numbers of Englishmen were quickly armed and trained to fight, supposedly to defend the realm against the Spanish attack. But there is no evidence of any threatened Spanish invasion at this time. Almost surely, this was a covert plan to protect against Essex's returning with his army, perhaps supported by Tyrone's army, in an attempt to seize the throne.

Essex did come, but not in force and without Tyrone. Defying the queen's orders once again, the desperate, unstable Earl crossed the Irish Sea and rode hard for London. He was accompanied only by the young Earl of Southampton and a small group of friends who could come to his aid if he was attacked on arrival.

Leaving his escort in London, he dashed headlong for Elizabeth's Nonsuch Palace in Surrey. Muddy, unshaven and disheveled from his long ride, he rushed into the palace. Unannounced, he pushed his way into the queen's own chamber, where her shocked ladies in waiting had been helping her dress. Her hair, now white, was down, and she was without the red wig and heavy makeup she regularly wore.

Frightened at Essex's intrusion and wild appearance and concerned that he may have been accompanied by a significant body of armed troops, the queen feigned pleasure at seeing him and bantered with him in a frivolous, teasing way. Finally, Essex was eased out, pleasantly surprised that, after all that had occurred, the queen seemed quite friendly.

Later that day, she met him again. This was a brief meeting, and her attitude was not the same. Still, it was not yet menacing. Perhaps she had heard that he was accompanied by armed friends, who might yet cause trouble. In any event, she simply directed him to make his report to the Council and to remain in his quarters. They never met again.

Elizabeth was now aware that definitive action must be taken. She could no longer continue this charade. She recalled Bacon's advice. If she was unwilling to embrace Essex and ignore his Irish debacle, his disobedience of orders and possible treason, she must confine him. Essex was still hugely popular. If desperate and free, he could be extremely dangerous. Elizabeth acted with caution. It would be prudent to make no immediate move that suggested the imposition of severe punishment on the popular Earl. Two days after his return, Essex was placed in the custody of Lord Keeper Egerton, a member of the Council who had been his friend. It was not freedom, but it was hardly the Tower.

After a time, Essex was induced by his friends to write an abject apology to Elizabeth for his conduct of the Irish campaign. It was sound advice, but an apology was not enough for her. It is probable that she was now aware of what he had really been planning in Ireland. Possibly, she also learned of his fathering Elizabeth Southwell's child and bribing Thomas Vavasour to take the blame. In any event, she kept the Earl comfortably confined.

Essex started a correspondence with James VI of Scotland seeking to persuade James to send Scottish troops or at least an ambassador to London with a demand that Elizabeth officially designate the Scottish king as her successor. He added, almost as an afterthought, that James' demand should also include freeing and reinstating Essex and dismissing Cecil and Elizabeth's other advisors.

James had been friendly with Essex and had been falsely persuaded by him that Robert Cecil was opposed to his succeeding Elizabeth on the English throne. But James was no fool. He may have liked Essex, but he was far too cautious to send troops or have an ambassador make any such arrogant demand of Elizabeth. Nor would he undertake any other ill-conceived gamble in aid of the mercurial Earl. James was not about to jeopardize his chances to become King of England, and he certainly realized that a demand to be designated Elizabeth's successor would enrage the queen and be counter-productive. He replied to Essex that he might send an ambassador to Elizabeth, but gave no hint as to what that ambassador might say.

After ten months in the custody of the Lord Keeper, Elizabeth finally allowed Essex to return to his own home. Lord Mountjoy had replaced him as commander of the Irish campaign. Mountjoy was a friend and former ally of Essex and the lover of Essex's sister, Lady Rich. Ironically, Mountjoy was achieving considerable success in suppressing the Irish rebellion, inflicting costly losses on Tyrone and adding to Essex's humiliation at his own failure on the same mission.

Perhaps Elizabeth felt that this public humiliation was, in itself, a significant punishment for the vainglorious

Earl. If so, it was not his only punishment. The Queen banned Essex from court, and, severest of all, she declined to renew his highly lucrative monopoly in importing sweet wine. Undoubtedly she calculated that this could penalize Essex in a way that would not arouse the public ire, since the people were never happy with the monopolies the Queen granted to various noblemen, allowing them to charge higher prices in the absence of competition. Essex pleaded urgently that this last punishment be withdrawn. His debts and expenses were staggering, and losing the sweet wine monopoly was a crushing blow. His pleas were unavailing.

On one fateful occasion, hearing a reference to "the Queen's conditions," he shouted "Her conditions? Her conditions are as crooked as her carcass!" The insult was repeated to Elizabeth, who must have been devastated by its cruelty, painfully contrasting it with the ambitious Earl's glowing references to her beauty. Undoubtedly, she now grasped fully what a supreme hypocrite he was and how foolish she had been to believe him — if she ever really had.

It has been argued that these cruel words, so hurtful to the queen, had been uttered when Elizabeth boxed his ears for turning his back on her. This seems unlikely. Her behavior at that earlier time would have been significantly more punitive and unforgiving had he hurled that ugly insult in the presence of others and after turning his back on the queen. Besides, nothing in that earlier incident involved her imposing any "conditions," making her use of that word in the earlier incident unlikely.

In any event, Elizabeth still took no precipitous action. She waited. As Essex grew more desperate, a group of rabid followers gathered around him, urging him to take bold action. They argued that his claim to the throne was better than Elizabeth's, that, with their help, he should seize it. They were mostly rash and hot-blooded young aristocrats, like the Earl of Southampton, as well as troublemaking swordsmen and disappointed office seekers doubtful of any future gain under Elizabeth.

Essex's feverish mind wavered from hour to hour, torn between inertia and rebellion. Even when he veered toward rebellion, he was not sure whether he intended to seize the throne himself or merely to "protect" Elizabeth by ridding her of the "evil men" who surrounded and advised her, like Cecil and Howard, allowing Essex and his allies to govern the realm "correctly" through the queen.

Finally, stirred by the feverish rhetoric of his followers, including his sister, Lady Rich, who derided his indecision as cowardice, Essex announced his readiness to act and, apparently, to seize the throne for himself.

Characteristically, his decision was made impetuously, without the kind of planning and preparation that might have allowed such a rebellion to succeed. No attempt was made to raise the sizeable army of retainers who owed allegiance to magnates such as Southampton and the young Earl of Rutland, also a part of Essex's clamorous mob of supporters. And, despite what was apparently said between Essex and Tyrone at their river parley, no effort appears to have been made to obtain the participation of Tyrone's forces or, other than the earlier and unsuccessful letter to the Scottish king, to acquire any other foreign support. Perhaps Mountjoy's efforts in Ireland prevented Tyrone from providing any aid to Essex; but there is no evidence that his aid was even sought. Essex had no more than 200 followers ready to march with him. He counted entirely on the citizens of London joining his coup once it began.

In what seems a frivolous attempt to raise citizen support, the Earl's allies arranged for the performance of Shakespeare's *Henry IV*, showing the overthrow and assassination of the reigning King, Richard II, by Bolingbroke, who took the throne as Henry IV.

Much later, Elizabeth told the historian, William Lambarde, that "this tragedy was played forty times in open streets and houses" and "I am Richard II, know ye not that." She grossly exaggerated the number of performances, but Essex's allies certainly intended the deposed King Richard to symbolize Elizabeth and to justify the overthrow of a reigning monarch. But performing the play was far too subtle a way to galvanize public participation in Essex's planned uprising.

The Council was deeply concerned at the activity surrounding Essex and the dangerous and unstable nature of the men gathered about him. The Chief Justice, the Lord Keeper, Sir William Knollys and the Earl of Worcester were dispatched to Essex's home to persuade him against committing any act of treason. Each of these men had been a friend of Essex, and Knollys was a relative as well. But when they arrived and tried to speak, they were shouted down and locked up as hostages by Essex's enraged partisans.

Now, there was no turning back. Armed and shouting their slogans, Essex and his inflamed followers entered the City, heading down Fleet Street toward the palace. They relied on attracting a throng of eager citizens to their cause as they moved through the streets.

But Robert Cecil had anticipated them. The forces raised to fight "the new Spanish invasion" had been assembled. Barricades were placed at strategic points in the streets, and Essex was officially proclaimed a traitor. Cecil even arranged for royal heralds to parade through the streets shouting that deadly proclamation. An attempt had also been made to persuade Londoners to stay behind closed doors, but there may have been no need for that. The dreaded word "traitor," loudly proclaimed by royal heralds, was probably sufficient to dampen the enthusiasm of most citizens. It was one thing to join in a protest march in support of the popular and charismatic Earl. It was quite another to participate in what was being officially proclaimed as a treasonous act. A man could be hung, drawn and quartered for that.

Whatever the reason, no one joined Essex and his followers as they passed through the empty streets, the Earl desperately shouting for the people to rally to his cause. Soon, a number of Essex's men began to drift away, undoubtedly realizing the likely penalty for being arrested as a part of a treasonous uprising.

Finally, realizing the game was up, Essex made his way to the river and from there returned by boat to his home. Arriving there, he found that his eminent hostages had already been released. Ultimately, he and his principal followers were arrested. This time, there were no half measures. The Earl went straight to the Tower.

Elizabeth told the French Ambassador, "A senseless ingrate has at last revealed what had long been in his mind." She probably knew what was "in his mind" well before he actually took to the streets.

In a later chapter, I'll discuss Essex's trial for treason, one of the great spectacles of the age. Ironically, the prosecution was led by his former friend and ally, Francis Bacon, whose career Essex had consistently tried to advance. Now, Bacon had achieved that preeminence — at Essex's expense. The evidence was overwhelming. Essex attempted, with some arrogance, to defend himself by attacking the character of his accusers, notably Cecil and Bacon. The attempt was an abject failure.

Essex was convicted in February 1601. Shortly thereafter, at the age of only thirty-four, he was quietly beheaded within the Tower grounds. It was said that this had been the Earl's own request. More likely, the queen's advisers considered a public execution, before an excited mob, too big a risk. Undesirable talk had spread quickly about the dramatic events at the execution of Mary Stuart, even though it was far from London, and attendance had been limited. Elizabeth was not likely to allow a similar performance in public and in London by the still popular Essex.

Many thought that, at the last minute, the Queen would grant Essex a reprieve — even forgive him, as she had so often in the past. This time, she did not. Perhaps she could not erase from her mind his cruel remark about her crooked carcass, or perhaps she fully grasped the danger he would always pose if allowed to live. Most likely, it was both.

Abroad, there was admiration for Elizabeth's resolve in executing the highly popular and dangerous Earl. As Henri IV of France put it "She only is a king. She only knows how to rule."

Six of Essex's co-conspirators were executed; but the Queen was surprisingly lenient toward Southampton and Rutland. A stay in the Tower plus a large fine was all they suffered. With Essex himself removed, perhaps Elizabeth felt that the focal point of the rebellion was gone and there was no need to create the disturbing spectacle of executing well known, titled Englishmen. The men themselves were contrite, and their powerful families interceded, pleading for mercy. Still, Southampton remained in the Tower until freed by James I after Elizabeth's death.

When Elizabeth discovered that a man had been blackmailing Essex by threatening to reveal letters he had written that were insulting and disloyal to the queen, she insisted on prosecuting the blackmailer. He was convicted and fined.

Ultimately, Mountjoy achieved complete success in Ireland (at least for the time), routing Tyrone's army and forcing the surrender of a Spanish force that landed there to aid the Irish cause.

A perilous threat had been averted. The nation seemed on a safe and sound footing. But Elizabeth was aging, although she continued to ride, hunt, walk in her garden and even dance. Certainly, her mental faculties and ability to charm were unimpaired.

A report of the French Ambassador gives us an intriguing and somewhat ambiguous portrait of the aging and still unpredictable queen. Because it is a remarkable, firsthand view of the queen, I quote it at some length.

> . . . *a gentleman from the Queen . . . led me across a chamber of moderate size wherein were the guards of the Queen, and thence into the Presence Chamber, as they call it, in which all present, even though the Queen be absent, remained uncovered. He then conducted me to a place on one side, where there was a cushion made ready for me. I waited there some time, and the Lord Chamberlain, who has the charge of the Queen's household (not as* maître d'hôtel, *but to arrange audiences and to escort those who demand them and especially ambassadors), came to seek me where I was seated. He led me along a passage somewhat dark, into a chamber that they called the Privy Chamber, at the*

head of which was the Queen seated in a low chair, by herself, and withdrawn from all the Lords and Ladies that were present, they being in one place and she in another. After I had made her my reverence at the entry of the chamber, she rose and came five or six paces towards me, almost into the middle of the chamber. I kissed the fringe of her robe and she embraced me with both hands. She looked at me kindly, and began to excuse herself that she had not sooner given me audience, saying that the day before she had been very ill with a gathering on the right side of her face, which I should never have thought seeing her eyes and face: but she did not remember ever to have been so ill before.

She was strangely attired in a dress of silver cloth, white and crimson, or silver 'gauze,' as they call it. this dress had slashed sleeves lined with red taffeta, and was girt about with other little sleeves that hung down to the ground, which she was for ever twisting and untwisting. She kept the front of her dress open, and one could see the whole of her bosom, and passing low, and often she would open the front of this robe with her hands as if she was too hot. The collar of the robe was very high, and the lining of the inner part all adorned with little pendants of rubies and pearls, very many, but quite small. She had also a chain of rubies and pearls about her neck. On her head she wore a garland of the same material and beneath it a great reddish-coloured wig, with a great number of spangles of gold and silver, and hanging down over her forehead some pearls, but of no great worth. On either side of her ears hung two great curls of hair, almost down to her shoulders and within the collar of her robe, spangled as the top of her head. Her bosom is somewhat wrinkled as well as one can see for the collar that she wears round her neck, but lower down her flesh is exceeding white and delicate, so far as one could see.

As for her face, it is and appears to be very aged. It is long and thin, and her teeth are very yellow and unequal, compared with what they were formerly, so they say, and on the left side less than on the right. Many of them are missing so that one cannot understand her easily when she speaks quickly. Her figure is fair and tall and graceful in whatever she does; so far as may be she keeps her dignity, yet humbly and graciously withal.

All the time she spoke she would often rise from her chair, and appear to be very impatient with what I was saying. She would complain that the fire was hurting her eyes, though there was a great screen before it and she six or seven feet away; yet did she give orders to have it extinguished, making them bring water to pour upon it. She told me that she was well pleased to stand up, and that she used to speak thus with the ambassadors who came to seek her, and used sometimes to tire them, of which they would on occasion complain. I begged her not to overtire herself in any way, and I rose when she did; and then she sat down again, and so did I. At my departure she rose and conducted me to that same place where she had come to receive me, and again began to say that she was grieved that all the gentlemen I had brought should see her in that condition, and she called to see them. They made their reverence before her, one after the other, and she embraced them all with great charm and smiling countenance.

In September 1601, when a Spanish force landed in Ireland, Elizabeth was characteristically short of money. She had sold land and some jewels, but more was needed to finance the fight against the Spanish in Ireland. She went before Parliament seeking an extraordinary subsidy for that purpose. Parliament was fully prepared to give her what she wanted. With some trepidation, however, one member of the Commons rose to speak against the Queen's grant of monopolies, like the one for sweet wines previously enjoyed by Essex. Similar monopolies had been granted in many essential products. They naturally resulted in higher prices to the consumer and were extremely unpopular with the public. Still, historically, they had been considered a royal prerogative; and the speaker was not proposing specific legislation to end them — just expressing an opinion.

Elizabeth must have realized the gross unfairness of this added benefit to the already rich and favored, and how unpopular the monopolies were with her subjects. Perhaps she even foresaw that, someday, Parliament would demand the end of this inequitable practice, in exchange for granting the tax-based subsidies sorely needed by the Crown. In any event, she realized the political wisdom of taking the initiative before that point was reached.

Without being formally asked, she quickly issued a promise to Parliament to end the most onerous monopolies. This occasioned an outburst of joy in the Commons. One member was even in tears. The body issued a warm thanks to the queen. Her response was vintage Elizabeth. "Thank me," she said, "when I have performed my promise."

In a remarkable three days, she had. The promised proclamation was signed and delivered to Parliament. She had given the Commons and the public what it wanted, but had done so voluntarily, preserving the royal prerogative to rule as she deemed fit.

In an atmosphere of joy and support for the queen, she agreed to receive and address a delegation of members at the Whitehall Palace. When the delegation was to be selected from among the members of the House of Commons, everyone wanted to go. Shouts arose of "all, all, all!" A pleased Elizabeth sent them a message. It would be crowded, but "all" could come. In an extraordinary gathering, 140 members of the Commons trooped to Whitehall to hear what the queen had to say.

This was Elizabeth's "Golden Speech", given on November 30, 1601, an address that has been treasured by Englishmen over the centuries.

There will never Queen sit in my seat with more zeal to my country, care to my subjects, and that will sooner with willingness venture her life for your good and safety than myself. . . . And though you have had, and may have, many princes more mighty and wise sitting in this seat, yet you never had, nor shall have, any that will be more careful and loving.

Not only was Elizabeth's speech received with joy and enthusiasm, it was then that word arrived of Mountjoy's smashing victory in Ireland, routing Tyrone and forcing the Spanish troops to surrender. It seemed Elizabeth's shining hour, in which she was both beloved and successful.

Over the ensuing months, however, the queen's physical condition materially weakened. In March of 1603, she became seriously ill; and, soon, it became apparent that this extraordinary woman, who had ruled England for so many years, was finally dying. Stubbornly unwilling to take to her bed, she lay for days on a pile of cushions heaped on the floor of her chamber. Robert Cecil finally told her that, to comfort an anxious public, she "must go to bed." The old fire blazed one more time. "Little man," she rasped, "is 'must' a word to use to princes?"

Finally, the end came and was announced. "This morning about three at clocke hir Majestie departed this lyfe, mildly like a lamb, easily like a ripe apple from the tree . . ."

It was March 24, 1603. The great Queen had reigned for the entire life of most Englishmen.

The nation went into mourning, and accolades came from virtually every poet, author and political figure. Francis Bacon pronounced her a "great Queen," for

> . . . this part of the island never had forty-five years of better times . . . not through the calmness of the season, but through the wisdom of her regimen. For if there be considered

of the one side . . . the constant place and security, the good administration of justice; the temperate use of the prerogative . . . the flourishing state of learning and . . . of the other side, the differences of religion, the troubles of neighbor countries, the ambition of Spain and opposition of Rome; and then that she was solitary and of herself . . . I could not have chosen one more remarkable or eminent . . . concerning the conjunction of learning in the Prince with felicity in the people.

Strangely, England's most famous author said nothing. Inexplicably, the renowned poet and playwright, William Shakespeare, made no comment on the great Queen's death. Had that author died before her? William Shaksper of Stratford on Avon was very much alive. Why did he not speak out? Had the true author been someone else, who paid tribute to the deceased queen in his own name and felt no need to make a public statement in the name "Shakespeare"? We do not know. We may never know.

The Elizabethan era, a wondrous and unique reign of forty-five years, had finally come to an end. The official religion of the English had been altered and established without a destructive civil war. England had defeated the mightiest nation in Europe and had emerged as a formidable sea power. Scotland no longer posed a threat, and the problems of Ireland seemed to be coming under control. France, Spain and the Empire remained potential adversaries, although fears of a Franco-Scottish or Spanish-Irish alliance appeared at an end. The

Netherlands remained a troubling problem, but seemingly less so than in earlier times.

The English had also enjoyed a period of relative stability. For the last 30 years of Elizabeth's reign, there had been no armed rebellion of any significant magnitude. Certainly, Essex's ill-fated march through the streets did not qualify as such.

England had also become a major economic power, fueled by an international market-based economy. London had been transformed from a second rate, backwater town into a bustling center of international trade. Ships of all nations crowded English wharfs, unloading cargoes from all over the world and loading English cloth and other English products for shipment and sale to ports and markets almost everywhere.

English ships, their voyages financed by private investment, plied the seas seeking trade and treasure. The great English trading companies were founded, including the Russia Company, the Levant Company, the East India Company and, just three years after Elizabeth's death, the Virginia Company, named for the "Virgin Queen."

Merchants and traders of many nations crowded the London Exchange, opened by Elizabeth in 1570 to facilitate international dealings in commodities and investments of every kind.

During Elizabeth's reign, the relationships between Crown, Council and Parliament were generally cooperative and efficient, as was the relationship between the Crown and the local government of the capital. The population of London and its suburbs had tripled from about 60,000 to around 180,000. The City was well managed by the Lord Mayor and the Court of Aldermen, with the support of the Guilds. Those critical organizations regulated apprenticeships and permission to trade and offered young men from the provinces the opportunity to work their way up to become artisans or merchants, owning their own shops and even holding positions of responsibility and honor in City or Guild governance.

Education had improved throughout the nation. Male literacy had vastly increased. Female literacy still lagged far behind, although it too had increased. The great universities at Oxford and Cambridge continued to turn out a generally well-educated leadership class. Printing had come into its own, particularly in London. Printers were everywhere in the capital, turning out books, tracts and other material at an ever increasing rate for a growing number of literate Englishmen.

The inns of court, which attracted hundreds of lawyers, judges and students of the law, created a fashionable and intellectual enclave in the Strand and Holborn areas of London. And, as we have seen, theaters were opened in the "liberties," the areas outside the jurisdiction of city government. The plays of Shakespeare, Marlowe, Ben Jonson and others were regularly performed there and in the provinces by troupes of actors, most of them sponsored by noblemen.

The plague periodically decimated the capital's population. Infant and child mortality remained overwhelming, venereal disease was rampant and, in London, deaths regularly outstripped births. Yet, the city's population increased because of the massive influx of men from the rural areas and from other nations.

There was still crime and poverty, and inflation remained a serious problem. But Englishmen were not starving or rioting in the streets and, in general, this was a period of optimism and national pride.

Everything considered, Elizabeth left England and Englishmen in far better condition than when she took the throne. She was an extraordinary woman, and she knew it. As she put it herself, "I thank God that I am endowed with such qualities that if I were turned out of the realm in my petticoat, I were able to live in any place in Christendom."

But she was more than an extraordinary individual. Will and Ariel Durant pronounced her "the greatest ruler that England has ever known." It would be difficult to quarrel with that assessment.

* * * * *

By 1603, most Englishmen had never known any monarch but Elizabeth. Now they would. The great Queen was succeeded by James I, the son of Mary Stuart, the once Scottish Queen and (probably) of her vicious husband,

Darnley. From the time of his mother's abdication in 1567, he had been James VI, King of Scotland.

While Elizabeth had not formally designated James as her successor, she was probably aware that Robert Cecil had quietly arranged, through "secret messages," for the Scottish king to succeed her when at last she died. In fact, Cecil began a secret, coded correspondence with James in 1601, two years before the death of the queen. It went without saying that Cecil would be handsomely rewarded by the new monarch.

Only with her last breath did Elizabeth supposedly agree explicitly to Cecil's plan, whispering so that only he could hear, "I will that a king succeed me, and who but my kinsman the King of Scots." Did she really say this? Probably not, but we will never know.

At the moment of the queen's death, Sir Robert Carey leapt on the first of a series of horses that had been waiting for him all across England. After a wild ride from Richmond to Edinburgh, made in an amazing three days, Carey was the first to tell James he was now King of England. Probably, his plan was to ingratiate himself with the new monarch before any potential rival could deliver the news.

Carey, a son of Lord Hunsdon and grandson of Mary Boleyn, was an accomplished diplomat, previously entrusted by Elizabeth to carry letters to the Scottish king. Ironically, it was this probable great-great-grandson of Henry VII, the first Tudor King, who proclaimed the end of the Tudor dynasty and welcomed the first Stuart monarch to the throne.

James VI of Scotland now became James I of England. He had an excellent claim to the throne now that Elizabeth, her siblings and his own parents were dead. He had other qualifications as well. He had been King of the Scots for 36 years, his ancestors had ruled Scotland since the fourteenth century and he was highly intelligent and well educated.

He was also a homosexual and had a number of male "favorites." Nevertheless, he was married to a Danish princess, with whom he managed to produce six children, two sons and four daughters.

James had been raised a Protestant, but was generally tolerant of Catholics. After the "gunpowder plot" of 1605, however, his attitude and treatment of Catholics hardened. This was a Catholic scheme to murder the king by blowing up the Westminster Palace as he opened the new session of Parliament on November 5, 1605.

The plot was uncovered when one of the conspirators wrote, warning his brother-in-law to stay away from Parliament that session. The recipient of the letter brought it to Robert Cecil, who took immediate steps to protect the king and Parliament. Guy Fawkes was captured in the cellar of the Palace about to light the fuse on enough gunpowder to blow up everyone who might be in or near the building. Since then, the holiday commemorating the event has been called "Guy Fawkes Day," and children seeking a holiday gift cry out "A penny for the old Guy."

During James' reign, the Puritan movement was reinvigorated and grew strong. But he resisted Puritan pressure to abolish the status of bishops, uttering famously "No bishop, no king!" He also directed preparation of a new version of the Bible, still known as the "King James Version." Thus, two of the most important volumes in the English language were created in James' reign, the King James Bible and the First Folio of Shakespeare's plays.

A serious spendthrift, James had a continuing battle with an increasingly powerful Parliament to obtain the funds to cover his extravagance. He also had trouble with some of Elizabeth's best men, notably Francis Bacon, who was stripped of his offices for taking bribes, and Sir Walter Raleigh, who, as we have seen, was executed supposedly for treason.

James died in 1625, succeeded by Charles I, whose stubborn defiance of a much more assertive Parliament led to civil war, his execution and an interregnum during which England was governed by Parliament and a "Protector," rather than a monarch.

* * * * *

Having summarized Elizabeth's life and reign, Part Two will explore the key issues about the great Queen that have been debated for centuries. By analyzing how she acted and dealt with respect to each separate issue, such as sex, marriage or murder, over the course of her lifetime, we can seek out patterns and proclivities evident over that entire period, and perhaps reach some conclusions that may not be evident from a purely chronological study.

Naturally, many events included in Part One will be revisited in Part Two, requiring some repetition.

Many of the questions considered in Part Two have no clear and provable answers. What I've provided are simply my own conclusions from the available evidence.

ILLUSTRATIONS

Queen Elizabeth I by Unknown English artist
© National Portrait Gallery, London

III

King Henry VIII after Hans Holbein the Younger
© National Portrait Gallery, London

IV

Katherine of Aragon by Unknown artist
© National Portrait Gallery, London

v

Anne Boleyn by Unknown English artist
© National Portrait Gallery, London

VI

Thomas Cromwell, Earl of Essex after Hans Holbein the Younger
© National Portrait Gallery, London

KATHARINE PARRE

King Edward VI by Workshop associated with 'Master John'
© National Portrait Gallery, London

Mary, Queen of Scots after Nicholas Hilliard
© National Portrait Gallery, London

Robert Dudley, 1st Earl of Leicester by Unknown Anglo-Netherlandish artist
© National Portrait Gallery, London

ET VIRTUTE

ÆT

Sir Walter Ralegh (Raleigh) by Unknown English artist
© National Portrait Gallery, London

XIII

Robert Devereux, 2nd Earl of Essex after Marcus Gheeraerts the Younger
© National Portrait Gallery, London

DA ... EXPECTAT

POTEST NEC V

REID

Queen Elizabeth I by Marcus Gheeraerts the Younger
© National Portrait Gallery, London

XV

PART TWO
ELIZABETHAN ENIGMAS

Chapter One

Virginity

I'VE STARTED MY ANALYSIS of the principal issues surrounding Elizabeth's reign with the question most frequently asked and debated. Was she in fact "The Virgin Queen?" Was that dramatic label true? Did this independent, passionate woman never have a sexual experience? Through most of her life, there were scandalous rumors of her erotic adventures. What was the truth? We can only try to reach a reasonable conclusion from the evidence available after four hundred years.

To being with, we can dispose of the theory that Elizabeth had some gross physical defect that prevented sexual intercourse. There is not the slightest evidence to support this claim, and there is considerable evidence to the contrary.

When Elizabeth was an infant, Henry VIII offered her in marriage to a son of the French king. The French sent two trusted representatives who gave the naked princess a thorough physical examination, after which they pronounced her completely free of any defect. Since the principal purpose of the examination was to determine Elizabeth's ultimate ability to bear children, it is likely that any gross vaginal abnormality would have been found and noted.

In 1566, there was talk of Elizabeth's marriage to the French king. The French Ambassador pressed her personal physician about her ability to bear children. "If the King marries her," replied her doctor, "I guarantee ten children; and no one in the world knows her constitution better than I do." Of course, the doctor was exaggerating and could have been lying. But his statement is evidence, even if not conclusive.

Later, when Elizabeth's marriage to the Duke of Alençon was being discussed, Burghley wrote a memorandum for his own eyes only, a practice he often followed. It evidenced the queen's continuing ability to conceive, which, of course, pre-supposed her ability to have sex.

Considering the proportion of her body, having no impediment or smallness in stature or largeness in body, nor no sickness, no lack of natural function in those things that properly belong to the procreation of children, but contrariwise, by judgment of physicians that know her estate in those things and by the opinion of women, being most acquainted with her majesty's body in such things as properly appertain to show probability of her aptness to have children even at this day.

Had Burghley written this memo for the French, we might have suspected an intent to mislead. But no one was to see it other than Burghley himself. He had no motive to shade the truth. Of course, part of what he wrote was hearsay provided by "physicians." Elizabeth's personal doctor might lie to the French Ambassador; but would he lie to a man as powerful as Burghley — about a matter of such importance? Conceivably he might, to protect the secret of someone even more powerful — the queen. But Burghley was no fool. In writing the memo for his own eyes only, Burghley must have considered that possibility and dismissed it.

Given the evidence of the French envoys who examined Elizabeth, the word of her physician, the Burghley memo and the absence of any evidence to the contrary, the theory that the queen had some structural abnormality can be dismissed as wholly unsupported by the facts.

There were many rumors of Elizabeth's sexual exploits. They started with Admiral Thomas Seymour. It seems clear that the young princess, teenage hormones raging, was highly attracted to the dashing and physically aggressive Admiral. Seymour's wife caught them in each other's arms, kissing passionately. Later, when Elizabeth's cofferor, John Parry, was interrogated, he provided the hearsay assertion that Kat Ashley said there had been even more between Seymour and the princess and that Parry must keep this secret, or Elizabeth could be "dishonored forever."

Parry, no tower of strength, was motivated to tell the royal interrogators whatever they wanted to hear. But, if Kat Ashley really said this to Parry, and if she was not exaggerating, what was this "even more" that could so dishonor the princess? Was it just heavy petting and fondling, or was it an outright sexual relationship. The former seems more likely. They were, after all, in the home of Seymour's wife, the former queen, Catherine Parr; and Kat Ashley was almost always present. It is doubtful they would have risked sexual intercourse under those circumstances. It is not, however, impossible. But then, Kat Ashley may never really have said what Parry told the interrogators.

Something seems odd about Catherine Parr's role in Elizabeth's relationship with Seymour. According to one report, Catherine joined the Admiral in tickling and fondling Elizabeth in the morning; and, in a bizarre episode redolent with psycho-sexual overtones, Catherine held Elizabeth firmly by the arms while her husband cut the princess's dress to shreds. Of course, there could be a relatively innocent explanation. Elizabeth's dress was black, because she was still mourning the death of her father. Perhaps cutting her dress off was simply a playful way of encouraging the princess to stop mourning and move on with her life. Perhaps. But perhaps not.

Catherine finally sent Elizabeth to live elsewhere. She did not appear to be angry, and the two remained on good terms. Did she send the princess from her home to protect her from Seymour, or to keep her husband from temptation, or was it because of growing concern about her own, possibly perverse involvement in their relationship? Or was it a little of each?

The next sexual "suspect" in Elizabeth's life was Robin Dudley, her childhood friend, whom, as queen, she made Earl of Leicester. They seemed to have loved each other for most of their lives. Certainly, Leicester was a handsome, lusty man, with the dark, dangerous looks that led to his being called "Gypsy."

To say Leicester was sexually active is a significant understatement. Even aside from whatever his relationship was with Elizabeth, he impregnated Lady Douglas Sheffield, who was married at the time, and apparently had an affair with her sister, as well. He certainly slept with Lettice Knollys before their secret marriage. His reputation as a seducer is evidenced by the fact that Lettice's father, who knew Leicester well, insisted that the couple go through a second marriage ceremony *in his presence*, to make sure the handsome Earl really married his daughter.

Later a scurrilous book was published entitled *Leicester's Commonwealth*. It repeated every rumor of the Earl's seductions and accused him of bedding almost all of Elizabeth's ladies in waiting, including a sexual affair with a mother and daughter at the same time.

There were, of course, many rumors of sexual intimacy between Elizabeth and Leicester. The Queen had a proclivity for fondling Leicester, even tickling him in public when he knelt for her to proclaim him an Earl.

They were frequently alone together, and were seen kissing on more than one occasion. Even after his wife's death, when suspicion and scandal created a new obstacle to their possible marriage, Elizabeth's personal relationship with Leicester — whatever it was — seemed to become even more careless of what others thought. Leicester was assigned quarters in the Palace adjoining Elizabeth's. He would enter her bed chamber and even "took upon himself the office of her lady in waiting, by handing to her a garment which ought never to have been seen in the hands of her master of horse." Despite the almost constant presence of ladies in waiting, it is by no means impossible that the two could have found opportunities to have sex.

The reports of foreign Ambassadors contain the assertion, or at least the strong implication, that Elizabeth and Leicester were lovers. The Spanish Ambassador wrote that "it is even said that her majesty visits him in his chamber day and night"; and his replacement wrote that he had heard "extraordinary things about this intimacy" and that the Council itself "made no secret" of the affair. And according to the Ambassador, Elizabeth admitted to him that she had great affection for Leicester and that she was "no angel."

In 1571, when Elizabeth's marriage to the Duke of Anjou was being discussed, the French envoy brought with him not only a portrait of the Duke, but also one of Mme. de Chateauneuf, supposedly Anjou's mistress. It was suggested that the lady might be a fine bride for Leicester. The jest at the French court was that, since Anjou was going to wed Leicester's mistress (i.e., Elizabeth), Anjou could at least offer his own mistress to Leicester.

On the other hand, there is significant evidence that all of the rumors, jokes and assertions were false. Confiding in her longtime friend and confidante, Kat Ashley, Elizabeth squarely denied that she had ever had sex with Leicester. She added, however, that, if she had wanted to, she didn't know who could forbid it.

In 1562, when Elizabeth appeared to be dying of smallpox, she swore, on what she probably considered her deathbed, that she and Robin had never been lovers. She said that, "Although she loved and had always loved Lord Robert Dudley dearly, as God was her witness, nothing improper ever passed between them." Given the widespread belief in damnation and hell, such deathbed statements were considered highly credible, since the dying person would not be likely to jeopardize her immortal soul in such a moment. Whether that would apply to someone as bold, free thinking and capricious as Elizabeth is a more difficult question.

What have been reported as Leicester's own words strongly suggest that he never had sexual intercourse with Elizabeth. Rumors were circulated about Elizabeth's having sexual affairs with both the Duke of Alençon and his representative, Jean de Simier. A jealous Leicester is said to have asked her directly "whether she was a maid or a woman." She is said to have replied that she was "still a maid."

One could always question the veracity of Elizabeth's response. But Leicester's asking the question is more significant. If accurately reported, it would certainly mean that, up to that point, she and Leicester had never had sexual intercourse. And, if the two had not made love by the time he asked the question, it is unlikely they did thereafter.

Why would Elizabeth have rejected what must have been erotic advances from Leicester, a handsome and sexually aggressive man with whom she seemed in love? The answer may lie in the risk of pregnancy. There were contraceptive devices in the 16th century, such as a hollowed out half lemon inserted vaginally as a diaphragm or a crude condom sewn from a pig's bladder or fine cloth. But these primitive devices were extremely unreliable. Even aside from religious principles and her desire to be perceived as England's "Virgin Queen," Elizabeth could not take any chance of becoming pregnant out of wedlock. She was surrounded on a daily basis with Ladies of the Bedchamber, Ladies of the Privy Chamber, Mistresses of the Wardrobe and Maids of Honor. It is unlikely that her even missing a period would have escaped notice; and, slim as she was, concealing an advanced pregnancy would have been impossible. Since pregnancy had to be avoided, she and Leicester could satisfy each other in other ways, and possibly they did.

The Queen was a healthy, passionate woman, who obviously cared for Leicester and was physically attracted to him. They may well have engaged in various forms of erotic contact short of sexual intercourse, ranging all the way from heavy petting to manual stimulation and even oral sex. Probably, however, they never made love.

But Leicester was not the only subject of ugly rumors about Elizabeth's supposed promiscuity. A legend was created that she had insatiable desires that she repeatedly gratified by having sex with her courtiers and even her servants. The Venetian envoy wrote "many persons say things (about Elizabeth) which I should not dare write." The Spanish Ambassador wrote that she served as "the hackney of her own vassals," meaning that they rode her at will and often. She was rumored to follow the practice of seducing handsome young men and keeping them in attendance upon her so that she could readily satisfy her sexual needs. This seems impossible; and the Spanish Ambassador was probably writing what his king wanted to hear.

Christopher Hatten, Thomas Heneage and Edward de Vere, the Earl of Oxford, were often named as sexual partners in these rumors. Elizabeth loved to flirt with these attractive courtiers, but it is highly doubtful that any of them were ever in her bed. Hatten loved Elizabeth all of his adult life and repeatedly told her so. But there is no indication that they were lovers. He swore they were not, and it is unlikely they were. Nor is there real evidence of an affair with Heneage.

The Queen was obviously attracted to Oxford, who was a bold and dashing man, highly intelligent, well read and widely traveled. She certainly enjoyed his company and, at one point, granted him a very substantial annual stipend. But, in 1485, Oxford's grandfather, a renowned military leader, had saved the day for Elizabeth's grandfather, Henry VII, at the Battle of Bosworth Field, allowing him to defeat Richard III and start the Tudor dynasty. In a sense, she owed her crown to Oxford's forebearers and, when he was in financial difficulty, her generous monetary assistance was not necessarily attributable to a sexual or even romantic relationship.

Oxford was acknowledged at the time to be a fine poet and playwright. Many believe he was the real author of the works attributed to William Shakespeare. If this was true and if the queen knew it, it would be still another reason for her largesse.

When Oxford impregnated Anne Vavasour, one of Elizabeth's maids of honor, he was sent to the Tower; and, on his release, he was banished from court. If Oxford wrote Shakespeare's sonnets, this may be the shame and disgrace to which the poet refers.

It has also been argued that Southampton was the illegitimate child of Oxford and Elizabeth and that Shakespeare's sonnets were written by Oxford about Southampton and the Queen, that Southampton was the "lovely youth" and even that Elizabeth was the mysterious "dark lady" of those famous verses.

It's a romantic idea; but there is no evidence to support it; and it is difficult to square with some of the sonnets. Sonnet 20, for example, calls the lovely youth "the master-mistress of my passion" and adds,

And for a woman wert thou first created;

Till Nature, as she wrought thee, fell a-doting,

And by addition me of thee defeated,

By adding one thing to my purpose nothing.

But since she prick'd thee out for woman's pleasure,

Mine be thy love, and thy love's use their treasure.

Obviously this double entendre was not written to the queen, or any woman. It is patently directed to a male, who was "prick'd . . . out for woman's pleasure"; but it is hardly something the poet would write to his own son.

There is also the fact that Oxford urged Southampton to marry his daughter, which, if the Earl were his son, would have had Oxford urging his two children to marry each other. Of course, it's possible that Oxford wasn't really the girl's father. But that too seems unlikely.

It has been suggested that Elizabeth had an affair with Sir Walter Raleigh. Raleigh was tall, handsome and highly intelligent. He rendered valuable military and naval service and ultimately named the Virginia Colony for Elizabeth. Obviously, the Queen found him attractive, and, after she discovered Leicester's marriage to Lettice Knollys,

Elizabeth and Raleigh were frequently together and seemed to delight in each other's company. Ultimately, however, Raleigh was sent to the Tower in disgrace for marrying and impregnating Bess Throckmorton, one of Elizabeth's Maids of Honor. At times, there was certainly a flirtation between Elizabeth and Raleigh; but it is unlikely that they carried on a sexual affair.

In short, there is no real evidence supporting the rumors of Elizabeth's promiscuity. Perhaps the best evidence to the contrary is the personal investigation conducted by Adam Zwetkovich, an envoy of the Emperor, as a necessary preliminary to the proposed marriage of Elizabeth to Archduke Charles, the Emperor's brother. The Emperor had instructed his envoy to proceed with the marriage negotiations only if, after a careful investigation, he was convinced that the English Queen was still a virgin.

These were Imperial orders, to be taken seriously and disobeyed at one's peril. Zwetkovich, who had no motive to lie, reported back to the Emperor that, as instructed, he had made "diligent inquiries concerning the maiden honor and integrity of the Queen," and found that there was no evidence whatsoever that she was no longer a virgin and that all the ugly rumors to that effect were "the spawn of envy and malice and hatred." Evidently the Emperor was convinced; and Zwetkovich was directed to proceed with the negotiations.

As a final chapter in Elizabeth's sex life, if she had one, we must consider the Earl of Essex. Certainly, the Queen was very attracted to the handsome, young Earl, and he won lucrative favors from her by constantly affirming her beauty and his love. Did he mean it? Not for a minute. But it seemed to work — at least until Essex made foolish, impetuous mistakes.

Was there a sexual component to their relationship? Although she was in her sixties, sex was certainly possible. Yet, somehow, it seems improbable. There is no evidence that it occurred.

On the other hand, the account of the French Ambassador, who met with Elizabeth during the same period, may suggest that the queen was at least still engaging in what she considered seductive behavior. If the translation of his remarks is accurate, was Elizabeth's pulling open her gown and revealing much of her body a sexual come-on? Probably not. Probably, opening her robe was just what she said it was, discomfort with the heat.

One other factor may complicate the issue of the queen's virginity — a young man claimed to be her son. There was historical precedent for this kind of situation. During the reign of Henry VII, two young men, Lambert Simnel and Perkin Warbeck, appeared separately in England. Each claimed to be one of the two sons of Edward IV, thought to have been murdered years before by their uncle, Richard III. Simnel was certainly not one of the missing princes. Warbeck could well have been, despite his ultimate "confession" that he was not.

Such a claimant appeared during the reign of Elizabeth. In 1587, the year before the Armada, a young

Englishman was arrested on a ship in Spanish waters. Considered a possible English spy, he was brought to the Spanish court, where he gave his name as Arthur Dudley. He claimed to be the illegitimate child of Queen Elizabeth and Robert Dudley, by this time the Earl of Leicester. He told an elaborate story about his childhood and subsequent adventures, interweaving his tale with the names of Leicester's aides and friends.

The young man told the Spanish he was a Catholic, and said that, despite the possibility of conflict between the two nations, he wanted to be "everybody's friend and nobody's enemy." He claimed he had been in Spain to visit the Shrine of Our Lady of Montserrat. The Spanish kept him under close observation, still considering him a possible spy. But unlike the typical handling of such suspects, King Philip took a personal interest in the young man's treatment. That is not surprising. If he had a colorable claim to be Elizabeth's son and was a Catholic to boot, he could have been valuable to Philip in a number of ways.

Pompeo Pellegrini, one of Walsingham's clandestine sources of information on events in Spain, reported that "Arthur Dudley" appeared to be around twenty-seven and that he acted like "the man he pretends to be," i.e., he acted like an Englishman of noble birth.

Sir Francis Englefield, an Englishman living in Spain, reported that the young man seemed accurate in relating facts and events concerning Leicester and others.

After being "debriefed," Arthur appeared to have stayed in various Spanish towns, at least until the failure of the Armada. After that, he disappears from recorded history. Possibly, he entered a monastery and remained there. Possibly, Philip decided that he was a spy and had him killed. We do not know.

Was "Arthur Dudley" simply a charlatan, posing as a royal bastard to attract attention, garner some Spanish coin and perhaps arrange an aristocratic, even royal marriage? Or did he dare to think that, if the Armada succeeded, Philip might consider placing him on the English throne.

On the other hand, he may have been one of Walsingham's double agents planted in or near the Spanish court to gather information. Or, was Walsingham or Burghley so Machiavellian and farsighted as to hedge England's bets by feeding the Spanish an aristocratic English Catholic who claimed royal descent, with the thought that, if the Armada succeeded, Philip might place "Arthur Dudley" on the English throne, and that, once he had the powers of a king, this royal "mole" might save Elizabeth and the Council members from execution or at least foster tolerance for the Protestant religion? Probably not. The young man may have been one of Walsingham's agents, but, if so, it is likely that Walsingham had far less elaborate plans for him.

Although it can't be proven one way or the other, "Arthur Dudley" was probably *not* the son of Elizabeth and Leicester. Aside from the likelihood that they never made love, if Arthur was twenty-seven in 1587, he was born around 1560. That was the year Leicester's wife was found dead at the bottom of a staircase; and both Leicester and the queen were suspected of having her killed.

To be pregnant out of wedlock would have been bad enough. But to be pregnant with the "love child" of the man whose wife he was suspected of murdering would almost surely have cost Elizabeth her throne, if not her life. This would be true whether the pregnancy occurred before or after the death of Leicester's wife. And there would have been no way to avoid others noticing, hinting or reporting that the queen was or had been pregnant and tying that fact to the suspected murder. Yet, there is not the slightest such hint or report in that period, not even in the writings of the Spanish Ambassador, who would have immediately and eagerly reported it.

In summary, we have, on one side, the rumors of Elizabeth's sexual exploits, plus her strong, impulsive, passionate nature, seemingly inconsistent with more than seventy years of virginity. On the other, we have her own "deathbed" affirmation that she never had "improper relations" with Leicester, as well as Leicester's asking if she was "still a maid," plus the conclusion of the Emperor's envoy after "diligent inquiries into her virginity," the absence of any direct evidence of a sexual liaison with anyone and the likelihood that those spreading rumors of scandalous behavior were, for the most part, motivated, as the Imperial envoy reported, by "envy and malice and hatred."

In a court of law, the judgment would certainly be for the Queen, that, in fact, she lived and died the "Virgin Queen." But we are not in a court of law, and you can draw your own conclusions. Those conclusions can never be verified. Elizabeth took the secret to her grave.

CHAPTER TWO

MARRIAGE

THE SECOND QUESTION most frequently asked about Elizabeth is why she never married. There were suitors, negotiations and promises galore, but never a wedding. Why? Were there times when she intended to marry, but simply changed her mind? Or did she never really intend marriage at all? Did she just pretend to consider one suitor after another, without ever intending to marry any of them?

Leicester reportedly said, "I have known her, from her eighth year, better than any man upon earth. From that date she has invariably declared that she would remain unmarried." Did her declarations to Leicester represent her true feelings on the matter? Or was he simply trying to rationalize her not marrying him?

Some writers have attributed Elizabeth's reluctance to marry to traumatic events in her life, such as the execution of her mother and of Admiral Seymour. Their theory is that these disturbing events caused her to associate marriage with death and thus to avoid it. Pronounced with authority, such pseudo-psychoanalytic theories can gain wide acceptance. They are usually not susceptible of objective proof or disproof. In this instance, however, the trauma theory seems of doubtful validity.

Why then wouldn't Elizabeth want to marry? Probably, there were two principal reasons. First, given the mores and tradition of the age, men were in control, and wives obeyed their husbands. Even if he was only called a "consort," rather than a "king," a husband with any degree of pride would not only want to participate in deciding important matters, he would probably insist on controlling such decisions. In her single state, Elizabeth had the final word. Married, that absolute control would have been severely eroded, if not wholly eliminated. And Elizabeth had great confidence in her own intelligence and judgment. She would have wanted to avoid ceding her power and authority to any man or even sharing it. Take any one of the many men named as potential husbands for Elizabeth, and it is difficult, if not impossible, to imagine her having been willing to rule jointly with him, much less to obey him in governing the realm.

Second, as Elizabeth must have seen it, a royal husband would sooner or later have liaisons with other women. Her father, Leicester, Philip, Alençon, Essex and almost every man she knew, married or not, was promiscuous or tried to be. Her husband would be royal, and royal advances were rarely rejected. Married, Elizabeth would have to bear the whisperings and malicious gossip time after time, particularly as she grew older and her husband chose one young mistress after another.

But, if Elizabeth never wanted to marry, why did she go through this strange dance of pretending she did, only to find excuse after excuse for not proceeding? There were at least three basic reasons.

First, there was the pressure to marry from the Council, Parliament and the public. Until much later in her reign, they were all anxious for Elizabeth to marry and produce an heir. Otherwise, they feared that her death would result in conflict and possibly civil war, with the danger of her being replaced by a militant Catholic.

Elizabeth managed to control her Council and face down Parliament; but the English people were a different matter. To them, marriage and childbearing were a natural thing for a woman and would eliminate any fight over the succession and a possible religious conflict on the queen's death. Although England was hardly a democracy, Elizabeth cared about the opinions of her subjects and strove to keep them happy, at least when it didn't conflict with what she considered her God given right to rule and to do what she deemed best for the nation. Appearing to consider offers of marriage could help satisfy the public and even Parliament and the Council.

Then there was religious pressure. England was torn between Catholics and Protestants. Many Catholics would have preferred Mary Stuart on the throne and a restoration of the old religion. While the Scottish Queen was alive, she was the focus of repeated Catholic plots to attain those objectives. When she gave birth to the future James VI of

Scotland, Protestants feared that this potential male heir would be raised a Catholic like his mother. This created increased pressure on Elizabeth to marry and have a child of her own, in order to insure a Protestant succession. As it turned out, Mary Stuart abdicated the following year, and her son James was raised as a Protestant.

Perhaps the most important reason for Elizabeth's seeming to consider one match after another was the need to keep England's potential enemies off balance. Spain was a rich and powerful Catholic nation that posed a real threat of invading England and overthrowing its queen. France too was primarily a Catholic nation, controlled much of the time by the lethally dangerous Guise family and the Catholic League. By marrying a Frenchman, she could lessen the danger from that source and create a barrier against the power of Spain. By marrying a Habsburg relative of the Spanish kings, she could forge a powerful alliance with Spain and the Empire, lessening any threat from them and deterring the French. By appearing ready to do one thing or the other, depending on the situation, she might keep both potential enemies at bay.

If she had made it plain that she would never marry, Elizabeth would have lessened the support of her own countrymen and would have seriously eroded her ability to deter both France and Spain from moving against her to put a Catholic on the throne.

For these basic reasons, it was tactically sound to involve herself, time after time, with various suitors, sometimes Spanish, sometimes French, sometimes from the Habsburg Empire, and to be perceived as inevitably moving toward marriage, even though she never quite got there.

Only by carefully examining Elizabeth's conduct with reference to her various suitors over the years can we make a more informed approach to deciding whether her conduct was based on the changing needs of a pragmatic foreign policy or simply reflected a frivolous inability to make up her mind.

The earliest suitor mentioned was the third son of the French king. These discussions began when Elizabeth was an infant. Such arranged marriages among royal children were not uncommon in the 16th century, although the actual betrothal and, certainly, the official wedding would not occur until much later. For example, Mary Stuart was betrothed to the French Dauphin as a young child and resided at the French court for years awaiting their marriage. In the case of Elizabeth, however, the religious inflexibility of the two fathers, Henry VIII and the French king, prevented this early match.

As a young woman, Elizabeth's first serious suitor was Admiral Seymour. After the death of his wife, he certainly intended to marry her if he could. Elizabeth had previously been attracted to the dashing Admiral; and, as we have seen, there had been kissing, fondling and perhaps even more between them. But marriage was something else. Elizabeth could not marry without the consent of King

Edward's Council. The will of Henry VIII provided that, if either of his daughters married without the Council's consent, she would forfeit her right to the succession. But Admiral Seymour was the uncle of the new, young king and the brother of Somerset, the Royal Protector. He was also funneling money secretly to his royal nephew in order to win his support. Apparently, he felt his chances of obtaining the Council's permission to marry Elizabeth were good. He was wrong.

Elizabeth's cofferer, Thomas Parry, told her that Seymour had inquired about her property and expenses, had suggested that they exchange properties and said that he was "about to have her." Parry pursued the matter with Elizabeth, asking "whether, if the Council would like it, she would marry with him?"

If Parry is to be believed, even at fifteen, Elizabeth already showed the sound judgment that characterized her in maturity. According to him, she replied, "When that comes to pass, I will do as God shall put in my mind." Of course, it never came to pass, and Seymour was executed for treason.

Before Elizabeth took the throne, several foreign princes were proposed as potential husbands, including the Habsburg Archduke Ferdinand and Prince Eric of Sweden. At that point, there was less pressure on the princess to marry and bear a child. She was not yet queen; and, in those early days, she could more easily remain firm in stating that she had "no wish to marry." Possibly that was her true feeling at the time, but no one really believed it.

Philip pressed Queen Mary to have Elizabeth marry Duke Emmanuel Philibert of Savoy, a staunch ally of the Empire. But Elizabeth was adamant in her refusal. Although angry, Mary followed sound advice not to be perceived as forcing her popular sister into a foreign match.

In 1558, when Elizabeth became queen, everything changed. Now, as the monarch, she was strongly urged to take a husband and bear children. At first, she continued to express her opposition to marriage. In a speech to Parliament in 1559 she said, "I have already joined myself in marriage to a husband, namely the Kingdom of England." Later that year she told Parliament, "And in the end, this shall be for me sufficient, that a marble stone shall declare that a queen, having reigned such a time, lived and died a virgin."

Nevertheless, the pressure to marry continued and increased. Parliament, the Council and the public all wanted it. As bright and perceptive as Elizabeth was, she must have concluded at some point that it would be wise to stop expressing a fixed intention to remain single and, instead, to show a continuing interest in the available matches, using her potential marriage for political advantage.

Philip of Spain, who had always found Elizabeth attractive, made an attempt, through the Spanish

Ambassador, to discuss their possible marriage. Elizabeth was well aware that the English public, being generally anti-Spanish and having seen Englishmen die fighting Spain's battles in the lowlands during Philip's marriage to her sister Mary, would find Elizabeth's marriage to the same Spaniard wholly unacceptable.

But Elizabeth took her time in responding to Philip's offer. She was negotiating with the French; and her negotiating position was considerably stronger if they faced the possibility of a royal Anglo-Spanish marriage. She told Philip's Ambassador, Count de Feria, that if she married at all, her preference would be Philip. That bought her some time. And, when she was ready to put an end to the possibility of marrying Philip, she sought to soothe his pride. She avoided an explicit rejection, and let it be known that she intended to remain Protestant and could never confirm the authority of the Pope to grant the dispensation that was necessary, since Philip had been married to her sister.

When Philip promptly married the daughter of the French king, Elizabeth teased the Spanish Ambassador that Philip could not have been very much in love with her, since he hadn't even had the patience to wait for a formal response to his proposal.

But, the problems inherent in marriage to Philip were less serious with regard to his Habsburg cousins, Archduke Ferdinand and Archduke Charles. The Habsburg Emperor, Ferdinand I, was, of course, allied with Philip, who was his nephew. But marrying one of the

Emperor's sons was not the same as marrying a Spaniard. They offered a promising and beneficial match, warding off the French and bringing England closer to Spain and the Empire, without the disadvantage of importing another Spanish king.

Elizabeth politely rejected the idea of Archduke Ferdinand, since he was reputed to be extreme in his religious views and ferociously anti-Protestant. But she seemed willing to pursue the idea of marrying his brother, Archduke Charles. A representative of Charles traveled to London for the discussions, only to be met with Elizabeth's numerous personal questions about the Archduke and by her insistence that she meet him before making any decision. The Spanish Ambassador wrote that, when the match with Charles was proposed to Elizabeth, "She went back again to her nonsense, and said she would rather be a nun than marry without knowing whom and on the faith of portrait painters." Perhaps she had in mind the part played by Holbein's flattering portrait in inducing her father to agree to marry the unseen Anne of Cleves. More likely she was just using this as an excuse.

Nevertheless, many thought that, one way or another, Elizabeth would ultimately accept the obvious advantages of a match with Charles. They were wrong. She wrote the Emperor that she did not yet wish to marry, although she recognized that, when she did, Archduke Charles would be the best possible husband. She left the door open. She almost always left marital doors open. What could occur in the future, she said, would be directed by God.

Sir William Pickering, once a candidate for the queen's hand himself, had predicted that the Archduke's suit would come to naught. He told the Spanish Ambassador that he was wasting his time pressing it, since "he knew she means to die a maid."

But, sensibly, Elizabeth was no longer making that outright declaration — at least publicly. She had realized the need to appear open to marriage and the strategic value of keeping both France and Spain off balance by appearing ready to marry a prince of, or allied with, first one and then the other.

And the foreign suitors were not limited to France, Spain and the Empire. There was Prince Eric of Sweden. Eric had been proposed as a husband even before Elizabeth became queen. Now, he wrote her passionate love letters in Latin and sent his brother, Duke John of Finland, to press the match.

Spain and the Empire were concerned that Elizabeth might accept Eric's suit, creating an Anglo-Scandinavian alliance of Protestant states. Their concern was needless. Elizabeth was well aware that, compared to a Spanish, Imperial or French match, Sweden offered little that could help England financially, militarily or politically.

Characteristically, however, the queen was in no hurry to allay the Spanish and Imperial fears. She withheld her response to the Swedish proposal until, finally, Prince Eric demanded Duke John's return. Eric suspected that, instead of acting as a loyal representative, his brother was having his own affair with the queen. There is no indication that such an affair occurred. Perhaps worse, however, the faithless Duke John proposed his own marriage to Elizabeth. Finally, he left England, with no commitment from Elizabeth to marry either brother. Prince Eric continued for years to have hopes for the match, but nothing ever came of it.

The Scots were also ready to play the marriage game. The Scottish Lords of the Covenant suggested that Elizabeth marry the Earl of Arran, at that time, heir to the Scottish throne. Marriage to Arran could have united the two kingdoms and helped to end French influence in Scotland. But Arran proved weak and ineffectual in the struggles against Mary of Guise; and, although Elizabeth met with him a number of times, she finally, though politely, rejected the match.

Marriage to one of the English suitors, William Pickering and Edward Courtenay, the Earl of Devon, was discussed and gossiped about. Such a marriage would have pleased Parliament and the public and might have produced an heir. But, like Arran, they each had notable character flaws; and, unlike a French, Spanish or Imperial match, the prospect of an English marriage would have had little value in advancing English foreign policy.

Robert Dudley was something else. For years, the queen's "dear Robin" was rumored to be a likely bridegroom, even though both his father and grandfather had been executed for treason, and Robin himself had been imprisoned in the Tower for supporting Lady Jane Grey. Soon after her accession, Elizabeth appointed Dudley her "Master of the Horse," an important position at court. This led Catherine de Medici to remark nastily that Elizabeth was about "to marry her horse-keeper."

Obviously, Elizabeth had very affectionate feelings for her "Robin"; and, on his wife's death, many anticipated that Elizabeth would marry him. Clearly, he entertained such hopes himself. But there was widespread outrage at the notion, and the suspicion and scandal associated with his wife's mysterious death made the match difficult, if not impossible — if Elizabeth had ever really considered it.

As we have seen, Dudley schemed to bring their marriage about, even suggesting to Philip of Spain (through the Pope and others) that, to avoid Elizabeth's making a French match, Philip should support her marriage to Dudley. In return, once Dudley was the royal consort, he would support Spanish policy and possibly even restore Catholicism as England's official religion.

None of this came to pass. Unquestionably, Elizabeth loved Dudley. But she recognized his faults. More importantly, she realized that marrying him would create bitter division among her courtiers and advisors, would be extremely unpopular with the people after the suspicious death of his wife, and would provide no real advantage to her or to England. She made her decision and told Cecil she would definitely not marry Dudley.

Having come to that firm conclusion, Elizabeth suggested that Dudley marry Mary Stuart, in which event, she would recognize Mary as successor to the English throne. Her idea was that, married to Dudley, Mary would calm down, be less of a threat to religious reform and perhaps even be a good queen. Elizabeth made Dudley Earl of Leicester, in order to give him greater status in Mary's eyes. She showed Melville, the Scottish Ambassador, a miniature of Dudley. On the wrapping, she had written "my Lord's picture." Was this a piece of theatre designed to show the Scots what a prize Elizabeth was relinquishing to Mary? Perhaps. Or perhaps it reflected Elizabeth's true feelings.

In any event, nothing came of the plan to marry the newly-made Earl to Mary Stuart. Mary chose, instead, the youthfully attractive Lord Darnley. Aggravated, Elizabeth protested to the Scottish Ambassador that "no woman of spirit would make choice of such a man" when she could have the bold and handsome Leicester. But it was to no avail. Mary had fallen in love with what Elizabeth described as the "lady faced" young lord, and they soon married. This union of two Catholic claimants to the English throne and the potential birth of their child posed a dire threat to the Protestant cause and brought added pressure on Elizabeth to marry. Negotiations for a Habsburg match with the Archduke Charles were resumed, but Elizabeth continued to give mixed signals and to demand a face-to-face meeting.

Meanwhile, Catherine de Medici suggested a match between Elizabeth and her eldest son, Charles IX, then fifteen and King of France. Leicester, still hoping he had a chance to marry the queen, attacked the idea of the French royal marriage, even though he felt sure public opposition would prevent it. He counted on the French realizing this and supporting his own suit, rather than risking Elizabeth's making a Habsburg match that would throw England into the arms of the Empire and Spain. At the same time, Leicester thought that, if negotiations for the match with Archduke Charles broke down, which he also believed was likely, the Spanish would back his own marriage to the Queen, rather than risk her marrying a Frenchman.

The Habsburgs sent a special envoy to ascertain Elizabeth's intentions regarding Archduke Charles. The Imperial envoy made it clear that Charles "would be again prepared to woo the illustrious queen, if he had clear indications of her intentions. He would not, as on the last occasion, suffer himself to be led by the nose." He had "great desire to see her" his envoy said. Elizabeth's response caught the envoy and her Council by surprise. "I have never said hitherto to anybody that I would not marry the Earl of Leicester." What? The Habsburgs thought that any idea of that foolish match had been put behind her. Probably, Cecil had told them so.

Almost surely, she did not mean what she said about marrying Leicester. She probably said it to throw the Imperial envoy off balance and to slow things down. But Cecil feared that Elizabeth might really marry her "Robin," whom Cecil then considered troublesome and dangerous. And Cecil was not alone in that belief. Leicester had his share of powerful enemies. Cecil's concern was increased by the fact that, as Leicester had hoped, the French were supporting his suit as a means of avoiding the Habsburg match.

Cecil prepared a memorandum on why the queen's marriage to Archduke Charles was far preferable to a marriage to Leicester. Marrying Leicester, he wrote, would not increase the queen's riches or her power. It would lead the world to believe the rumors of their having had an improper relationship. And Leicester, Cecil wrote, sought nothing but to advance and enrich himself and his friends and tended to offend everyone else. He was deeply in debt and still suspected of murdering his wife. Finally, Cecil wrote, he was the kind of husband who would constantly resent Elizabeth's status and power.

Elizabeth knew all this. It was why she had probably decided not to marry Leicester. But that did not prevent her from terrifying everyone with the prospect, including Cecil and the Habsburgs.

The potential match with Archduke Charles proceeded slowly, in fits and starts. Elizabeth's decision remained elusive. While acknowledging Charles as a splendid prospect, she began raising problems concerning his religion. She insisted that, no matter what he said publicly, he must swear secretly to abandon Catholicism.

As Elizabeth must have foreseen, Charles' brother, now the Emperor, found this unacceptable. "The religion [Charles] was brought up in should be permitted him," and this, he demanded, "must be winked at by the Queen."

Nevertheless, the discussions continued. Parliament put all the pressure it could on Elizabeth to force her to marry someone, or at least to name a successor. She resented this pressure on what she considered a matter of personal choice and one well within her royal prerogatives. She argued that naming a successor would simply create a focus for plotting and rebellion; and, as to marriage, she pointed to her continuing negotiations with the Archduke Charles.

Still, she continued to insist that Charles travel to England and cautioned that, even if he did, she could not promise an affirmative answer. The Habsburgs were unwilling to have Charles travel there possibly to be inspected and rejected; and there the matter rested. Negotiations continued, but slowly. The Emperor wrote to his brother that Elizabeth "seems to regard it as profitable to create delays somewhere or somehow in order to gain an advantage." He was correct.

On one occasion when Elizabeth was professing her desire for Charles to come to England, so that the match might proceed, the Spanish Ambassador played a joke on her. He whispered to her that Charles was already at her court in disguise. Elizabeth became highly distressed. "She turned white," the Ambassador wrote, "and was so agitated that I could not help laughing to see her." It was one thing to pretend longing to meet a suitor who was far, far away. It was quite another to contemplate his being right there at court, expecting a firm and final answer.

When Mary Stuart became a captive of the Scottish Lords of the Covenant, the pressure on Elizabeth to marry lessened. The Imperial representatives took the position that Archduke Charles would accompany Elizabeth to Anglican services, but that he must have his own private chapel for Catholic mass. With the pressure to marry decreased by the diminished threat of Mary Stuart, Elizabeth firmly refused the Imperial demand, saying it would violate English law.

Probably she had concluded long before that, if they married, Charles would gradually insist on openly practicing his religion and that he would demand a role in decision making, a process in which he would be strongly influenced by Spain and the Empire. Whatever her reasons, Elizabeth's adamant stand against a private Catholic chapel put an end to the match.

The Queen had done it again. The Spanish Ambassador saw it clearly. Elizabeth, he said, wanted everyone to be in love with her, but would never be in love with anyone sufficiently to marry him.

But the world of politics and religion in the 16th century could change rapidly. First came the rebellion of Catholic Northern lords designed to free Mary Stuart and place her on the English throne. Then, in 1570, the Pope issued his bull excommunicating Elizabeth, freeing her subjects from any allegiance to her and authorizing them to kill her without sinning. This was followed in 1571 by the Ridolfi Plot, which had Elizabeth's overthrow and death as its aim and which not only involved English conspirators, but had demonstrable Spanish backing.

It seemed an appropriate time for Elizabeth to play the marriage card again. The suggestion was made to the Imperial Court that perhaps discussions of a match with the Archduke Charles should be resumed. This time, however, the Habsburgs were understandably unwilling.

Meanwhile, relations with France seemed to be improving. At this point, Catherine de Medici, acting through her son, Charles IX of France, had seemingly halted the religious war between the French Catholics and the Protestant Huguenots. Catherine's party, the "Politiques", appeared to be the most tolerant Catholic party. They seemed to have attained at least temporary ascendancy over the militantly Catholic Guise family and the Catholic League. But Catherine's younger son, Henri, Duke of Anjou, was perceived by the Politiques to be a tool of the Guise family and likely to stir up renewed trouble.

One solution was to marry Anjou to Elizabeth. An English alliance would be a desirable protection against Spain, always France's principal rival. Catherine de Medici was a daughter of the once preeminent Florentine family. The strategies of Machiavelli were a part of her birthright. She had married one French king and was ultimately the mother of three others. From her point of view, placing her second son Anjou next to Elizabeth on the English throne was eminently desirable.

There was also good reason for such a match from the English point of view. English relations with Spain had deteriorated because of English seizure of Spanish treasure ships and Spain's involvement in the Ridolfi Plot. An Anglo-French alliance could deter Spanish military adventures against England. And, with a French prince sharing the English throne, the French were not likely to fight for the claims of Mary Stuart. A rapprochement with France seemed sensible; and a match with Anjou seemed a good way to achieve it.

Moreover, if Anjou did not marry Elizabeth, there was a risk of his going through a proxy marriage to Mary Stuart, creating a new French-Scottish alliance that would seek to rescue Mary and place her on the English throne.

With those considerations in mind, Elizabeth kept the possibility of marriage to Anjou alive, hinting, discussing, and, sometimes, even seeming to agree to the match. When the French Ambassador met with Elizabeth, she said that, if she did decide to marry, it could only be to a man from a royal house, with a rank suitable to her own. The Ambassador used what seemed the queen's deliberate opening to point out that Anjou was "the most accomplished prince in the world and the only person worthy of marrying her." Elizabeth understood that Anjou had been brought up as one "not averse to the Protestant religion," but she expressed concern about his age. He was only nineteen at the time. When the Ambassador said that Anjou "Bore himself already like a man," Elizabeth replied, "He will always be younger than me." Leicester, who was present and sought to appear in favor of the match, jested, "So much the better for you."

But there were troubling reports about Anjou. "He is completely dominated by voluptuousness," wrote the Venetian Ambassador. He is "covered with perfumes and essences. He wears a double row of rings and pendants in his ears." Not only that, Anjou's habit was to attend balls dressed as a woman, in full makeup and low-cut gown. Elizabeth certainly realized that proclivity would not sit well with the English.

Moreover, Walsingham reported to the queen on Anjou's true religious views. "You have been persuaded that he has a leaning to the new religion and might be brought to adopt it. Undeceive yourself. He was born a Catholic, he has lived the declared champion of Catholicism. Believe me, he will live and die in this faith."

Elizabeth intended to keep the discussions going for as long as she could, but the more she learned about Anjou, the less she fancied the idea of marrying him. Nevertheless, when one of her ladies was tactless enough to say that marriages are best between people near the same age, Elizabeth's pride was wounded. "Nonsense!" she retorted angrily, "There are but ten years difference between us." In fact, the difference in years was eighteen.

Keeping the matter open for political reasons, Elizabeth created the impression that she was ready to accept Anjou's proposal should he make one. He did, informally and hedged with conditions. She instructed Walsingham, then Ambassador to France, to ask for further talks. She "thankfully accepted" Anjou's proposal in principle and suggested the use of her sister Mary's marriage treaty with

Philip of Spain as a starting point for further negotiations. At the same time, however, she pointed out that Anjou's form of religion was contrary to the law of the land.

Anjou then sent an envoy with a formal offer of marriage and a portrait of himself. The French conditions were that he be crowned "King" to rule jointly with Elizabeth, that he be granted an allowance of £60,000 per year and that he and his household be allowed freely to exercise the Catholic religion.

Surprisingly, Elizabeth appeared to go along with all but the religious condition, which was unacceptable. Probably, none of these one-sided, arrogant conditions were acceptable to her; but that is not what she said.

Burghley believed that Anjou would ultimately yield to Elizabeth's position on the subject of religion. As he cynically put it Anjou "would not lose a queen with a kingdom for a priest's blessing of a chalice."

Burghley was wrong. Catherine de Medici made it clear that Anjou demanded the right to practice Catholicism openly, with all of its ceremonies. Elizabeth tried gamely to keep the matter open, still fearing that Guise influence would send Anjou to Mary Stuart. But that risk had to be faced. The Anjou match was at an end.

At this point, Catherine de Medici, still hoping to see one of her sons sharing the English throne, proposed a new idea. Her youngest son, the Duke of Alençon, might be an even better husband for Elizabeth, since, on the subject of religion, he was "a much less scrupulous fellow."

There were decided advantages to this match. There was the continuing theme of deterring Spain with the threat of an Anglo-French alliance. In addition, as his mother had said, Alençon was not a rigid and devout Catholic like his brother. According to her, he had been quite tolerant of the French Huguenots. And, unlike his brother, Alençon did not go about in female attire.

Moreover, since the French king, Charles IX, was without children, his brother, Anjou, was next in line to the throne. Anjou's becoming King of France, while sharing the English throne, would have created serious problems. Alençon, as the youngest brother, was less likely to face that situation.

Thus began twelve years of an on again-off again courtship between Elizabeth and Alençon. During that period, Elizabeth gave the impression that she was smitten with her "frog," and used every device and dodge to keep the suit alive, while never totally committing. At first, she seemed quite receptive. But, probably, her real goal, at the time, was to bring about an Anglo-French mutual defense treaty, which might hold off the Spanish, without the necessity of her actually going through with a French marriage.

Some of the pressure for such a marriage was relieved in April 1572, when Charles IX gave up on Mary Stuart and signed a mutual defense treaty with England, without waiting for Elizabeth to marry his brother. This was the Treaty of Blois. Given that pact, Elizabeth felt much less need to move toward a French marriage. Although she continued to express delight at the idea of marrying Alençon, she did not hurry into a commitment.

There were also political reasons for delay. The Dutch were again in open revolt, and the French seemed ready to intervene there against the Spanish. To Elizabeth and the English merchants, French control of the Netherlands would be worse than Spanish. Another powerful reason for delaying any French match was the public's attitude toward the St. Bartholomew's Day Massacre of August 1572. As we have seen, Catherine de Medici and her oldest son, Charles IX, acquiesced in the assassination of Admiral Coligny, which was followed by the slaughter of French Huguenots, first in Paris and then throughout France.

That horrifying episode of religious genocide provoked a strong anti-French reaction in England. It increased the popular opposition to a French marriage for Elizabeth and created doubt that the French, controlled then by the Catholic party, would come to the aid of Protestant England if it was attacked by Spain. And, although the English public didn't know it, Elizabeth may have been aware that Coligny was shot with a gun from Alençon's own arsenal.

Under the circumstances, Elizabeth sought better relations with Spain, deferring any thought of marriage to Alençon. Their marriage discussions were also deferred by Alençon's brief imprisonment for conspiring with Huguenot friends. Then, in 1574, the likelihood of marriage to Alençon seemed further diminished by Anjou's taking the French throne as Henri III on the untimely death of their brother Charles IX. Alençon was now next in line to the throne, with the title Duke of Anjou. To avoid confusion, however, I'll continue to call him "Alençon."

At this point, Alençon showed a side of himself that must have given Elizabeth further pause. After seeming for years to be pro-Huguenot, Alençon accepted a cynical offer from his brother, now the French king. Alençon would receive the valuable duchies of Anjou and Touraine, if he would end all tolerance for the Protestant side. Not only did he turn away from the Huguenots, he led troops against them. By 1576, the chances of Elizabeth marrying Alençon had seemed to evaporate.

But, once again, the international situation changed. Spain was enjoying success in the Netherlands and was becoming more belligerent. Perhaps even more dangerous, Catherine de Medici appeared to be pressing Alençon to make a Spanish marriage. A Franco-Spanish alliance would, of course, be a disaster for England. Once again, there was need for Elizabeth to revive talks of a French marriage.

It was a fair bet that Alençon and his mother would prefer his sharing the English throne to whatever match could be arranged with France's arch-rival Spain. If Elizabeth could appear, once again, ready to marry Alençon, the Duke's Spanish marriage plans could be derailed, and any attack by Spain might be deterred by fear of a new Anglo-French alliance.

Discussions of the Alençon match were revived in 1579 and continued through 1581. They were stimulated on a personal level by Simier's visit to London, by his disclosure of Leicester's marriage to Lettice Knollys and by Alençon's own romantic journeys to visit and woo his "beloved." They were given heightened political impetus by Philip's conquest of Portugal, the growing success of his lowlands campaign and the fact that Henri III of France (formerly the Duke of Anjou) had proved a more moderate ruler than had been feared.

Walsingham readily grasped the political implications of the revived marriage talks. He wrote,

The negotyacion of [Alençon] *here taketh greater foote than was first looked for and receaveth no smaule furtheraunce up* [on] *occasion of the decayed state of things in the Low Countryes for that Her Majestie, forseeing that yf the King of Spain come once to have his will there he will prove no very good neythbour to her.*

Elizabeth herself realized the important political interests involved. On Alençon's arrival in England she wrote to Burghley, "Let me know what you wish me to do." She was seeking his advice on politics, not romance. The resumed negotiations for the Alençon match proceeded rather slowly; but, despite strong popular opposition, they seemed headed toward a royal marriage.

As time passed, however, the political situation shifted again. The need for a French marriage began to appear less pressing. Elizabeth agreed with Alençon to provide money for his Netherlands campaign on condition that he would oppose the then pro-Spanish Guise faction in France. Possibly she believed that the investment might sufficiently serve England's needs. If Alençon was an ally, dependent on English funding, perhaps he needn't be her husband. And, Alençon's vast popularity among the French might keep his royal brother from supporting the idea of a Spanish assault on England. Relieving Guise pressure for that idea by giving Alençon money might lessen the need for Elizabeth to marry him — at least for the time being.

The reasons for and against moving toward marriage with Alençon were complex and difficult to evaluate. Apparently, however, Elizabeth made her decision, one that may have involved a clever feint in one direction and a seemingly decisive move in the other. She played out the dramatic scene of kissing and exchanging rings with Alençon, suggesting they were, or were about to be, wed. Then she told him sorrowfully the next day that she could not marry him after all — at least not now.

That feint at marriage allowed Alençon to save face and blame Elizabeth's "change of mind" on the frailty of women. Ultimately, as we have seen, the Duke was given a significant sum of money and politely escorted from the realm.

Philip of Spain was not surprised. He wrote to his ambassador that he had been convinced from the beginning that Elizabeth would never accept Alençon's suit.

Had Elizabeth ever really intended to marry Alençon? Probably not. Most probably she was playing a political game through all those years, trying to keep the French close and the Spanish off balance, promising a French marriage, while, at the same time, keeping Parliament and her Council at bay and the people appeased. The English were opposed to the match with Alençon; but, with Elizabeth continuing to discuss it and appearing to favor it, they could not accuse her of refusing to marry.

And yet, when we look at her poetry at the time, perhaps we see something else. In 1582, the year Alençon left England for good, this is what Elizabeth wrote:

> *I grieve and dare not show my discontent;*
>
> *I love, and yet am forced to seem to hate;*
>
> *I do, yet dare not say I ever meant;*
>
> *I seem stark mute, but inwardly do prate.*
>
> *I am, and not; I freeze and yet am burned,*
>
> *Since from myself another self I turned.*

My care is like my shadow in the sun—

Follows me flying, flies when I pursue it,

Stands, and lies by me, doth what I have done;

His too familiar care doth make me rue it.

   No means I find to rid him from my breast,

   Till by the end of things I be suppressed.

Some gentler passion slide into my mind,

For I am soft, and made of melting snow;

Or be more cruel, Love and so be kind.

Let me float or sink, be high or low;

   Or let me live with some more sweet content,

   Or die, and so forget what love e'er meant.

– ELIZABETHA REGINA.

Is Elizabeth saying something very different from what we might otherwise conclude? Was the "love" she hoped to "forget" love for Alençon? Had she really wanted to marry him, but decided it was not the right course for England or for herself?

Perhaps; but probably not. When she wrote the poem, Elizabeth may have been thinking about someone else entirely. Some lines, like "His too familiar care," might suggest Leicester or even Raleigh. But others, like "I love, and yet am forced to seem to hate" do not suggest either of them — not in 1582. Elizabeth had learned of Leicester's marriage to Lettice Knollys three years before in 1579, and his disobedience in the Netherlands campaign did not occur until 1586. She did not learn of Raleigh's marriage to Bess Throckmorton until 1591. There would seem no reason why she was "forced to hate" either Leicester or Raleigh in 1582, when she wrote the poem. In 1582, the poem could not have been about Essex; since they did not meet until 1584, when Leicester brought him to Court. Possibly the poem was just an example of Elizabeth's creative mind and was not biographical at all. There is also another possibility. Elizabeth seems to have disclosed her poem to others. Was it simply another way of seeking to mollify the French by suggesting a continued but vain love for Alençon? Maybe. In any event, the poem remains one more mystery about this enigmatic queen.

Probably, Elizabeth had decided early on that she would never marry, never share her rule with any man. Her pattern of behavior over the years supports this view. While she might have talked, in her early years, about staying "a maid" forever, she realized soon enough that to continue that unpopular stance openly and as a matter of serious policy would be politically dangerous, perhaps suicidal.

The Queen certainly grasped that a potential marriage could be a significant political weapon. She was aware that her people generally opposed both a French and Spanish match. But, she could — and did — use the threat of one or the other or even an Imperial match to keep both the French and Spanish at bay. Had she married anyone — even someone she loved — or made it clear she would remain a virgin for life, that potent weapon would have been lost. I doubt that she was prepared to lose that weapon, knowing how vital it was to the safety of her realm and herself.

Can we know with certainty that this was her thought process or that her intention didn't change capriciously from year to year or even day to day? No. She made no deathbed "confession" of what she had intended and left no dispositive writing on the point. Possibly there were times when Elizabeth really intended to marry, but simply couldn't make up her mind. Somehow, that seems unlikely.

CHAPTER THREE

MURDER

THIS WAS A VIOLENT AGE. Elizabeth did not shrink from the sight of blood and death — at least not the blood and death of animals. She loved the hunt, which could be extremely brutal. And, like her subjects, she even enjoyed bear baiting, a bloody fight to the death between a chained bear and a pack of vicious dogs.

When she deemed it essential, Elizabeth was ready to send men to die in battle. She was generally reluctant to engage in military ventures, but that was not an antipathy to violence. Principally, it was her concern about the economic and political cost of such ventures and her inability to control her commanders once they were in the field.

But what about murder? Did Elizabeth sanction that form of personal violence when it suited her needs — or desires? Did she advocate its use — even profit by it?

She has been suspected of complicity in at least one murder, the mysterious death of Robin Dudley's wife in 1560, the second year of Elizabeth's reign. The circumstances of her death have led to centuries of analysis and debate and at least one play, Sir Walter Scott's *Kenilworth*. They could serve as the basis for an Agatha Christie plot.

The Queen was in love with Dudley; that seems clear. But Dudley was married to Amy Robsart, a Norfolk heiress. They were frequently apart for months, and it was obvious that Dudley was far more interested in the glamorous Elizabeth and the prospect of his becoming Consort or king, than in his long suffering, provincial wife. Could Dudley obtain a divorce? There appeared to be no grounds; and, if, somehow, Dudley could put aside his wife in order to marry the queen, the Council, the clergy, the nobility and, most importantly, the public would be outraged. Pursuing that course could even lead to Elizabeth's losing her crown. Was there another way?

On September 8, 1560, Amy was staying at Cumnor Place, the manor house of Sir Anthony Forster, a business associate of Dudley. A few miles from Oxford, Cumnor Place had been built in the fourteenth century. It was actually owned by George Owen, who leased it to Forster.

Amy, then 28, had sent all of her servants to a local fair at Abingdon. They were to be gone the entire day. Somehow, sometime that day, Amy fell down a flight of stairs, breaking her neck. Or at least it seemed so, since her body was found at the bottom of the stairs with her neck broken.

In England and throughout Europe, Dudley was suspected of arranging his wife's murder in order to marry the queen. Elizabeth was suspected of being complicit in his criminal plan in order to make their marriage possible.

Dudley was "cleared" by a local inquest that found Amy's death an accident. But that finding did little to end the widespread rumors of his guilt — and the queen's. Certainly, the circumstances of Amy's death were suspicious. According to the Coroner's Report, written in Latin, Amy not only had a broken neck, but also two head wounds, which the Report adds would be called "dynts" in English. A "dynt" typically referred to a wound caused in combat, as by a sword or pike.

Evidently, the coroner probed such wounds with his thumb to measure their depth. One "dynt" in Amy's head was a quarter of a thumb deep. That was bad enough. But the depth of second "dynt" was an extraordinary *two thumbs*. That second wound would certainly have fractured Amy's skull and penetrated deep into her brain, causing massive damage. It would have been a fatal wound, even if her neck had not been broken.

Could that devastating wound have been the result of a fall down the stairs? It seems most unlikely. Amy did not fall down a long, straight stairway. It was only a few steps; and the staircase was apparently "dog-leg" in structure, described as a "pair of stairs" consisting of "eight steps."

Moreover, the Coroner's Report said that Amy's body was "without any other marks or wound." If she had fallen down the stairs, wouldn't there be bruises, abrasions or cuts on her arms, legs, back or chest?

Strangely, when Amy's body was found, her skirt was not in disarray. It was neatly tucked around her legs, and a hood was in place on her head. Those facts also seem inconsistent with her falling down the stairs. With a head wound two thumbs deep, would her hood still be in place? It seems unlikely, if not impossible.

Was Amy attacked by an unknown assailant, who then placed her body at the bottom of the stairs, rearranging her clothing in a bizarre nod to propriety and replacing her hood in the hope of covering the grievous wound to her head?

Modern medicine has provided a possible explanation for Amy's broken neck. If, as appeared to be the case, Amy had metastasized breast cancer, malignant lesions could have formed in her neck, weakening the bone and causing a fracture if she fainted or tripped. Possibly the bones could even have fractured spontaneously as she descended the stairs. But that would not seem a credible explanation for a head wound two thumbs deep or the absence of cuts, bruises and abrasions elsewhere on her body or the pristine state of her clothing.

Conceivably, more facts could have been determined if Amy's remains had been exhumed and examined. She was buried in the Cathedral of St. Mary the Virgin in Oxford. Unfortunately, the floor of the Cathedral was excavated in 1946, and the multitude of disparate bones was so mixed in the soil that it would be difficult to separate out what might be the remains of any particular individual. And, even if this could be determined by DNA analysis, it would not be likely to establish the cause of death.

The actual staircase down which Amy fell may well be located in an ancient farmhouse in Lower Whitley, near the former site of Cumnor Place. The local legend is that the staircase was moved to the farmhouse in 1811 when Cumnor Place was torn down, but that it is still haunted by Amy's ghost.

On a sunny summer afternoon, I visited Lower Whitley Farm to inspect the staircase. Running its entire length is a massive, ornately carved banister more characteristic of a manor house like Cumnor Place, than the rustic farmhouse that is its present location. Apparently, this is the staircase in the southwest corner of Cumnor Place that led from the ground floor up to Amy's personal quarters. The staircase itself is wooden and it is consistent with reports that the one down which Amy fell had a "dog-leg" design. It makes repeated turns of 90 degrees through flights of stairs and intermediate landings. The lowest flight of stairs consists of five steps, leading from the ground floor to the lower landing. At a 90-degree angle from the lower landing, three more steps lead up to the upper landing. Thus, it is "a pair of stairs" consisting of "eight steps."

Given the sharply-angled turns and landings of the staircase, it would have been impossible for Amy to have fallen down more than one set of these steps; and, since she was found at the foot of the staircase, that set of steps had to be the lowest flight, which consists of only five steps — if, as seems likely, this is the staircase down which she fell.

As the following diagrams show, no one could have fallen down the three steps from the upper landing to the lower, bounced to the left all the way across the lower landing and then somehow turned left again at a 90-degree angle to tumble down the final set of five stairs.

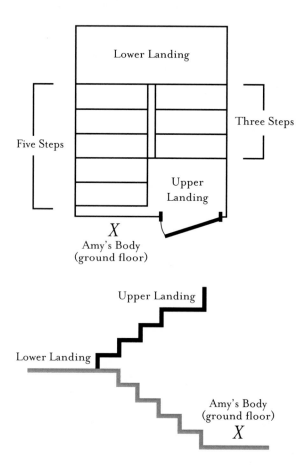

If Amy had fallen from the upper landing, her fall would have been down only three steps and it would have stopped at the lower landing. She could not have rolled across the lower landing, making a 90-degree turn to plunge down the last flight of stairs.

It has sometimes been assumed that Amy fell down a totally different staircase at Cumnor Hall, a circular stone staircase near the northern front of the manor. That staircase descended from a gallery sixty feet long, rather than from Amy's personal quarters. Hitting her head on stone has been given as a possible explanation for Amy's severe head wounds. But a wound two thumbs deep into Amy's brain is not likely to have been caused by striking her head on a step or bannister, even one with a hard, stone surface. And if she tumbled down a stone staircase, we would expect bruises and abrasions, and there were none.

Unfortunately, the Coroner's Report does not provide the surface size of the head wounds or their shape or the part of the head in which they were located. But, to create a head wound two thumbs deep would seem to require the downward stroke of a pike or a powerful stab with a sharp and heavy dagger, probably in the more vulnerable part of the head, such as the base of the skull or the side of the head just above the ear. A blow from a blunt instrument would not have been likely to penetrate two thumbs into the skull. And a fall down some steps, even if stone, would be most unlikely to cause a head wound of that extreme depth.

It was reported that Amy fell down "a pair of stairs" consisting of "eight steps," and described as "dog-leg" in structure, while a contemporary sketch of the circular stone staircase shows that it had twelve or thirteen steps, not eight. These descriptions seem inconsistent with the stone staircase; but they are consistent with the wooden staircase moved from Cumnor Place to Lower Whitley Farm. That one is, indeed, a "dog-leg" staircase; and, although the bottom flight had only five steps, the upper flight had three steps. It could certainly have been described as "a pair of stairs" consisting of "eight steps."

It might be argued that one flight of the stone staircase could have had only "eight steps." But the sketch doesn't appear to show that; and it was the "pair of stairs" that had "eight steps," not one flight of those stairs. In any event, isn't it more likely that, being alone, Amy was descending from her own private quarters, rather than from the unoccupied "long gallery" on the opposite side of Cumnor Place?

Amy's personal quarters at Cumnor Place were on the "first floor" (the second floor in American terminology). If the staircase at Lower Whitley Farm is the one down which Amy fell, the jury's assumption was probably that her own apartment led to the upper landing of the staircase, that, leaving her apartment, she fell down all eight steps of the "pair of stairs" between the upper landing and the ground floor. But, even on that assumption, one would expect the jury to have realized that she could not have fallen down the three step upper flight, rolled across the lower landing, and then tumbled at a 90-degree angle down the five step lower flight, and that, if she fell at all, it would have been down only one of the "pair of stairs."

Of course, it's possible that the jury never really visited Cumnor Place and were simply told that it was "a pair of stairs," consisting of "eight steps."

If, as seems likely, Amy fell down only the bottom five steps, what does that tell us? First, it eliminates suicide. One does not commit suicide by throwing oneself down five steps — or, for that matter, even eight steps.

Second, while it would not be impossible, it is unlikely that Amy broke her neck in an accidental fall. It would require extraordinary bad luck to break one's neck by falling down only five steps. And, if there had been such a fall, even the result of a spontaneous fracture, we would not expect to find a wound penetrating her skull and brain to a depth of two thumbs. We would also expect to find other abrasions, bruises and cuts. We would also expect Amy's skirt to have been in disarray, rather than neatly arranged. And, in light of the severe wound to her head, we would expect her head gear to have fallen away, rather than remaining properly placed on her head.

That devastating head wound, the absence of bruises or abrasions on her body, the conformation of what is probably the staircase and the condition of her clothing all seem to make murder the likely cause of Amy's death — that someone plunged a pike or dagger into her head, then broke her neck with a wrenching twist of her head, placed her at the bottom of the stairs, carefully (and stupidly) rearranging her skirt around her ankles and putting her headdress properly in place on her head.

Amy's head wounds would have bled profusely. Yet, there was no report of blood stains. Was there blood on Amy's clothing? We don't know. Probably what the coroner's jury saw, and the coroner examined, was Amy's unclothed body. So far as we know, her clothing was not inspected for blood or brain tissue.

If Amy's death was murder, the prime suspects would be Dudley, Elizabeth and Cecil. Each of them had the means and the opportunity to bring about Amy's death — acting, of course, through others. Each could have readily found someone prepared to kill her for a relatively modest payment or simply out of loyalty.

But what about motive? Dudley had a strong motive for seeing his wife dead, but not under these suspicious and scandalous circumstances. If, as was reported, Amy was extremely ill with breast cancer, her murder would have been against Dudley's interests. As an innocent widower, he might have had a chance of marrying the queen. As a suspected murderer, that chance was greatly diminished, especially with the queen suspected of complicity in the crime.

Leicester's Commonwealth, a scurrilous publication issued years after Amy's death, accused Dudley of trying to have Amy poisoned even before he arranged her fatal "fall." But *Leicester's Commonwealth* was replete with extreme and unsupported accusations against Dudley, many of which are of doubtful validity.

On the other hand, according to a report from Alvaro de la Quadra, then the Spanish Ambassador, Cecil had confided in him the day before Amy's death that Elizabeth meant to marry Dudley, that "they" were claiming falsely that his wife was ill and intended to kill her and that she was on guard against poison. Presumably by "they," de la Quadra meant Dudley and Elizabeth, although he could have meant Dudley and unnamed accomplices.

Cecil's blackening Dudley's name with such an accusation would not be surprising. Cecil never trusted Dudley, who seemed to be pushing Cecil aside as the queen's closest advisor. And, after Amy's death, Cecil desperately opposed Elizabeth's marrying Dudley. He threatened to resign if she planned such a marriage.

The day before Amy's death, Cecil may also have feared that Dudley would somehow obtain a divorce and seek Spanish support for his marrying Elizabeth, even agreeing to see Catholicism restored in England. Naturally, Cecil would have wanted to prevent that, possibly even lying to de la Quadra to deter Spain from favoring such a match. But if the "they" who Cecil said might kill Amy included Elizabeth, the disloyalty inherent in that statement would seem very much out of character for Cecil. Certainly de la Quadra would pass on that harsh accusation to Philip, giving him a further excuse for seeking to overthrow the "heretic" queen.

It is conceivable that, in his determination to turn de la Quadra against Dudley, Cecil felt that the Spanish would be more likely to believe the accusation if he implicated the queen. But passing on such a story could have done severe harm to Elizabeth and to England — particularly Protestant England; and it seems wholly unlike Cecil to have done that. Another possibility is that the "they" who might kill Amy did not include Elizabeth at all.

It has been assumed that Cecil actually said the things attributed to him by de la Quadra. But de la Quadra's report may have been inaccurate or exaggerated, or even intentionally false. He was often unreliable and inclined to malicious comments. This could be one. De la Quadra's report was made on September 11th, after he had learned of Amy's death. He may have had only a vague recollection of what Cecil said days earlier; and his reconstruction of their conversation may well have been influenced by the news of Amy's death. Or de la Quadra may have simply made the conversation up, telling the Spanish king whatever he wanted to hear — true or not.

In later years, it was rumored that Dudley, by then Lord Leicester, had poisoned the husband of his mistress, Lady Douglas Sheffield. When Lord Sheffield was on his way to London to institute divorce proceedings on the ground of his wife's adultery with Leicester, he suddenly grew ill and died. Poisoning was considered probable; and Leicester seemed the likely suspect. Nothing was proved, but the rumors persisted, as did rumors that Dudley's men had unsuccessfully tried to poison Amy Robsart.

It could be argued that Dudley, an ambitious and sometimes unscrupulous man, would not have hesitated to commit murder to attain his goal — becoming Royal Consort, or even King. And he did not behave as if he believed Amy's death precluded a royal marriage. On the contrary, he went forward to press his case for marrying Elizabeth, even though Amy's death and the resulting scandal made the match unlikely, if not impossible.

On the other hand, Dudley wrote letters just after Amy's death asking that a jury of substantial men "search thoroughly and duly by all manner of examinations, the bottom of the matter" and that their inquiry "have no respect for any living person." We have only copies of these letters; but, if they are not fakes, deliberately contrived to create a false impression of Dudley's innocence, they seem inconsistent with his guilt.

One might reason that, if Elizabeth wanted to marry Dudley badly enough, she might have schemed to cause Amy's murder or that she might at least have tacitly condoned it. But nothing in Elizabeth's conduct supports that inference. Despite her strong and lasting affection for Dudley, and Cecil's possible remark to de la Quadra, Elizabeth probably never intended to marry him. And, if she had wanted to marry him, the circumstances of Amy's mysterious death, and the widespread suspicion and scandal it created, would have been a powerful deterrent to doing so.

This was only the second year of Elizabeth's reign. A weakened England with a depleted treasury, no standing army and not much of a navy, faced the enormous might of France, Spain and the Empire. Mary Stuart had become Queen of France and the French were strongly allied with the Scots. There remained vast support for the Catholic cause in England and, thus, a serious risk that an unstoppable movement could arise to replace Elizabeth with her cousin Mary Stuart, who already claimed to be the rightful Queen of England.

It is a distinct possibility that, if Elizabeth had married Dudley after his wife's "murder," neither the English public nor the nobility, nor the European powers would have permitted her to remain on the throne. Elizabeth was no fool. She would have been fully aware of that danger; and it seems virtually impossible that she would have acquiesced in a plot to murder Amy as a way to marry Dudley.

There were, however, two pieces of evidence that have been taken as suggesting Elizabeth's complicity. First, de la Quadra's report of September 11th also stated that, returning from a hunt, Elizabeth told him "Robert's wife is dead or nearly so." The Ambassador wrote that the queen asked him to say nothing about this. He added that "since this was written the death of Lord Robert's wife has been given out publicly."

De la Quadra does not date his conversation with Elizabeth; and it has often been construed as dispositive evidence of a statement by the queen *even before Amy's fall*, showing her knowledge of a criminal plan to murder Amy. It is not.

Saying that Amy was "dead or nearly so" doesn't make sense. If Amy had actually died, Elizabeth would surely have known. Possibly, saying Amy was "nearly" dead, implying that this was from disease, could have been a clumsy attempt to cover up a murder. But it could also have been an innocent reference to Amy's breast cancer, which was thought to have reached an advanced stage. Possibly, de la Quadra was not sure whether Elizabeth said Amy was dead or that she was nearly dead.

According to de la Quadra, Cecil had said Amy was not even ill; but de la Quadra's report may have been exaggerated or entirely false or the statement may have been part of Cecil's determined attempt to turn the Spanish against Dudley. And, even if Dudley had been spreading a false story about his wife's being seriously ill, it is still possible that Elizabeth believed him and spoke of Amy's condition to de la Quadra.

What de la Quadra reported as the Queen's remark has been construed to mean "Amy has been killed or is about to be." But that would seem the last thing Elizabeth would have said if she knew Dudley was planning the murder of his wife. It would have been particularly moronic to say such a thing to the Spanish Ambassador, who would repeat what she said to his king, and probably to all of Europe.

Moreover, de la Quadra does not report that Elizabeth's statement was made before "the death of Lord Robert's wife," as has frequently been assumed. What he says is that it was made before the news of Amy's death "*has been given out publicly*" — a very different thing. Amy fell on September 8th. It was not until September 11th that Elizabeth announced that Amy had died of a broken neck.

If, in her conversation with de la Quadra, Elizabeth was referring to Amy's broken neck, rather than to her having a terminal illness, their conversation probably occurred *after* Amy's fall on the 8th, but before Elizabeth's announcement on the 11th. De la Quadra's letter was dated September 11th. His previous letter was on September 4th, so his conversation with Elizabeth was probably no earlier than the 4th and no later than the 11th — if it occurred at all.

If the queen had really said that Amy was "dead *or nearly so*," since Amy was found late on the 8th, the queen's remark could conceivably have been on the 9th, if a hurried and inaccurate report had reached the queen from Amy's home in Oxfordshire. But that seems improbable. If Elizabeth simply said that Amy was "dead," the remark could have been on the 9th, 10th or even the 11th.

The assumption that Elizabeth's supposed remark to the Spanish Ambassador was necessarily before Amy's death on the 8th, and that it shows Elizabeth's prior knowledge that Amy was to be killed, makes no sense at all, but it is the kind of misperception that, once expressed, is repeated for centuries as fact.

The second piece of "evidence" supposedly pointing to Elizabeth's guilt — or at least indicating her motive — is even weaker and significantly so. Supposedly, she was heard to say to a torchbearer in a holiday parade that she would make Dudley "the best that ever was of his name." Since Dudley's father had been a Duke, only by making him a king could this become true; and Elizabeth could not make him king if he was still married to someone else.

That the queen would make such an indiscreet, personal statement in the public streets, and to a torchbearer, is patently unbelievable; and, in any event, it is not clear who supposedly heard it or if it was accurately reported or whether this was supposedly said before or after Amy's death. If after her death, it would have been foolish and out of character, but no indication of guilt. If before Amy's death, and if Elizabeth was in on a plot to murder Dudley's wife, it would have been the height of stupidity to say this. And, again, Elizabeth was certainly not stupid. This bit of secondhand hearsay is worthless as evidence of Elizabeth's guilt.

Even today, however, there are those who believe that Dudley was guilty of murdering Amy, even if Elizabeth was not. Would a modern jury find "reasonable doubt" as to Dudley's guilt? Very likely, particularly given his letters urging a thorough inquest and the alternative scenario provided by modern medical theory. Would a jury find "reasonable doubt" as to Elizabeth's complicity? Almost certainly. Even if there was a murder, there is no reliable evidence to implicate the queen. Certainly, de la Quadra's report on what Elizabeth or Cecil supposedly told him would be insufficient for a conviction.

But what about Cecil himself? He had the means, the opportunity and possibly the motive. He mistrusted

Dudley and may have been concerned about the possibility of his successfully obtaining a divorce. After Amy's death, he vehemently opposed Elizabeth's marrying Dudley and was desperate to stop the match. Before Amy's death, was his concern so intense that he would arrange to have her murdered, expecting that Dudley would be blamed and that the resulting scandal would prevent the marriage? His statement to de la Quadra that Dudley (and possibly Elizabeth) might commit such a crime could have been part of such a plan — spread the rumor that "they" are planning to murder Leicester's wife, so that, when she dies, the scandal will extend to Europe as well as England, and a marriage to Leicester would be impossible.

The scandal that would follow Amy's death would probably have served Cecil's interest by frustrating any plans of Dudley and Elizabeth to marry. But, Cecil couldn't be sure of that. Arranging Amy's death could possibly have had the opposite effect. It would have freed Dudley to marry and created the risk that an impetuous and passionate Elizabeth might have married him, regardless of the scandal and the public's reaction. A desperate Cecil may have taken the gamble; but this is sheer speculation. We have no real evidence of Cecil's guilt, and he too would surely be acquitted by a modern jury.

Dudley had a number of dedicated enemies, who, theoretically, could have had Amy killed in an attempt to destroy his reputation and prevent his marrying the queen. But these men were the sort much more likely to kill Dudley, himself, than to kill Amy in an attempt to damage her husband's reputation. They were not that subtle.

There is also the possibility of suicide. Amy's sending her servants away for the day might support that theory. But throwing herself down a short flight of stairs in the hope of dying seems an extremely unlikely way of committing suicide. And, Amy was devoutly religious. Suicide was a mortal sin that would deny her a Christian burial in consecrated ground and condemn her soul to purgatory, if not hell. She would be even less likely to commit that grievous sin if she expected imminent death from disease. Conceivably, she could have taken an overdose of her medication, either accidentally or intentionally, and, trying to walk in an over-medicated state, fell to her death. But that too seems unlikely, given the short flight of stairs, the deep wound to her head and the fact that her clothing appeared to be rearranged.

There is also the possibility that someone heard Elizabeth make an offhand remark to the effect that Amy was an annoying obstacle to her happiness. The knights who slaughtered Thomas Beckett misconstrued a casual remark by Henry II ("Won't someone rid me of this troublesome priest?") as a plea by the king to have Beckett killed. Similarly, Amy's killer may have acted in the moronic belief that he was doing just what the queen wanted.

After centuries of speculation and the disappearance of the evidence, we will probably never solve this mystery. We can, however, conclude that Elizabeth's complicity in murdering Dudley's wife is most unlikely.

* * * * *

It has been speculated that, when the English and Scottish Protestants were having great difficulty besieging Leith Castle, the pro-French Regent, Mary of Guise may have been poisoned with Elizabeth's knowledge and assent. There is no evidence to support this. Sanctioning the assassination of a reigning monarch, or her lawful Regent, would have been inconsistent with Elizabeth's strongly held views. She may, of course, have rationalized killing the militantly pro-French Regent on the ground that her death would contribute to England's security. But all we have is a "maybe," not nearly enough for an indictment, much less a conviction.

It seems clear that, after Mary Stuart's conviction, Elizabeth did seek to have her assassinated in order to avoid the need for a royally sanctioned execution. It has been reported that she asked Sir Amyas Paulet, then Mary's guardian, to kill her and that he refused, responding, "God forbid that I should make so foul a shipwreck of conscience or leave so great a blot to my poor posterity, to shed blood without law or warrant." Since Paulet refused to kill Mary, we would, at most, have had the queen soliciting a murder that was never committed.

And there were certainly extenuating circumstances. Mary had already been convicted of plotting the queen's murder and had been sentenced to death. The choice was between a quiet assassination, which would have been understood and overlooked by European monarchs, or the formal witnessed execution of an anointed ruler, approved and ordered by the English queen, an act they would angrily deplore. A quiet killing would certainly have been in Elizabeth's interest, and seemingly in England's interest as well.

Moreover, another fact is generally overlooked. Paulet had signed the Bond of Association that bound him on his oath to kill anyone who plotted to harm the queen. Certainly, Mary had engaged in such a plot. Ironically, Paulet is considered noble for refusing Elizabeth's request that he kill Mary. But, Paulet was violating his own, freely given oath and was forcing his queen to be blamed for an act that would generate rage and revulsion almost everywhere but England.

Elizabeth was understandably concerned about the potential danger of a hostile European reaction if Mary was executed by royal command. Since Elizabeth had the lawful right to order her beheaded, was it so much worse to ask that she be quietly killed, if that would better serve England's interests?

In any event, as to murder, itself, the evidence does not support the charge that Elizabeth was guilty of murdering anyone.

Chapter Four

Executions and Torture

A JURY WOULD CERTAINLY ACQUIT ELIZABETH of the charge of murder. But how do we judge the executions she ordered or those carried out in her name? Today, opponents of capital punishment would label them "judicial murders"; and, often, they were unnecessarily and hideously brutal. Most, although by no means all, were punishment for acts that were patently treasonous or were otherwise justifiable by the laws and mores of the time.

The executions of the Duke of Norfolk, Mary Stuart and the Earl of Essex certainly belong in that category. Norfolk, then the only English Duke, conspired to rescue Mary Stuart, marry her, overthrow Elizabeth and put Mary (and himself) on the English throne. Although Norfolk's indecision kept him at home, other northern peers, led by the Earls of Northumberland and Westmoreland, acted to restore Catholicism and carry out Norfolk's plan. They took to the field with their numerous retainers, raised others and attempted unsuccessfully to rescue Mary, after which they planned to march on London and overthrow the queen.

Although he took no part in the fighting, Norfolk had clearly conspired to commit treason. He did so again in the Ridolfi Plot that finally led to his execution. Without question, his execution was consistent with the law. Still, Elizabeth repeatedly revoked his death warrant before she reluctantly permitted his beheading. Despite Norfolk's traitorous acts, his death hardly shows her as bloodthirsty or vengeful.

The same can be said for the execution of Mary Stuart. Mary was the focal point of plot after plot to depose and kill Elizabeth, put Mary on the throne and restore Catholicism. She fell into a trap, providing dispositive evidence of her conspiracy to commit treason. She approved a plot calling for Elizabeth's assassination. She was tried by commissioners appointed by the queen and, although she was not allowed an attorney, her guilt was demonstrable. Perhaps she would have been convicted even if the evidence of her guilt had not been so strong. But it was.

And, even though the Council and the people cried out for Mary's prompt execution and her continued existence threatened Elizabeth's crown and life, Elizabeth delayed and agonized at extraordinary length over ordering Mary's death. Burghley wanted Mary's execution to have the color of legal process. He wanted not only a trial and conviction, but also an execution with the formal approval of the monarch.

The last was the point on which Elizabeth disagreed. From her point of view, there were sound reasons for equivocating about Mary's execution. All European rulers deplored the idea of executing an anointed monarch; and there was certain to be a hostile reaction to Mary's beheading from the Kings of France and Spain. Cynically, they preferred a quiet assassination. As we have seen, so did Elizabeth.

The order for Mary's execution leads to one of the unsolved issues of Elizabeth's reign. On February 1, 1587, after a long period of indecision, Elizabeth sent for William Davison, her newly appointed Second Secretary. In Davison's presence, she signed the warrant for Mary's execution and instructed him to have the Lord Chancellor affix the great seal to it, making it official.

Without delay, Davison did as she instructed. The following day, he saw the queen and told her the warrant had been sealed, as she had directed. According to Davison, she asked "Why such haste?", but in no way indicated that the warrant should be held by him, rather than delivered.

Davison gave the signed and sealed warrant to Burghley, who called an emergency meeting of the Council on February 3rd. The ten members present voted unanimously to send the death warrant immediately to Fotheringhay Castle, where Mary was held. That very day, the warrant was given to a trusted courier who rode hard for Fotheringhay. The Council decided to keep their dispatch of the warrant confidential until Mary was executed. The headsman was instructed to travel in disguise, his axe concealed in a trunk. Ostensibly, the secrecy was to protect the queen and the execution process from a desperate act by pro-Mary fanatics. Possibly, the real reason was to keep Elizabeth from knowing the execution was imminent, lest she change her mind.

Five days later, on February 8th, the execution took place. Apparently, the queen learned of Mary's beheading on February 9th, the day after it occurred. She went into a towering rage. Soon, the story was circulated that Elizabeth had ordered Davison to hold the death warrant until she gave him further instructions, and that he had violated her order. It seems clear this story emanated from the queen herself. It certainly didn't come from Davison; and only the two of them knew what had really been said.

Davison was dismissed, tried, imprisoned in the Tower and sentenced to a heavy fine. Angrily, the queen blamed Burghley as well and cut off all contact with him. Then she wrote to Mary's son, James VI of Scotland, describing the execution as a "miserable accident."

After a few weeks, the queen resumed her working relationship with Burghley. But, the truth may lie in the queen's subsequent treatment of Davison. He remained in the Tower for only eighteen months. Elizabeth kept Davison at a distance and even expressed continued anger at what she claimed he had done. But his fine was apparently forgiven and, while he no longer held his post as Second Secretary, he continued to receive the salary and perquisites of that office.

Elizabeth could easily have executed Davison to lend her story credibility. Certainly her father would have done that without giving it a second thought. The fact that Davison was spared and treated rather generously suggests that she never gave him the order she claimed. If she had been telling the truth, and Davison had really disobeyed a direct royal order to hold the warrant, sparing him from a traitor's death would have been an extraordinary and seemingly unbelievable act of clemency and kindness.

Considering all the facts, Elizabeth's conduct in the matter of Mary Stuart was hardly tyrannical. Mary was clearly guilty of acquiescing in Elizabeth's overthrow and death. She was lawfully tried, convicted and sentenced to death. To avoid a violent reaction from European rulers, however, assassination seemed the wisest course. When Sir Amyas Paulet refused to kill Mary, Elizabeth arranged matters so that, to the fullest extent possible, she could deny that she authorized Mary's death. While hardly commendable, this pragmatic solution was probably the soundest course of action – for England as well as Elizabeth.

We need not spend much time questioning the guilt of Essex. For a time, he may have been undecided as to his goals; but it is clear that, in the end, when he stormed through the streets with his armed adherents, he intended to depose Elizabeth or, at the very least, remove her from effective governance and make her his puppet.

That her overthrow was part of his plan was shown by the confessions of Essex's co-conspirators and by their arranging for production of Shakespeare's *Henry IV*, featuring the deposition of Richard II, the reigning king. Their thinking was that the play would show the public that overthrowing a monarch could be justified, leading Elizabeth to cry out later "Know ye not that I am Richard II?"

Essex's own conduct at his trial supported the inference of his guilt. Dressed all in black, he seemed to mock the proceedings, grimacing and tugging at his co-defendant's sleeve when something struck him as bizarre or humorous. Instead of trying to prove his innocence, he attacked the character and motives of his accusers. He accused Robert Cecil, the queen's Principal Secretary, of supporting the claim of the Spanish Infanta to the throne of England. To add authenticity to this serious charge, Essex claimed that Cecil's treasonous conduct had been discovered and reported by a member of the Council.

Unseen, Robert Cecil had been observing the trial from an alcove. In a moment of high drama, he stepped forward and demanded to know which Council member supposedly made this extraordinary accusation. Surprised by the sudden appearance of the man he despised, Essex turned for an answer to his co-defendant, Southampton, obviously the source of the story. Pressed to respond, Southampton named Sir William Knollys. One can imagine the furor and excitement that followed this exchange.

At Cecil's demand, Knollys was immediately found and brought before the court. He was not told what had been said, so that he had no time to consider his answer or to discuss it with anyone. Under questioning, Knollys flatly contradicted the claim of Southampton and Essex. He described their charge against Cecil as "slanders upon the Secretary, whereon he is as clear as any man present."

Similarly, Essex accused his prosecutor, Francis Bacon, of bearing him malice. Bacon, the Earl's longtime friend, replied, denying the accusation,

I loved my Lord Essex as long as he continued a dutiful subject, and I have spent more hours to make him a good subject to Her Majesty than ever I did about my own business.

Essex's smear tactics failed utterly. Undoubtedly, they angered the men who would decide his fate; but they would have reached the same verdict anyway. The evidence of his guilt was overwhelming. Essex was found guilty of high treason and sentenced to death.

After his trial, Essex confessed to the acts of which he was accused and even to having urged the Scottish king to send troops into England to force Elizabeth to do the Earl's bidding.

Essex's treason was manifest and blatant. His betrayal of the queen was deplorable. Certainly the law — and even the morality of the time — called for his execution. Here again, Henry VIII would have killed him the first time he disobeyed a royal order, as when he continued to make unworthy knights, appointed Southampton Commander of the cavalry, failed to attack Tyrone or even when he turned his back on the monarch. If anything, Elizabeth had been far too lenient with Essex in the past — and she knew it. This time, she did not hesitate in signing the death warrant. Of course, unlike the executions of Mary Stuart and the Duke of Norfolk, beheading Essex caused Elizabeth no concern about the reaction of the great European powers. They could only be pleased.

There were other executions in Elizabeth's reign that were not so justifiable, even by the law and mores of the time. A notable example was the execution of Edmund Campion.

Campion was an Oxford graduate who had been a celebrated scholar and orator. His skill had been noted and praised even by Elizabeth and by Leicester, to whom Campion dedicated his *History of Ireland*. William Cecil described Campion as "one of the diamonds of England." But this "diamond" left England; and, after training at Douai and other seminaries, he became a Jesuit, and one of the first Jesuits seeking to rekindle English Catholicism.

Shortly after his return to England, Campion wrote, "my charge is to minster the sacraments, to instruct the simple, to reform sinners, to refute errors and, in brief, to cry alarm spiritual." Lest these words be erroneously construed, he added that he had been forbidden by his Jesuit superiors "to deal in any respect with matters of state or policy of this realm."

Nevertheless, Campion was charged with treason and convicted. There was some indication that his fellow priests had circulated at least one pamphlet asserting that Elizabeth was not the lawful queen. But Campion himself, in an audience with Elizabeth, acknowledged that she was, although insisting that she, like everyone else, was subject to the Pope.

Essentially, the "treason" of which Campion and two other priests were convicted was coming to England to urge Elizabeth's subjects to return to the "True Church." Parliament had passed a statute making it treason to induce a person to withdraw allegiance from Elizabeth by converting that person to Catholicism.

Campion would have admitted inducing such conversions, but he undoubtedly would have denied urging anyone to withdraw allegiance from the queen. As the law was applied, however, it was assumed that any conversion of an Englishman to Catholicism necessarily meant denying full allegiance to the queen by subordinating her will to that of the Pope.

When Campion returned to England from abroad, he knew that torture and execution probably awaited him. But, he stood ready to

> . . .carry the cross . . . while we have a man left to enjoy your Tyburn or to be racked with your torments or consumed with your prisons. The expense is rekoned, the enterprise is begun; it is of God, it cannot be withstood.

Evelyn Waugh in his 1935 biography of Campion said "martyrdom was in the air of Douai. It was spoken of and in secret prayed for, as the supreme privilege of which only divine grace would make them worthy."

On the scaffold, about to die, Campion said

If you esteem my religion treason, then I am guilty; as for other treason, I have never committed any, God is my judge.

Walsingham's agents didn't see it that way, and they could be brutal in enforcing religious laws, as well as in seeking information. Although she had previously respected — even admired — the scholarly Campion, Elizabeth must have given her approval to his execution. After such events as the Northern Rebellion and the papal bull excommunicating her, she may have decided that the threat to her rule and her life posed by militant Catholics required draconian measures. Still, Campion's execution is difficult to justify.

Priests were one thing. The common people were another. Unlike Mary, Elizabeth was extremely reluctant to burn or otherwise execute ordinary citizens for religious offenses. When an aggressively anti-Catholic Parliament decreed the death penalty for citizens who refused twice to take the Oath of Supremacy, Elizabeth simply ordered that no citizen should be asked a second time.

Elizabeth did order the burning of three militant Catholics and two Dutch Anabaptists, a sect that refused to baptize their children and espoused other "heretical" views. But her record with respect to that barbaric practice cannot be compared with her sister's. Mary burned 300 Protestants in a five-year reign, for an average of 60 immolations per year or one every six days. Over her 45-year reign, Elizabeth burned five "heretics" for an average of one every nine years. Even so, that was five too many. And Elizabeth ordered many questionable executions by means other than burning. One hundred twenty-three Catholic priests were executed in her reign. While they were not burned at the stake, most were hung, drawn and quartered, a death more gruesome, although probably less painful.

* * * * *

The execution of priests and the burning of even five heretics was a harsh application of a bad law. Nevertheless, it was the law as interpreted by the queen's judges, and, as so interpreted, it had been violated. The execution of Dr. Rodrigo Lopez was something else. It was probably the execution of an innocent man. Did the queen know he was innocent or at least that he might be? Probably; but it remains another mystery.

Dr. Rodrigo or Ruy Lopez was a Portuguese Jew, who had converted to Christianity. He came to England, where he established a successful medical practice. Having received his medical training in Portugal, he seems to have been a highly skilled practitioner. He was probably more advanced in his methods than his English colleagues, whose ministrations often caused death or disability, rather than preventing it. Lopez's practice was so successful that he became the physician to Leicester and other English notables. He is said to have cured Walsingham of kidney stones. In 1586, he became Elizabeth's own chief doctor. She liked and admired Lopez, calling him her "little ape."

Dr. Lopez's wife, Sarah, was a Portuguese Jewess, who surely was a convert like her husband. She had to be. England's Jews had been expelled by Edward I; and, except for converts to Christianity, they were not admitted into England until the government of Oliver Cromwell in the 17th century. The records of St. Bartholomew's Parish show that Sarah Lopez bore the doctor seven children, three of whom apparently died when very young.

Although thriving in England, Lopez remained highly interested in Portuguese politics. Philip of Spain had made himself King of Portugal by the strength of Spanish arms. But his claim to the Portuguese throne was subject to question. There was a rival candidate, Don Antonio, whose aim was to oust Philip and the Spanish from Portugal. This, of course, was consistent with the aims of Elizabeth and her advisors, who wanted to see Portugal and its powerful maritime fleet independent of Spain. Dr. Lopez and most of London's Portuguese Jewish converts backed Don Antonio, whose mother was a Jewess who, like them, had converted to Catholicism.

When the Spanish army invaded Portugal to place Philip on the Portuguese throne, Don Antonio had raised a resistance force, but was unsuccessful in defending his country against Spanish power. He fled first to France and then to England, where at some point he became involved with Dr. Lopez, who spoke five languages and acted as Don Antonio's interpreter.

Until the defeat of the Armada, Elizabeth had tread carefully concerning Don Antonio, not wanting to inflame Philip. After the English victory, however, she became more aggressive. She provided part of the financing for a fleet under Sir Francis Drake that landed Don Antonio and a small force in Portugal. They had some minor military successes. But the Portuguese did not rise up in support of Don Antonio, as had been expected, and the English force was not strong enough to take heavily fortified Lisbon without the backing of a popular uprising. Characteristically, Essex, who was part of the expedition, challenged any man in Lisbon to come out and fight him in a personal duel. No Portuguese champion came forward. The English had to withdraw; and a disappointed Drake brought Don Antonio back to England.

Given his language skills, Lopez could be useful in various other countries. Even the queen called upon the doctor to foster her relationship with the Ottoman Sultan, whose forces she hoped to unleash against the Spanish, rationalizing that Protestants and Muslims were natural allies against the "idolatry" of Catholicism. The Sultan, however, was occupied elsewhere, battling other European powers and menacing Vienna.

At some point Lopez appears to have become involved in espionage work for Walsingham. Evidently, his mission was to convince the Spanish that he would commit acts in their interest for large sums of money. In carrying out this plan, Lopez established and maintained contact with Spanish agents.

For example, a Spanish agent wrote to Mendoza, the Spanish Ambassador to France, suggesting that, for a price, Dr. Lopez would kill Don Antonio by substituting poison for his regular medicine. It is likely that, if Lopez really said this, it was a ruse, engineered by Walsingham, to let the Spanish believe the doctor was a man whose nefarious services were available to them at a high price. This was at the very time Lopez was vigorously raising money for Don Antonio's cause in London and urging Elizabeth to back his invasion attempt. And Don Antonio was never poisoned, even though Lopez, as his personal physician, had many opportunities to poison him.

But, fate cruelly intervened in Lopez's espionage career and his life. In 1590, when Walsingham died, many of his secrets died with him. One of those secrets may have been that Lopez was following Walsingham's instructions in pretending to the Spanish that, for enough money, he was prepared to carry out their schemes.

During this period, Essex was engaged in a rivalry with Burghley and his son for influence with Elizabeth. One way Essex sought to prove his value to the queen was in establishing his own international espionage network operated by his then ally, Anthony Bacon, and, for a time, Walsingham's former operative, Thomas Phelippes. Much of the information obtained by Bacon's network pertained to Spain and Spanish intentions.

Apparently, Lopez had been supplying information on the Spanish, but doing so through Walsingham. After Walsingham's death, the doctor may have supplied that information to Burghley or his son, or even directly to the queen. Now, Essex sought to replace them all as the source of the queen's international information. If Essex perceived Lopez to be a competitor in this arena, it would surely have annoyed the Earl, who was not a man to suffer annoyance lightly.

Moreover, Essex accused Lopez of spreading malicious rumors about him. We do not know the truth of this accusation, or what the rumors supposedly were. But, the unstable and vainglorious Earl was not a man to be crossed – certainly not by a Portuguese Jew.

Whether for these motives, or to impress the queen, or weaken Burghley or possibly even out of a sincere belief, Essex turned viciously on Lopez and produced "evidence" that he argued showed not only that Lopez was a Spanish agent, but that he was planning to poison the queen.

Lopez had clearly been involved in contacts with suspected Spanish agents, probably at the behest of Walsingham. A message was found indicating that the doctor was to receive a large sum of money for something he was to do; and a courier was arrested with an encrypted letter referring to a large price to be paid to an unidentified person for "pearls."

Essex argued that it was Lopez to whom the money was to be paid and that "pearls" was a code name for murder of the queen. In fact, pearls had sometimes been associated with Elizabeth. They were considered a symbol of virginity, and a well known portrait of her done in 1583 shows her wearing a double strand of pearls with a much larger pearl hanging from a jewel over her heart.

Despite this "evidence," both Burghley and his son believed Lopez to be innocent. His house was thoroughly searched, and nothing incriminating was found. They questioned him, and were convinced by his responses. Burghley wrote to his son that "in Lopez falling I see no poynt of treason intended to the Queen but a redynes to make some gayn to the hurt of [Philip]." After Burghley explained his views to the queen, she rebuked Essex, calling him "a rash and temerarious youth to enter into the matter against the poor man, which he could not prove, but whose innocence she knew well enough." Essex was humiliated and furious.

After sulking for two days in his home, the Earl was determined to produce something that would convince the queen of Lopez's guilt. His own honor and reputation were at stake. He directed that the "interrogation" of the two agents with whom Lopez had dealt be pursued more vigorously. Probably tortured horribly on the rack, the two "confessed" that Lopez was prepared to do what

Philip of Spain directed and that this could have included poisoning the queen. Of course, if Lopez was working for Walsingham, this is what the Spanish agents were supposed to think.

This new "evidence," while hardly compelling, was considered more than sufficient in the 16th century, especially when taken with the letter about "pearls." Charges of treason were brought against Lopez. He was sent to the Tower, tried, convicted and sentenced to death. Elizabeth must have acquiesced in his being tried, but she may still have had doubts as to his guilt. She ordered that Lopez not be removed from the Tower for execution.

Using a ruse, Essex arranged to have the doctor brought out from the Tower. The Earl's men seized Lopez and rushed him to the scaffold. He suffered the horrible fate of untitled traitors. He was hung, but cut down while still alive. Then, as he watched in agony, his genitals were sliced away and he was disemboweled ("drawn"). His body was then cut into four pieces ("quartered"), which were hung on iron spikes in the city as an example and deterrent to its citizens.

The method of execution was one of the critical class distinctions then prevalent in England. Commoners convicted of treason faced this barbarous form of death. Convicted noblemen, like Essex, Norfolk and Northampton, were granted the comparatively humane death of beheading.

It is reported that, before being butchered, Lopez cried out from the scaffold that he loved the queen "even more than he loved Jesus Christ." Coming from a converted Jew, the crowd took this as bitter irony. Perhaps it was.

There is no evidence that the queen reacted angrily to Essex's conduct in removing Lopez from the Tower and having him quickly killed. On the contrary, she gave Essex a substantial sum of money shortly after the execution, leaving her views and actions highly ambiguous.

Why had the queen changed her mind and permitted this brutal execution of a man she knew and respected and as to whose guilt she apparently had serious doubts? We do not know. She was afraid of being assassinated, which was a very real danger; and she may have been convinced by the "confessions" of the two spies that she should take no chances. Perhaps, after agonizing over the matter, she elected to sacrifice Lopez in the interests of her own security. Perhaps, she also decided cynically that saving Lopez was not an issue on which to defy and humiliate the hugely popular Essex.

What were the true facts? We cannot know for sure. Possibly Walsingham hit on the idea of having Lopez offer to poison Elizabeth, so that the Spanish would not hire some real poisoner to do the job. And, of course, Lopez would have simply stalled, negotiated and never carried out the assignment. This plan, like many of Walsingham's espionage capers, would have been unknown to the queen and probably to the Council as well. The problem for Lopez, of course, was that, when Walsingham died, there was no one to prove his innocence.

Did Essex really believe in Lopez's guilt? It's possible. But one version of the events paints a very black picture of Essex's role. Godfrey Goodman, the Bishop of Gloucester, wrote a history in the early years of King James' reign. According to Goodman, it was not Walsingham, *but Essex himself* who asked Lopez to pretend to the Spanish that, in return for a sizeable payment, he would poison the queen. The plan was designed to prevent the Spanish from hiring real assassins who might actually kill her. Goodman wrote that Lopez agreed with Essex to carry out the plan and began to exchange a series of letters with the Spanish.

According to Goodman, Essex became angry at Lopez, first, for giving espionage information directly to the queen, rather than passing it through Essex, and, second, for saying derogatory things about the Earl. These things, Goodman wrote, led Essex deceitfully to accuse Lopez of planning to poison Elizabeth and then to pursue the doctor's execution.

While Essex was certainly capable of such hideous duplicity, it seems more likely that it was Walsingham who created the plan for Lopez to pretend to be a poisoner and that neither Essex nor the queen was aware of the plan, leaving Lopez effectively defenseless on Walsingham's death.

Whichever theory is correct, we can fault Elizabeth for permitting Lopez's conviction and not preventing his cruel death, once Essex had him removed from the Tower — assuming there was sufficient time for her to intervene.

She did, however, show some posthumous kindness. Rather than imposing a forfeiture of Lopez's property, as would have been customary, Elizabeth allowed the doctor's assets to go to his wife Sarah, who must have needed them to support their four remaining children.

This was not the only instance of Elizabeth's generosity toward the wives and families of men whose activities were deemed criminal. When Michael Tempest, a participant in the Northern Rebellion of 1570, fled to France to escape capital punishment, Elizabeth provided an annuity of £20 to his wife and family. And, although the Earl of Arundel died in the Tower, having been imprisoned and attainted for plotting to restore the authority of the Pope, Elizabeth gave his widow a pension of £8 per year.

Elizabeth did suggest to Burghley that the Babington plotters be subjected to a death even more painful than usual. They were hung, but cut down quickly, then butchered in a particularly painful way. But, after the first group of plotters were executed in this brutal way, Elizabeth apparently changed her mind, or her anger cooled. She ordered the remaining plotters executed somewhat more mercifully.

Elizabeth must also have given her consent to hanging hundreds of northern rebels. Evidently, she found it easier to impose capital punishment on faceless multitudes than on an individual she personally knew and easier to execute those who threatened her throne and her life, than those who opposed her religion.

If angry enough, Elizabeth could certainly take bloody action short of execution. An example was John Stubbs, whose right hand was brutally chopped off. Using a heavy mallet, the executioner drove a cleaver through Stubbs' wrist until his hand was severed from his arm. His crime was publishing a tract virulently attacking the Duke of Alençon and his proposed marriage to Elizabeth.

Whether or not Elizabeth really intended to marry Alençon, she wanted the French and Spanish to think so. She was well aware that the Alençon marriage was unpopular with her subjects. Someone like Stubbs fanning the flames of their discontent could generate a firestorm of anti-Alençon opinion, making it difficult — even dangerous — for her to seem about to marry the French Duke.

Elizabeth needed a severe deterrent against such inflammatory rhetoric. Her father would have executed Stubbs without a second thought. Elizabeth considered that idea, but rejected it. To her, striking off his right hand seemed a balanced course, brutal yes, but not by the standards of the time.

Stubbs' own reaction to the punishment — doffing his hat with his left hand and crying out "God save the Queen!" — suggests that, like the average Londoner, he did not find her decision unusually cruel. Probably he realized he had been lucky to escape with his life.

Considering all the evidence, we can conclude that, for the age, Elizabeth was not particularly "bloody" in imposing punishment. Yes, she sanctioned beheadings, hangings, drawings and quarterings — even a handful of burnings. But, for the most part, the executions she ordered or permitted were consistent with the law and mores of the time, rather than the vengeful, arbitrary killings ordered by her father.

And it was a brutal age. Even Henry VIII's numerous executions and the cruel record of "Bloody Mary" pale beside the multitudes killed for their religious beliefs by the French and the Spanish.

But what about torture? The torture of prisoners, suspects and potential enemies had gone on for centuries — long before the Tudors. It continued long after them and still exists in many countries — even developed countries, when they feel sufficiently threatened. Not surprisingly, torture occurred in the reign of the Tudor monarchs, and even in the reign of Elizabeth. At least some torture had her tacit, if not explicit, approval, particularly when her throne and her life were threatened.

The principal torture device used in Elizabethan times was the rack. This was a fearsome device on which the turning of a winch caused the victim's arms and legs to be slowly pulled from their sockets, causing excruciating pain. Often, the victim would say whatever he thought the torturer wanted to hear, just to end the pain. Those who employed the rack either didn't realize that the information they received from its agonized victims was potentially unreliable — or, more typically, they didn't care. Ordinarily, the goal was to obtain a "confession" or incriminating "evidence." Who cared if the confession or evidence was false?

Other forms of torture were also used, such as placing a circlet of knotted cord on the prisoner's head just above the eyes, inserting a stick under the cord and twisting the stick, forcing the knots to bite excruciatingly into the skull. A similar effect could be achieved by compressing the head with an iron band. Another common approach was to tear off the fingernails with pliers or to drive spikes under them.

A less obvious form of torture was to stand the prisoner with his back against a wall with his hands manacled to the wall as high above his head as his arms would reach. After a short time, this became unbearably painful. Unlike the rack, this mode of torture had the advantage of leaving the victim unmarked and apparently undamaged, giving greater credibility to his confession.

Walsingham certainly used torture as a means of obtaining both information and confessions. It seems clear that Essex continued that practice after Walsingham died, as, for example, using the rack to obtain the statements incriminating Dr. Lopez.

Was Elizabeth aware of this practice? Certainly in some cases. Probably not in others. It is conceivable, for example, that she was not aware that the "evidence" the Spanish agents provided against Lopez was obtained by torture.

Lawyers were often designated as commissioners to attend torture sessions. Thomas Norton, a lawyer who frequently attended such sessions, wrote a book in defense of Elizabethan torture. Norton insisted that no one was ever tortured unless a warrant authorizing it was signed by at least six members of the Privy Council and that no one was ever "tormented for matter of religion nor asked what he believed of any point of religion, but only to understand of particular practices for setting up their religion by treason or force against the Queen." Norton may have believed this; but the facts do not support it.

Walsingham had once confided in Burghley "Without torture, I know we shall not prevail." He meant what he said. For example, as Edmund Campion stood on the scaffold, it was noted that he had no fingernails. They had been ripped out by driving spikes under them. He had also been tortured on the rack three times in an attempt to learn the whereabouts of his fellow priests. He was so crippled by that agonizing process that, at his trial, he was unable to raise his right hand to take the oath.

Did Elizabeth know of Campion's torture? We don't know. There were reports that she was present on one occasion when he was questioned, but this may not have been a torture session. Even the reports of her presence may not be true. It has also been reported that she directed that Campion be well treated. That may also be untrue, given the extent of the torture to which he was subjected. Perhaps, she gave such an instruction knowing it would be ignored, but intending her concern for Campion to be reported. If so, she may have deliberately avoided learning what was actually done to him.

A letter from the Queen gives us a glimpse of her attitude to the use of torture in connection with prisoners thought to have aided the revolution planned by the Duke of Norfolk.

Right trusty and well beloved, we greet you well, and finding in traitorous attempts lately discovered that neither Barker nor Bannister, the duke of Norfolk's men, have uttered their knowledge in the under proceeding of their master and of themselves, neither will discover the same without torture; forasmuch as the knowledge hereof concerneth our surety and estate, and that they have untruly already answered, we will and by warrant hereof authorize you to proceed to the further examination of them upon all points that you can think by your discretions meet for knowledge of the truth. And if they shall not seem to you to confess plainly their knowledge, then we warrant you to cause them both, or either of them, to be brought to the rack, and first to move them with fear thereof to deal plainly in their answers. And if that shall not move them, then you shall cause them to be put to the rack, and to fe[el] the taste thereof until they shall deal more plainly, or until you shall think meet. And so we remit the whole proceeding to your further discretion, requiring you to use speed herein, and to require the assistance of our lieutenant of the Tower. Given under our signet the 15th of September 1571.

This letter tells us a few things about the queen's views on torture. Of course, it shows that she sometimes sanctioned its use. But it also shows a reluctance to employ actual torture if the threat of its use would produce the desired results; and, even when used, she apparently wanted it applied first in moderation ("to feel the taste thereof") to see if a lesser degree of pain would yield the information, without the need to apply the full excruciating measures of which the rack was capable.

That reluctance, in itself, was remarkable for the time. Most 16th century monarchs would have given no thought to sparing a suspect even a moment of pain, particularly if the suspect was thought to have acted or plotted against the monarch's throne or life.

Perhaps it was compassion on Elizabeth's part or perhaps she was wise enough to realize that utterances induced by extreme pain were often unreliable. If it was the latter, it tells us something else — that perhaps she wasn't interested in obtaining a confession that was false and made simply to avoid more pain. If so, that would certainly not be an attitude shared by many of her contemporaries or even by many rulers and interrogators of later periods who simply wanted a confession — regardless of its truth.

On the other side of the ledger, we have the fact that Walsingham employed Richard Topcliffe as his chief "interrogator" or, to put it more plainly, "torturer." Topcliffe was a twisted man who took enormous pleasure — probably even sexual pleasure — in inflicting pain on others and in devising new and excruciating ways of causing that pain. He even installed torture devices in his home to continue his work after hours on "special cases."

Topcliffe was a sadist before that term was even invented. He engaged in much the same sort of conduct attributed later to the Marquis de Sade. For example, after using torture to force Anne Bellamy, the daughter of a prominent Catholic family, to betray every member of that family, Topcliffe raped her, impregnated her and then forced her to marry one of his servants.

It would be difficult to believe that Elizabeth was not aware of Topcliffe's reputation. He seems to have been widely known and feared. The best that we might think is that perhaps she was unaware of the full extent of his appalling viciousness or of the psycho-sexual component of his behavior. And, even if she knew, perhaps she considered his fearsome reputation an effective and acceptable deterrent against plots that threatened her life.

We cannot clear Elizabeth of the charge of sanctioning torture. The most we can say for her is that she apparently had some reluctance to use it and may have tried to avoid it, if other methods would suffice. For a 16th century monarch that is not too bad.

CHAPTER FIVE

ESPIONAGE

ELIZABETH IS SOMETIMES CRITICIZED for relying heavily on spies, double agents and dirty tricks of the espionage trade. She did this primarily through Sir Francis Walsingham and his intelligence organization. Had she not done so, she probably would not have survived.

Walsingham, Elizabeth's spy master, was born in 1532, the son of a successful barrister. He graduated from Kings College at Cambridge, a bastion of militant Protestant belief and teaching. Throughout his career, he was inclined to stress the importance of aiding and promoting Protestant causes and vigorously suppressing Catholicism.

After leaving Cambridge, Walsingham traveled extensively in Europe, becoming fluent in both French and Italian. When he returned to England, he began the study of law at Grey's Inn. On Mary's accession, however, he feared arrest or worse for his Protestant views. He returned to Italy, where he was appointed to the faculty of the University of Padua.

When Elizabeth took the throne, Walsingham returned to England. He became a member of Parliament and ultimately developed a relationship with Cecil, who had just become the new queen's Principal Secretary.

Apparently, Walsingham's first foray into the field of spying and security came in 1568, when he wrote Cecil about Robert Stewart, who was hoping to persuade Elizabeth to intervene on behalf of the Huguenots in France. Walsingham did not endorse Stewart's plea, but he pointed out that the man might have valuable information.

Walsingham followed this up with another, even more security-conscious message. He forwarded to Cecil a letter from an Italian contact listing suspicious people who had traveled to England in the preceding three months and warning that the queen should check her food, bedding and furniture to avoid being poisoned. It was believed at the time that one could be killed by contact with poison-infused bedding or furniture. Possibly that belief was accurate.

Later in 1568, Walsingham learned, through the same Italian contact, that the Bishop of Rennes, then the French Ambassador to England, was encouraging a Catholic "uprising" against Elizabeth. On receiving this report, the queen declared the Bishop *persona non grata*, requiring him to leave England at once. He was replaced by a French Ambassador more sympathetic to Elizabeth and to the Protestant cause.

Next, Walsingham told Cecil that "he had arranged with the Lord Major of London to have weekly reports made of all strangers who took lodgings in the city." By this time, Cecil realized that, with Walsingham's keen intellect, extensive contacts on the Continent and knowledge of European languages, he was the ideal person to organize Elizabeth's protection from the many and varied threats she faced. Evidently, these communications were the beginning of the working relationship between Walsingham, Cecil and the queen that functioned successfully for many years.

Walsingham proved vigorous and efficient in ferreting out threats against Elizabeth, repeatedly warning Cecil and the queen about them, as well as urging and actually taking forceful measures to prevent their success. He constantly battled for greater recognition of the dangers that faced the nation and the queen. On December 20, 1568, for example, he wrote Cecil

> *I beseech your honour . . . that I may without offense*
> *conclude that in this division that reigneth among us, there is*
> *less danger in fearing too much than too little, and that there is*
> *nothing more dangerous than security,*

by which he meant complacency.

Walsingham was convinced that the powerful Guise family in France intended to replace Elizabeth with Mary Stuart and would stop at nothing to achieve this. He believed that Philip of Spain shared that intention. At some point, this may have been Philip's state of mind. At other times it was not. Undoubtedly, Philip would have preferred that a Catholic rule England. He certainly had his differences with Elizabeth; and, at times, he may have supported plots in favor of Mary Stuart. Certainly Mary hoped so. Yet Philip was always deeply concerned about French power and the danger of putting pro-French Mary on the English throne.

Still, Elizabeth was a Protestant queen, a "heretic" in the minds of Spain, the Empire, the Pope, French Catholics and even many Englishmen. She faced real and continuing threats from many quarters. It was Walsingham's job to stave off those threats and to protect the queen and the religious settlement she represented.

Walsingham was, of course, wary of Mary Stuart and those who supported her. When the Duke of Norfolk was put forward as a potential husband for Mary, Walsingham published a pamphlet strongly opposing the marriage. His position was ultimately adopted by Elizabeth, who forbad the match.

After Norfolk was arrested and the rebellion of the Catholic northern Earls was quashed, Walsingham set about investigating the overseas backing for Norfolk and the rebellion. He discovered that the focal point was Roberto Ridolfi, a Florentine banker. Ridolfi was an agent of the Vatican, apparently in the pay of both Spain and France. He had become active in England and had even established secret access to an employee in Cecil's household.

Ridolfi was arrested and held for a time in Walsingham's home, during which Walsingham may have turned Ridolfi into his own agent. He left for Rome after an audience with the queen, using a passport she had personally signed. Either Ridolfi had become a double agent or Walsingham simply calculated that they could learn more by leaving him at large and observing what he did and who he met.

In 1570, Walsingham was made Ambassador to France. He had not been anxious for the post, but, while there, he continued and expanded his espionage activities. By this time, he had agents throughout France and even a key informant in the Spanish Court. Through his agents and contacts, he was able to discover the plans of Elizabeth's Catholic opponents throughout Europe. For example, he discovered that the Guise family planned to arm the Irish Catholics and to marry the Duke of Anjou to Mary Stuart.

In the Spring of 1571, Walsingham was following Ridolfi's trail. An arrested Englishman informed him that Ridolfi had "instructions from Mary and a group of her friends in England to arrange with the Duke of Alba, the Pope and the King of Spain for armed intervention on her behalf."

Then Walsingham learned more. He wrote William Cecil (by then Lord Burghley)

I am given secretly to understand that Ridolfi had letters of credit given him by the Spanish Ambassador with the Duke *of Alba; whereupon he had a long conference with the Duke and was dispatched in post to Rome with letters of credit to the Pope, as also with letters of credit to the King of Spain promising to be in Madrid the 20th of the present month. Touching the matter of secrecy committed unto him I can learn nothing as yet, notwithstanding I thought it my part to advertise your Lordship of this much who perhaps by other advertisements can give some guess what the same importeth.*

Ultimately, the information generated by observing the conduct and contacts of Signor Ridolfi helped Walsingham and Burghley to defeat the plot that bore his name.

By this time, Walsingham was convinced that the queen could never be safe as long as Mary Stuart was alive. He wrote "So long as that devilish woman lives, neither her majesty must make account to continue in quiet possession of the crown, nor her faithful subjects assume themselves of their lives." For years, he continued to argue that, for Elizabeth to live, Mary must die. And it wasn't just the danger to Elizabeth and England. He also wrote Burghley "I fear that so long as that woman liveth there will never grow good accord in Scotland."

In 1573, Walsingham returned to England, where he was made a Principal Secretary and a member of the Privy Council. His influence was now extensive, and he had established a security and espionage network throughout Europe and beyond. Walsingham received reports from twelve different places in France, nine in Germany, four in Italy, four in Spain, three in the low countries and one each in Constantinople, Algiers and Tripoli.

One of the most dangerous plots discovered and defeated by Walsingham was the 1576 scheme of Don John and Philip to convey an invading army from the lowlands to England, using the ruse that they were "seeking shelter from storms." Walsingham warned Elizabeth, she raised a strong defensive force and the Spanish troops sailed, but not to England.

From 1580 onwards, Walsingham uncovered several English Catholic plots against Elizabeth, and many recusants (those who did not conform to the law requiring attendance at Protestant services) were arrested. Some were executed where there was evidence of their plotting against the queen. And priests were executed for attempting to convert Englishmen to Catholicism, which was deemed an attempt to end their allegiance to the queen. But aside from those actively involved in "treason," as defined by existing English law, Elizabeth tended generally to be lenient in matters of religion, at least compared to her sister Mary or Henry VIII. Walsingham vehemently disagreed with that leniency.

In 1583, Walsingham's French informants uncovered the Throckmorton Plot, another scheme organized by the Guise family and English Catholics to overthrow Elizabeth and put Mary Stuart on the throne. The two English leaders of the plot were Francis Throckmorton and Lord Henry

Howard. Mendoza, the Spanish Ambassador, was also deeply involved. Walsingham learned that they planned for England to be attacked by four hostile armies, one led by the Guise family, the second comprised of pro-French Scottish troops, the third a Spanish army and the fourth a contingent led by the Catholic Duke of Bavaria.

Moving swiftly, Walsingham closed down the scheme. Throckmorton, Howard and other conspirators were arrested and executed. Walsingham had long mistrusted Mendoza, having written to Burghley back in 1574

What Mendoza bringeth is not unknown, but men of judgment think the chief end of his coming is to entertain us with Spanish compliments to lull us asleep for a time, until their secret practices be grown to their due and full ripeness.

Now Walsingham had the pleasure of personally telling Mendoza he had 15 days to leave England and would never again be welcome. The four hostile armies never materialized.

The plots against Elizabeth usually revolved around the Guise family or the Pope or were in the name of Philip of Spain. Over the years, Walsingham was able to foil every plot that did not stop or fail on its own — a remarkable record.

By 1585, Walsingham had uncovered so many plots focused on making Mary Stuart queen that Elizabeth was persuaded to put her under stricter confinement. Yet, still another such plot was discovered. This time, Elizabeth was to be poisoned by Dr. William Parry, a reputable physician. Dr. Parry too was caught and executed.

Finally, as we have seen, by leading Mary and her conspirators to exchange letters in beer kegs sent to and from Mary's place of confinement, Walsingham was able to prove her personal involvement in a deadly plot. This time, she was clearly involved in encouraging a plan to assassinate Elizabeth to put herself on the throne.

After Mary was tried and sentenced to death, Walsingham vigorously urged her prompt execution. He argued that Mary was the principal danger to Elizabeth's crown and life.

> *The number of Papists, Atheists and malcontents will marvelously increase in respect of the hope they will conceive that the said Scottish Queen shall come to the crown . . . Now, touching the perils that are to ensue either by the K. of Scots or by the K. of Spain by a particular consideration of them, it will appear they are nothing equal to the peril that is likely to grow from her.*

Still, Elizabeth avoided taking the essential action. Finally, on February 1, 1587, Walsingham uncovered still another plot to assassinate Elizabeth using a massive amount of gunpowder. At last, Elizabeth signed the death warrant, and, whether or not she really ordered it, Mary was finally executed. Undoubtedly, Walsingham breathed a sigh of relief.

Walsingham tended to shape his reports to coincide with his own strongly held views on the Guise family, the Spanish and Catholics in general. But, Elizabeth was highly intelligent and keenly aware of the geopolitical situation. She was able to use the information supplied by Walsingham to great advantage, while making her own judgments about what should or should not be done.

Walsingham's organization performed another critical function in obtaining intelligence about the Armada. He learned as early as 1586 that the Spanish fleet was not ready and that a significant element of that fleet was not fit for the choppy seas of the Channel, being designed for the far calmer waters of the Mediterranean.

Walsingham devised a plan to cut off the vast amount of money Philip needed to support the Armada. While Spain was a wealthy country, Philip's expenses were huge and he was dependent upon bankers and financiers in Genoa and Florence to supply loans. Working through contacts in the London financial community, Walsingham was able to prevent or delay much of the funding on which Philip was counting.

Desperate, Philip turned to the Vatican. The Pope was willing to fund an attack on England's heretical queen; but, from Philip's point of view, the conditions left much to be desired. The Pope would lend him one million gold ducats. But one-half was to be paid only if and when the Spanish troops actually invaded England, and the other half was to be paid in installments every two months after the invasion, on condition the Spanish were still there.

In effect, Philip got nothing until his army effected a massed landing on English soil and, even then, half of the loan depended on the army's successfully holding that position for months. This was not much help to Philip, who needed the funds to meet the enormous costs of preparing the Armada before any invasion could occur.

Finally, however, Philip's ability to finance the Armada was saved by something beyond Walsingham's control, the arrival of Spanish treasure ships from the West Indies bearing more than enough gold ducats to do the job.

Although his attempt to cut off Philip's funding did not succeed, Walsingham gave the English enormously helpful information. In 1588, through a spy in Rome, he was able to obtain a copy of the actual Spanish invasion plan, which Philip had sent to the Pope. Walsingham pushed all of his sources ever harder for more and more information. He looked not only to his regular operatives, but also to traveling merchants and even the French Ambassador to Spain. His spies continued combing the Spanish coast for information.

This quest for intelligence paid off. Walsingham and the English commanders knew the size, force and tonnage of the Spanish ships that would comprise the Armada. They knew the personnel who would command and man those ships and their planned strategy to close with the English ships, grapple, board and capture them in hand-to-hand fighting. This allowed the English to avoid closing with the massive, high-sided Spanish galleons, and to rely on their skillful gunnery, superior seamanship and better designed ships to defeat the Spanish fleet.

Elizabeth became the iconic symbol of the Armada's defeat, and the English navy was given much of the credit. But the critical intelligence work that played such an essential role in producing the victory was done by Walsingham and his espionage organization.

Perhaps one can look upon the work of such spies, double agents and informers with a jaundiced eye. But, without the information supplied by the tireless and unceasing efforts of Walsingham, it is probable that Elizabeth would have been overthrown and killed.

Walsingham died in 1590, having lived to see Spain greatly weakened, England in a strong position internationally and Elizabeth protected and very much alive. Perhaps the most fitting tribute to Walsingham's enormous contribution to the safety of England and of Elizabeth is that, when Philip of Spain received a written report of Walsingham's death, he wrote in the margin "good news."

After Walsingham's death, Elizabeth relied on intelligence supplied by Burghley and by Anthony Bacon's network of overseas contacts. Much of Bacon's information was filtered through Bacon's friend Essex, who used it in an attempt to make the queen dependent on him and who undoubtedly tried to put his own political "spin" on the information he supplied.

Burghley took over the services of Thomas Phelippes and other former agents of Walsingham. Essex persuaded Phelippes to work for his new intelligence network; but the combination was not successful, and Phelippes returned to Burghley's service, continuing on as a major player in the intelligence organization of Robert Cecil.

Throughout her reign, Elizabeth was protected by active and generally efficient intelligence operatives. Yes, she was aided by nasty tricks of the espionage trade, particularly as employed by Walsingham and aides like Phelippes. Had this not been so, it's not likely she would have survived.

Chapter Six

Piracy And Worse

IN 1493, POPE ALEXANDER, the "Borgia Pope", acted as arbitrator of a vast territorial dispute between Spain and Portugal. He drew a longitudinal line and awarded everything east of that line to Portugal and everything west of it to Spain. Portugal got what is now Brazil, but the entire balance of what is now Latin America went to Spain. After all, the Pope, whose name was really "Borja," was Spanish.

The Spanish colonies proved to be immensely profitable sources of gold, silver, spices and other valuable items. Those colonies and the ships carrying their riches back to Spain became a tempting target for English "privateers" typically authorized by Elizabeth and sometimes even financially backed by her.

To the Spanish, Elizabeth was not only guilty of heresy that eroded the strength of the True Church, she was guilty of piracy that eroded Philip's pocketbook. The truth of the charge may depend upon one's definition of "piracy." When a virtual state of war exists between two nations, with the more powerful nation planning to invade the weaker, if the weaker nation stops and boards ships of its powerful enemy, removing their treasure in an attempt to cut off the means of its own destruction, is that "piracy"?

If so, Elizabeth was an aider and abettor of piracy. And, of course, the English "privateers" carried out such raids even when no Spanish invasion of England was planned, and at times when it would have been a gross exaggeration to say that a state of war — or even a "virtual state of war" — existed between the two nations.

Elizabeth had long encouraged such "commercial" ventures by English captains. These ventures played a part in developing the skills in fighting at sea that served the English so well in later years.

Elizabeth's first act of "piracy," from the Spanish point of view, was not really "piracy" at all. In 1568, three Spanish ships traveling to the Netherlands with cargoes of gold were forced by the threat of real pirates to put in at an English port. Elizabeth took the gold and refused to return it to the Spanish, basing her claim on "the law of the sea." As it turned out, the Spanish didn't even own the gold. It belonged to Genovese bankers who intended to transfer title to the Spanish when the ships reached Antwerp. The Duke of Alba planned to exchange the gold for cash to pay his troops. Evidently, Elizabeth decided to frustrate that plan. She kept the gold and apparently assumed the obligation to pay the Genovese bankers. If so, the bankers were presumably content. Philip, of course, was not.

Later, however, Elizabeth went beyond seizing ships driven to English ports by storms or turning a blind eye to raids on Spanish shipping by "privateers." She actively promoted and personally invested in such ventures. For example, along with Leicester, Walsingham and Hatton, Elizabeth was an investor in Francis Drake's voyage that circumnavigated the globe. It has been reported that Elizabeth ordered Drake not to tell Burghley of his proposed venture. This seems most unlikely, given the illustrious group of investors and the obvious preparation for the voyage. In any event, Drake did not merely go on a round-the-world voyage of exploration. When he returned to England three years later, the holds and decks of his ship were crammed with tons of gold, silver and jewels, the spoils of bold raids on Spanish treasure ships and Spanish ports in the New World.

Even after deducting Drake's own share, the gigantic treasure trove netted the shareholders a massive return of 4700 percent on their investment. Not only did this enrich Elizabeth and the other investors, it deprived Spain of much-needed revenue. And, the risk of future raids made loans from European bankers more expensive and difficult for Philip to obtain. That, in turn, impeded Spanish progress in mounting an invasion of England and in pressing Philip's Netherlands campaign.

The Spanish demanded that Elizabeth return the treasure seized by Drake. Naturally, Elizabeth refused. She calculated that, under the circumstances, Philip would suffer these losses, and possibly even negotiate a real peace, rather than start an expensive war.

The name of Drake's ship was appropriately changed from *The Pelican* to *The Golden Hind*. When Elizabeth went aboard for Drake's investiture as a knight, she joked that she had found a golden sword to decapitate him "for turning pirate."

And this was not the only English raid on Spanish ships and colonies. Drake, his cousin, Hawkins, and others carried out other daring raids. Sometimes, they used deception, rather than attack. On landing in the Spanish colony that is now Venezuela, Hawkins assured the local authorities that he was a personal friend of the Spanish king. Then he helped himself to the king's treasure.

Even when the privateers returned to England without having captured a treasure ship, it was generally because Philip had ordered the shipments stopped to avoid the losses. But this too delayed the Spanish king in refitting his navy, left him unable to pay his troops in the Netherlands and even caused failures among his bankers, making it even more difficult for him to obtain loans. All to the good, thought Elizabeth.

Investing in privateering became commercially fashionable in London. The ventures were risky, but often hugely profitable. Even careful and conservative Robert Cecil invested. Certainly the queen did, and not only in the voyages of Hawkins and Drake. In 1592, for example, Elizabeth and other investors had financed Raleigh when he captured the giant Portuguese galleon *Madre de Dios*, loaded to the gunnels with jewelry, ivory and spices.

Elizabeth also adopted a policy of stopping, searching and stripping the vessels of any nation trading with Spain. Her primary objective in carrying out this policy was to deprive Philip of the means to attack England or at least to delay such an attack and, hopefully, to bring Philip to the negotiating table. More than anything, Elizabeth wanted peace. Peace could save lives and money and possibly even her throne.

Thus, peace was always Elizabeth's basic policy. Ironically, her form of "piracy" furthered that policy, in that it lessened Philip's ability to wage war. Of course, it was also a way to enrich herself and thus promote the economic stability of the nation. Her subjects clearly preferred privateering to higher taxes. Whatever Elizabeth's motives, the outraged Spanish considered her conduct criminal and vigorously condemned it.

Finally, Philip hit on the idea of accompanying his treasure ships with fighting galleons. With the inception of these formidable convoys, English privateering became less profitable, and, for a time, tended to taper off.

However, after Philip's death in 1598, the English were less fearful of Spanish retaliation; and, despite the convoys, they were not so careful to restrict their raiding to "privateers." In 1602, for example, Sir Richard Leveson, leading a royal squadron flying the English flag, captured a massive, richly laden Portuguese carrack, even though it was protected by shore batteries and Portuguese warships.

In summary, Elizabeth was more than complicit in acts that, by any reasonable definition, would be considered "piracy." For the most part, this was a calculated risk taken in aid of state policy — not only to help meet England's need for revenue, but, at least during Philip's reign, to deprive Spain of the financial resources necessary to mount an invasion of England and possibly to lead Philip to the negotiating table, rather than to war.

But Elizabeth could justly be accused of something worse than piracy. This was the slave trade. Hawkins was not only a bold privateer, he was a part-time slave trader, apparently with the acquiescence and even aid of the queen. Of course, Elizabeth sought to avoid the stigma of imposing involuntary servitude on others. She reportedly told Hawkins that "she hoped the Africans would not be carried off without their consent, which would be detestable." Did she really believe the Africans volunteered for their new positions? It's not likely.

On the other hand, slavery had existed for many centuries and was generally accepted, even among educated, Christian folk. Yes, it was horrible and disgraceful. But, perhaps we should not be too quick to impose 19th century enlightenment ideas on a 16th century monarch. And, it does appear that, at some point, Elizabeth stopped condoning the slavery voyages; and they seemed to stop, replaced by the more lucrative attacks on Spanish treasure ships.

Chapter Seven

Miserliness

ELIZABETH HAS SOMETIMES been described as an obsessive penny pincher who cared more about saving money than promoting English interests. This is an unfair characterization. There were instances in which she is reported to have engaged in what could at least be called callous behavior on financial matters, as when she appears to have ignored the plight of unpaid soldiers and sailors after the fighting ended. And she has been accused of fiscal vindictiveness in refusing, on Leicester's death, to forgive his massive debts, leaving them to be faced by his widow, her old "rival" Lettice Knollys. Did the queen have the authority to cancel private debts? It seems doubtful. What about the rights of the creditors? Of course, Elizabeth could have paid the debts herself, but not doing that seems far less blameworthy.

To assess the charge of miserliness we need to examine the fiscal situation the queen faced and how she dealt with it. Unquestionably, Elizabeth was extremely careful and often difficult about expenditures. I have no doubt that, early on, she read and absorbed Machiavelli's *The Prince*. There, he advises that a successful ruler

> *ought not to fear the reputation of being mean* (Machiavelli meant "frugal") *seeing that, with his economy, his revenues are enough, that he can defend himself against all attacks and is able to engage in enterprises without burdening his people . . . for there is nothing wastes so rapidly as liberality* (Machiavelli meant "free spending"), *for even when you exercise it, you lose the power to do so and so become either poor or despised . . . Therefore it is wiser to have a reputation for meanness, which brings reproach without hatred, than to be compelled through seeking a reputation for liberality to incur a name for rapacity, which begets reproach with hatred.*

Elizabeth probably took these words to heart. Her spendthrift successors, James I and Charles I would have done well to have followed them. In any event, Elizabeth had significant other reasons for her inclination to be extremely careful about money.

The queen's resources were large, but not unlimited. At times, they were dangerously short of what was required to meet the nation's needs. Certainly there were occasions when she stubbornly refused to follow the recommendations of her Council, because she considered the cost too great. Usually, she was right. One key aspect of her reign, not so widely written about, was her thorough understanding of England's financial situation and her prudent management of the nation's finances.

In the 16th century, the ordinary needs of the nation were the private responsibility of the monarch, rather than of Parliament or the people. The queen's ordinary funds came primarily from the revenues of crown lands, customs duties, collected fines and ecclesiastical payments that had previously gone to Rome. Out of these ordinary revenues, Elizabeth had to meet all of her personal needs, maintain a lavish court and bear the cost of the entire English government. Taxation was not the customary means of meeting those "ordinary" expenditures.

For extraordinary expenses, such as a threatened war or other military or naval ventures, Elizabeth could call on Parliament for a subsidy funded by the imposition of a tax. But, until later in her realm, Elizabeth was generally reluctant to go to Parliament for money, lest it begin making demands in return. And she was always reluctant to see taxes imposed on her subjects, recognizing how unpopular such levies were.

And Elizabeth was canny enough to let Parliament play its historic role, so that, when taxes were necessary, they appeared to be imposed by Parliament, rather than the queen. Decades later, Charles I, less attuned to political realities, tried to govern and levy taxes without Parliament. He lost his crown and his head.

Given the many demands upon her treasury, Elizabeth's revenues were sometimes substantially less than the nation's interests required. Her ordinary revenues, during most of her reign, averaged £200,000 per year (about $150 million in terms of today's dollar). Over the first thirty years of her reign she received an average annual subsidy from Parliament of only £50,000. Out of that £250,000 of available funds, she had to meet all the costs of government, maintaining her court, defending the realm and paying the cost of any foreign military ventures. When taxes and ordinary revenues were insufficient, she was required to sell assets or borrow to meet the shortfall, and those loans had to be repaid.

The fiscal situation was often precarious. To begin with, Elizabeth inherited a debt of £200,000 from the reign of her sister Mary; and the costs of military campaigns early in Elizabeth's reign totaled £450,000. But Elizabeth expended the time and effort to understand financial issues and handled them with prudence and sound judgment. When she took the throne, she soon realized that, in the reign of her father, brother and sister, English coins had been debased to the point that foreign merchants would not accept them in trade, insisting on payment in gold. In 1560, by a bold and ingenious measure, Elizabeth and Cecil ordered all English coins to be turned in and exchanged for new coins that would reflect their true value, a value everyone would accept.

When the demand for new coins exceeded the available metal at the mint, Elizabeth turned to the London goldsmiths, who melted down old coins to make sufficient new ones. A massive amount of coinage was exchanged, and a serious monetary problem was solved. It was an extraordinary fiscal achievement.

In addition to demonstrating a sophisticated knowledge of economic issues, Elizabeth cut her expenses wherever she could and tried to save money by avoiding expensive foreign wars advocated by her Council. Her reputation for fiscal prudence was such that she could actually borrow money from European bankers at lower interest rates than Philip of Spain. Philip had greater sources of revenue, but was considered a less reliable borrower.

By 1584, Elizabeth had managed to pay off the deficit inherited from her sister, to meet the nation's extensive needs and to put aside savings of £300,000. However, between the massive cost of fighting the Armada and supporting the Dutch insurgents, her savings were reduced to only £55,000.

In 1589, she faced still greater demands. Henri III of France was assassinated, and the heir to the throne was Henri of Navarre, a Protestant and near victim of the St. Bartholomew's Day massacre. France's Catholic League opposed this Protestant heir taking the throne as Henri IV, and there was danger of the League's turning to Spain for aid in the civil war that was about to start. When Henri sent an emissary to London pleading poverty and seeking financial assistance, Elizabeth responded with a substantial grant. It was vital to England's interests that Henri be supported against the Catholic League and any Spanish encroachment. Reluctantly, Elizabeth allowed English troops to come to Henri's aid. Funding both Henri IV and the English expeditionary force ultimately cost Elizabeth nearly £400,000 — a massive sum, considering the nation's other needs.

Substantial sums were needed periodically to put down Irish rebellions and to support the Dutch rebels. The queen also paid a regular "pension" to the Scottish King James VI and even sent him extra payments to help him battle Catholic insurgents. And, of course, there were other pressing needs like refitting the navy and paying numerous office holders. And, in this age of pomp and display, it was essential that Elizabeth's court appeared splendid in every respect, lest she be viewed as a second class monarch.

In addition, Elizabeth felt the need to make generous grants and loans to valuable peers and officials. Hatton, for example, died owing the queen £56,000. Leicester borrowed £21,000, and Burghley's son-in-law, the Earl of Oxford, received a large annual grant from the queen, enabling him to maintain a lifestyle appropriate to his position and family. But, his grandfather had led the Tudor army that put Elizabeth's grandfather on the throne, and, having been praised for his poems and plays, Oxford *might* have written or co-written the works attributed to William Shakespeare. If he did, Elizabeth probably knew it.

By 1590, the queen's savings had been entirely used, requiring her to sell off crown lands, which, in turn, reduced her annual income. It also required her to demand forced loans from wealthy peers and to engage in the distasteful practice of seeking double and even triple or quadruple subsidies from Parliament, which meant raising the taxes on her subjects.

Elizabeth's share of the loot from Spanish treasure ships helped temporarily. So did the increased Parliamentary subsidies. By 1601, however, the Irish situation was turning dangerous again, with a menacing Spanish landing. The government was in desperate need of funds. Elizabeth was forced to sell off more crown lands and even personal jewelry in an attempt to stop the monetary hemorrhage.

By the end of her reign, in order to meet her fiscal responsibilities, Elizabeth had been forced to divest herself of virtually all of the property her father had gained from the Church by the English Reformation, plus a substantial part of her jewelry.

The reality was that the basic responsibility for governing and defending the nation had fallen on the queen herself; and, as a matter of long-term economic policy, her tight-fistedness had not only made sense — it had been vital to the nation's welfare. It was certainly not a means of preserving her personal wealth.

Elizabeth was fiscally careful, because she was bright enough to realize that she had to be if England was to be defended, properly governed and well served. In sum, the charge of miserliness is unfair or at least grossly exaggerated.

Chapter Eight

Capriciousness

PERHAPS THE CHARGE most frequently leveled at Elizabeth is that, faced with numerous decisions, she procrastinated and then changed and re-changed her mind, driving her advisors to distraction.

For example, although Walsingham was intensely loyal to Elizabeth, her delays, changes of mind, repeated "consultations," and the inaction they caused, sometimes created such extreme frustration that Walsingham could not refrain from speaking out. In an extraordinary letter he sent her in January 1575 he wrote

> *For the love of God, madam, let not the cure of your diseased state hang any longer on deliberation. Diseased states are no more cured by consultation, when nothing resolved on is put into execution, than unsound and diseased bodies by only conference with physicians, without receiving the remedies by them prescribed.*

Very few Englishmen could speak with such candor to the queen. But, by this time, she knew Walsingham's worth and understood his frustration.

Elizabeth did frequently delay, "consult" and change her mind. But, rather than mere caprice, this tendency to postpone and alter her decisions may, at least in large part, have been a deliberate tactic. Elizabeth had unwavering confidence in her own intelligence and judgment. She wanted the important decisions to be hers, to fit with her own view of the world and her own policies on how to deal with the myriad problems that arose during her reign. She was unwilling to delegate such decisions to men who were often affected by self-serving pride and hubris.

This was one of the reasons for Elizabeth's reluctance to be drawn into military adventures. Sending a force into battle inevitably meant ceding control to commanders, who could be arrogant, vainglorious and self-serving. It meant a loss of her own ability to direct the actions of her armies in the field or of her ships at sea, even when the national interest — even the national existence — depended on the decisions being made.

Elizabeth also realized that making fixed and firm decisions on any important issue meant turning the matter over to men to carry out those decisions, and that they would necessarily exercise discretion in doing so. Once this occurred, Elizabeth's ability to control events was necessarily lessened, if not eliminated.

One way to keep such men off balance and continually focused on the queen was to establish a reputation for changing her mind. If a royal decision was subject to being changed at any time, the men who were to carry it out would be far more inclined to stay closely in touch with her, heeding her thoughts and moods, lest the decision they were charged with carrying out be suddenly reversed.

Moreover, the likelihood of changes of the royal mind tended to slow down the process of taking action and to avoid sudden, impulsive and aggressive moves. Elizabeth almost always preferred a policy of inaction where that was possible. She often found that, with the passage of time, seemingly insoluble problems were somehow solved, and crises disappeared that had previously seemed to require quick, vigorous and expensive action. By acquiring a reputation for changing her mind and being unpredictable, her general policy was served, and impetuous, costly and irreversible moves could be avoided.

Often, Elizabeth's delays and changes of mind were based on changing circumstances. Sometimes Elizabeth would spend to aid the Dutch rebels and sometimes she would not. Sometimes she would help the French and sometimes attack them. Sometimes she would seek amicable relations with Philip and sometimes engage in conduct that she knew would enrage him. But this was the result of a constantly changing political situation and a deliberate attempt to keep potential enemies guessing as to what she would do and how she would do it. At least, for the most part, it was not the frivolous inconstancy with which she has often been charged.

For example, Elizabeth feared the Spanish acquisition of a deep water port on the Channel coast from which the Spanish fleet could more readily embark an invasion force. Whenever the Spanish threatened to take such a port, Elizabeth would be more inclined to fight in the lowlands or to help the Dutch rebels or the French to fight there. Otherwise, unless attacked, she would be reluctant about aggressively aiding either the Dutch or the French and preferred a policy of seeking peace with Spain. And, despite the English preference for the Dutch rebels, when it appeared that, by defeating the Spanish, the lowlands would become a dependency of France, she would lessen or withdraw her support.

Other powerful and successful rulers exhibited inconsistency in their policies. Philip of Spain wanted England to become Catholic, and the Spanish sometimes joined in plots to free Mary Stuart and put her on the English throne. But, much of the time, that was not at all what Philip wanted. His rivalry with France was often more important to him than the contest between the old religion and the new. Mary Stuart, who had been raised in France, whose mother and the Regent was Mary of Guise and who had been married to the deceased French king, was closely connected to French interests and staunchly pro-French. Sometimes, Philip was ready to overlook this danger. But, generally, he was reluctant to undertake actions that would put Mary on the English throne for fear of a powerful Franco-English alliance.

While Philip was sometimes aggressive in supporting and protecting Spanish interests, he suffered the piratical attacks of Drake and Hawkins on Spanish treasure ships without starting a war. Like Elizabeth, he was reluctant to undertake a costly and dangerous conflict with England, until, later in life, when religious issues may have taken on greater importance to him. By then, Mary Stuart had been executed, so that her pro-French views were no longer a concern, and the threat of an Anglo-French alliance seemed diminished. Only then did the Armada sail.

A prime example of royal inconsistency is, of course, Henri IV of France. A committed Protestant and leader of the Huguenots, he fought many battles against French Catholic forces. When he saw that it was the only way to unite the French, take Paris and reign effectively as their king, he switched and became Catholic. As he cynically put it, "Paris is well worth a mass."

So, perhaps we judge Elizabeth too harshly when we accuse her of inconsistency. She had many factors to balance, and they varied dramatically from time to time. Sometimes the danger came from the Spanish, sometimes the French. Always the urging of her Council to take robust military action had to be balanced against the enormous financial drain of a war and the possibility that she could find some way to solve the problem short of a military solution.

Sometimes, potential allies like the rebels in the Netherlands, or Henry IV in France had to be supported, other times not. Often, delay itself resulted in the problem disappearing, the danger dissipating, the men and money saved; and what better way to achieve delay than by a changing of the royal mind.

One area in which Elizabeth sometimes dreaded making a firm decision was ordering an execution. Her procrastination in signing and giving effect to death warrants for the Duke of Norfolk and Mary Stuart are examples. Fictional accounts portraying her as similarly reluctant to order the beheading of Essex are almost surely untrue. But she certainly appeared to be against the execution of Dr. Lopez and perhaps even had doubts about executing Edmund Campion.

To understand and appreciate the complexity of the decisions Elizabeth faced, the stakes involved in those decisions and the awesome responsibility that went with making those decisions, I'll dissect just one hypothetical issue as she might have done. Assume that she was called upon by her Council to send troops to aid the Dutch rebels, because the Spanish appeared to be gaining the upper hand in the Netherlands. She had to bring her intelligence and experience to bear in approaching the complex and critical decisions she faced. Probably, her thought process would have been like this:

If I intervene, how will Philip react? Will this bring on an expensive and dangerous war with Spain? Can I win such a war against Spanish power — with the kingdom, my religion — even my life at stake? And, if I can win it, can I do that without facing bankruptcy?

If I do not intervene, will the rebels turn in desperation to the French? If so, will French commercial domination in the Netherlands severely damage the English economy?

If I do not intervene in the lowlands and the Spanish prevail, will they acquire a deep water port on the Channel, enhancing their ability to mount a successful invasion of England at a time of their choosing?

If I do intervene, how much will it cost? Can I afford to bear that cost, meet my obligations to the bankers and still maintain a proper court and effective government? Parliament will probably grant me the funds, but will they ask something in return? What might it be? And parliamentary subsidies come from taxing the people. The harvest has been poor, prices are high. Will they bear the added levies without unrest . . . or worse?

Will the campaign expand and be prolonged, so that I find myself in a war without the ability to pay my soldiers? Can I send troops to the lowlands for only a limited period and with limited objectives? Is that worse than not sending them at all?

And if I do not send them, will that be taken as a sign of impotence or cowardice by Spain? By France? By the Pope? By the people? Will that make my potential enemies more aggressive? More willing to attack?

If I do intervene, who will command our forces? Once they are in the field, free from my constraints, the commanders will do whatever they please, even if it's contrary to my explicit orders.

And, if I appoint one man to command, others will react with jealousy, anger and continued bitterness, creating harm in ways I cannot foresee.

What if I simply delay my decision, then make it and quickly change it, only to delay it again? Might not many of these problems be avoided simply by not making a final, unchangeable decision?

Let's think it out. If I postpone the decision, or, having made it, quickly reverse it, I won't have to rely on a commander. I won't incur any cost in lives or treasure. I can pay the bankers promptly and maintain the government. I can avoid an immediate war with Spain, while continuing to pose a realistic threat. To them, I'm a woman with a woman's tendency to change her mind from day to day — even from hour to hour. They can't be sure I'll stay out of the fight. I could change my mind tomorrow. And, if the Spanish seem likely to seize a deep water channel port, or the French seem ready to dominate the lowlands, I can still intervene — although perhaps with less effect. But, considering all the factors, isn't the wisest course to procrastinate and keep my options open? While I may seem capricious to my advisors, undoubtedly annoying — even infuriating them, I will remain unpredictable to my enemies and a force with which they must reckon.

Perhaps this kind of reasoning explains why the queen so often delayed key decisions and changed her mind after making them. Perhaps she realized that, in many cases, the need for a decision simply disappeared.

* * * * *

We have already discussed the issue of marriage and Elizabeth's seeming indecisiveness and changes of mind with regard to suitor after suitor. This also seems more likely the result of calculated policy and the changing international situation, rather than the inability to make up her mind.

There is, however, one instance of Elizabeth's change of mind on such a matter that has often been cited as an example of her extreme capriciousness. After years of on-again, off-again marriage negotiations, Elizabeth, in the presence of others, kissed the French Duke of Alençon on the lips, exchanged rings with him and announced that they would be wed. Based on earlier custom, the Duke thought they were wed. At least that's what he wrote his brother. Yet, the very next day, Elizabeth told him she would always love him, but, sadly, could not marry him.

Was that really capriciousness or was Elizabeth simply trying to create that impression? If, after all those years and all those negotiations, she had announced to Alençon that she had simply decided not to marry him, the inference would have been drawn in France and elsewhere that she had played the Duke for a fool and had never really intended the marriage. That inference would have generated greater humiliation and anger on the part of Alençon, as well as dangerous hostility on the part of the French, who would consider themselves insulted and deceived.

On the other hand, that unfortunate and dangerous inference might be avoided if Elizabeth appeared to be simply a woman torn by feminine emotions, perhaps even a bit unstable, a woman who adored Alençon and longed to marry him, but suddenly got "cold feet," grew fearful and wary, and, as she so often did, changed her mind.

Did she deliberately stage that charade? We will never know, but it seems a likely explanation for her behavior. If so, it apparently had the desired effect. William Camden reported that, after Elizabeth's dramatic "change of mind,"

> the Duke returning himself after he left her in his chamber, pluketh off the ring, casteth it upon the ground, taketh it up again, rayleth on the lightness of women and the inconsistancie of islanders.

Wasn't his railing on "the lightness of women" better than his concluding (and France agreeing) that he had been deliberately deceived, strung along for years with false promises designed to keep all of Europe off balance?

Certainly, there were some contradictory aspects to Elizabeth, herself. She was hugely bright and highly educated. She loved poetry and music, and reading the classics was one of her greatest pleasures. She showed sympathy for the plight of other humans and seemed fond of horses and other animals. Yet she sometimes sanctioned torture and brutal executions. And, she adored hunting, showing no sympathy for the terrified foxes who were usually torn apart by the dogs. She even relished bear baiting, a "sport" in which a chained bear was attacked by a pack of ferocious dogs, the bear swatting at the dogs with his deadly claws, the dogs tearing at the bear's legs and leaping up to rip out his throat, until, finally, the bear or the dogs lay dead, drenched in blood.

But, given the standards and mores of the 16th century, were these really inconsistencies? Elizabeth would not have said so.

Elizabeth, tall, slim and regal, could be extremely feminine and decorous. Yet, sometimes, she could be most indecorous, publicly flirting with and teasing her favorites, fondling Robin Dudley in public and even tickling him during the formal ceremony in which he was created Earl of Leicester. There was her humorous remark to the kneeling Lord Oxford that, after all his years away from England, she had quite forgotten his embarrassing fart. She gave her friends nicknames, like "Eyes," "Lids" and "Pigmy." She regularly swore like a sailor — or, more accurately, like her father. Her favorite oaths were "By God's wounds!" or "By God's sacred limbs!" or salty references to other parts of the Lord's sacred body. On one occasion, Elizabeth's language to the Spanish Ambassador about the Duke of Guise was so utterly "foul" that the Ambassador was unable to report her words to his king.

Her temper was legendary. It could flare up in an instant. Although she was generally fond of her ladies in waiting and protective of them, from time to time, she would rage at them, sometimes even striking one for some foolish act or omission. We know from her godson, John Harrington, that

> She walks much in her privy chamber, and stamps her feet at ill news, and thrusts her rusty sword at times into the arras in great rage.

And, of course, we know of the famous scene in which she boxed the Earl of Essex's ears when he turned his back on her.

Were her sudden rages a lack of personal control or were they a device used to intimidate and control others? Probably, it was a little of each.

In summary, we see in Elizabeth a complex, secretive woman full of seeming contradictions and mood swings. Yet, evaluating the evidence as a whole, much more of her conduct appears planned and staged policy, rather than the result of emotional weakness, uncertainty or neurosis. And, one thing is clear: on those occasions when she felt that firm and resolute action was called for, she could be as decisive and unwavering as her father.

Perhaps it would be fair to say that such occasions were rare. But, there is this: given all the instances in which Elizabeth delayed making a decision or changed her mind, it would be difficult to point to even one such instance that, in the long run, brought about a significantly adverse result for England.

CHAPTER NINE

DUPLICITY

THE ANSWER HERE IS EASY. Elizabeth was duplicitous. She had to be. Facing constant threats of invasion, insurrection, disloyalty, deposition and even death, it would have been foolish, in most situations, to be open about her true feelings, plans and intentions. And Elizabeth was rarely foolish. Her position was analogous to that of a military commander. An essential skill in warfare is the ability to mislead an opponent, feinting left and attacking right, feigning weakness and retreat only to launch a crushing counterattack. We do not criticize military leaders for being "duplicitous." Yet Elizabeth needed that same skill, and it served her well.

Today, democratic governments are supposed to be transparent. Our leaders are supposed to operate openly and honestly, reporting to the people with total candor. Whether they really conform to that standard is another question. But Elizabeth ruled in a different age under very different circumstances. Not so long before her reign, Machiavelli had written that the successful ruler should create the impression of goodness and faithfulness, but must, in reality, emulate the fox, for he

who has known best how to use the fox has come to a better end. But it is necessary to know how to disguise this nature well and to be a great hypocrite and liar.

Elizabeth's responsibilities were very different from those of an American president or contemporary English prime minister. Her obligation was to rule, not to carry out the wishes of the people, the Parliament or even her own Council. Hers was the responsibility to protect the nation and, of course, to protect herself. Deception and duplicity were essential to her success.

There are many instances of Elizabeth's duplicity. I could not begin to cover them all. Certainly, she lied to Mary when she assured her dying sister that, as queen, she would remain a good Catholic, just as she had falsely pretended to be a practicing Catholic during Mary's reign. Had she not done so, she would probably not have become queen or even survived.

It would be hard to avoid the conclusion that Elizabeth was duplicitous on the issue of potential marriages. Her on again, off again matches with Archduke Charles and the Duke of Alençon are prime examples. Did she ever really intend to go through with those marriages? Probably not. But rekindling the possibility from time to time met her political goals, both domestic and foreign.

In the summer of 1570, she tried to avoid conflict with France by promising to pursue negotiations to restore Mary Stuart to the Scottish throne. At the same time, she was assuring the supporters of Scotland's King James that the negotiations would never succeed.

And, was she disingenuous when she blamed her secretary, Davison, for bringing about Mary Stuart's execution and called it a "miserable accident" in her letter to Mary's son? Probably. But, here again, there were sound reasons for creating that impression, considering the horror and outrage at Mary's beheading that arose in Europe and Scotland.

Obviously, Elizabeth practiced duplicity in dealing with Spain and France, just as they practiced it in dealing with her. In the dangerous world in which she lived, she could hardly do otherwise. To grasp the level of duplicity practiced between rival monarchs, one need only review Philip's detailed instructions to the Duke of Parma on how to deceive the English by pretending to negotiate while the Armada was being prepared to attack them.

Parma was to begin by demanding that the English apologize for Drake's raid on Cádiz. Then, Philip instructed his nephew:

> *When you have got this, you are to act as if you were completely deceived by it, and pretend to believe anything they tell you: you will then renew the negotiations, name commissioners, and propose a meeting on neutral territory. As for powers . . .*

say that you have had full powers for many months, but cannot exhibit them until conditions worthy of my acceptance have been offered. Say this only for the sake of appearance. It is the best way to take them in, so that the peace commissioners may meet. But to you only, I declare that my intention is that these negotiations shall never lead to any result, whatever conditions the English may offer. On the contrary, the only object is to deceive them, and to cool them in their preparations for defence, by making them believe such preparations will not be necessary. You are well aware that the reverse of this is the truth, and that on our part there is to be no slackness but the greatest diligence in our efforts for the invasion of England, for which we have already made abundant provision in men, ships and money.

Although we enter thus into negotiations, without any intention of concluding them, you can always get out of them with great honour by taking umbrage about some point of religion, or the other outrageous proposals they are likely to make . . . Thus you will proceed, now yielding on one point, and now insisting on another, but directing all to the same object — to gain time while preparations for the invasion are completed.

It would be difficult to find many clearer examples of duplicity than this. Yet, history doesn't label Philip as a particularly duplicitous monarch.

At least Elizabeth was somewhat more subtle in playing the game of international duplicity. But was she disingenuous in dealing with her own people? Sometimes. We have seen how she led them to believe that she was preparing to marry one suitor after another, probably intending no such thing. But maybe the best example of Elizabeth's deceiving the public was the episode in 1599, with Essex nearing the end of his failed Irish campaign, when word was spread that the Spanish were about to launch another massive armada to invade England, depose the queen and restore the nation to Catholicism. The Spanish were supposedly coming with tens of thousands of seasoned troops on hundreds of mighty galleons. The great English naval heroes were dead or aged. Who could stop the ferocious Spanish?

Immediately, the order went out to muster Englishmen into a newly-formed citizens' army to resist the threatened invasion. The nation responded with enthusiasm. Men from all over England, particularly from London, were given arms and a hurried training.

Of course, the new armada never came. It never existed. But how could English intelligence have been so faulty? There were the usual spies in Spain. The hundreds of ships and thousands of men were either there in the harbor of Cádiz or Ferrol or they were not. Were the English spies blind or drunk? Not likely.

The probable explanation is that Elizabeth and Cecil deliberately spread the frightening rumors of a new armada, well aware that they were false. Why would they do that? The answer lies in one word . . . Essex.

Essex had failed in his mission to destroy Tyrone, and he faced a hostile, angry Elizabeth. But he still had a strong following of hot-blooded officers and was still immensely popular with the public. He had also made countless knights, contrary to Elizabeth's explicit orders — even more than in his prior campaigns. These newly knighted men also tended to be staunch supporters of the mercurial Earl.

There were rumors and probably intelligence reports from Ireland that Essex was planning to bring his army back to London to force the queen to treat him with respect and to rid herself of her advisors and even that Tyrone would join with Essex's army in a march on England, possibly to put Essex on the throne, in exchange for a free hand in Ireland.

How could Elizabeth prevent this? Trying to muster an army to fight the highly popular Essex would have been difficult and divisive. Inducing Englishmen to flock to that cause in great numbers might have been impossible. Meanwhile, the nation would have been torn apart with dissension.

How then to quickly put England at arms, ready to protect London and the queen? The best way would be if a citizen army became necessary to defend England against a new and terrifying Spanish Armada — to spread rumors that such an invading force was coming, so that Englishmen would proudly and gladly rush to arms.

Seeing that newly assembled force protecting the capital and the queen might just be sufficient to deter

Essex from playing the high stakes game of launching his own "invasion" — high stakes, because, if he failed, his head would be on the block.

This plan would have made sense for Elizabeth and Cecil, and there is other evidence supporting it. If there had really been a massive armada out there, wouldn't Elizabeth's first act have been to recall the sizeable English army still in Ireland? The Irish problem could be dealt with later. With a new armada sailing up the Channel, the queen would want those thousands of trained troops available for home defense.

But Elizabeth did the opposite. She gave Essex firm written orders that he was not to return to England with his army until he had fought and defeated Tyrone.

That order cannot be squared with the threat of an oncoming Spanish invasion. But, if the talk of an invasion was a sham, designed to create the impression that England, and especially London, was armed and prepared to fight, and the point was to *keep* Essex in Ireland, the written order for him to stay there makes perfect sense.

Was this Elizabeth's plan all the time? Probably. Was it duplicity? Absolutely. Did it work? Yes. Essex violated her order by returning to England in an attempt to persuade her he was not at fault. But he came with only a handful of friends, without his army and without the support of Tyrone.

Would he have behaved differently had he not thought England was armed and prepared for battle? We'll never know.

Yes, Elizabeth was duplicitous. She had to be — and she was good at it.

Chapter Ten

"Favorites"

ELIZABETH HAS BEEN ACCUSED of having "favorites." Many monarchs did. To some, notably Edward II and James I, the term "favorite" meant a homosexual lover — Piers Gaveston in the case of Edward II and a variety of young men in the case of James I (despite his having a wife and fathering six children). But, the female lover of a male ruler was typically called a "mistress," rather than a "favorite."

Elizabeth did have "favorites," men she found attractive and whose careers she advanced. But, with the possible exception of Essex, it would be unfair and inaccurate to say that they didn't do their jobs well and didn't deserve the honors and rewards she bestowed on them. In general, she appointed competent men to positions in which they served competently.

Burghley gave her splendid service for decades, as did his son Robert in later years. Walsingham's work as her spymaster and security chief was superb and probably saved her life on a number of occasions. He received some properties from the queen, but was still hounded by creditors up to the time of his death. None of these men could properly be characterized as a "favorite."

On the other hand, Leicester was a favorite in the classic sense. He certainly had his self-serving moments, as when he supported the marriage of Mary Stuart to the Duke of Norfolk or when he tried to enlist the Spanish in his own attempt to marry Elizabeth or when, contrary to the queen's orders, he accepted the position of Governor General of the Netherlands. But, favorite or not, he rendered valuable service for years on the Council and probably worked himself to death in vigorous preparations to defend England against the Armada.

Edward de Vere, the Earl of Oxford, could possibly be called a "favorite" as well. He received substantial rewards from the queen. She found him attractive, but, as we have seen, she owed her crown to his ancestor's defeat of Richard III at the Battle of Bosworth Field. And, if, as some contend, he was the real author of the Shakespeare Canon, it's likely that Elizabeth knew it and rewarded him for that reason as well.

Oxford had lived in Burghley's house as a youth. He married Burghley's daughter, Anne Cecil. But the marriage was not a happy one. Oxford suspected that Anne was bearing another man's child. He refused to see her and remained apart from her for years, much of that time in Europe. Ultimately they reconciled and had two more children. Within a year of the birth of the second child,

Anne died. It has been argued that she was the model for Ophelia in *Hamlet*, that her brother was the model for Laertes and that the loquacious Lord Chamberlain, Polonius, was based on Burghley himself. Even if true, it would not necessarily follow that Oxford wrote the play.

Christopher Hatton was a handsome young man in love with Elizabeth for years. Plainly, she found him attractive, and he too was a "favorite." But he served the queen well in a number of offices, including Captain of the Queen's Bodyguard; member of the Privy Council and, ultimately, even Lord Chancellor. Although considered a comparative lightweight by some, Hatton was supremely loyal and was generally deserving of the advancements and rewards he attained.

Raleigh could also be described as a favorite. Tall and handsome, the queen appeared to find him attractive both physically and mentally. After she learned of Leicester's marriage to Lettice Knollys, she had Raleigh constantly by her side. She granted him the monopoly on importing sweet wine as well as prestigious living quarters on the Strand overlooking the Thames. But he gave her brave and effective service, as, for example, in the successful raid on Cádiz. There are those who believe that the queen was in love with Raleigh and that they were lovers. But that may overstate her feelings and misconceive their relationship. It's possible, but unlikely.

Certainly, the men on whom Elizabeth relied to protect England and advance its causes at sea — men like

Drake, Howard and Hawkins — were more than competent and, for the most part, hugely successful.

We know the most about Drake, whose bold and lucrative "privateering" and vast explorations (including even San Francisco Bay) have brought him lasting fame. But Howard led a raid on Cádiz; and, as Lord Admiral, he commanded the English fleet against the Armada. Hawkins also "privateered" with success and revolutionized ship construction and naval warfare. He was another of the commanders who led the fleet against the Armada. While they had the queen's admiration and gratitude, none of these seafaring heroes could fairly be called a "favorite."

With the exception of Essex's Irish campaign, Elizabeth avoided fielding large armies, as her father had. Her military actions tended to be limited in scope, a remarkable feat in a ruler whose kingdom was surrounded by hostile and dangerous adversaries. In those limited campaigns, Mountjoy, Sussex and Hunsdon proved themselves competent and successful commanders. Mountjoy and Sussex were not "favorites." Possibly Hunsdon could be considered one; but then he was the queen's "Cousin" (or, more likely, her half-brother).

But what of Essex? He was certainly a classic "favorite" almost from the time he was introduced to court as a handsome teenager. Very clearly, Elizabeth found the young Earl attractive and delighted in his company. And he did receive very significant rewards and honors. It would be difficult to say, as we did about the others, that Essex earned and deserved them.

Essex was certainly bold and physically courageous, and, while his actions in "fighting" for Henri IV, or in the Azores fiasco or in his failed Irish campaign were hardly praiseworthy, he did fight well in the Netherlands and in the raid on Cádiz. Still, he was basically unstable and unreliable and had a vicious, paranoid streak that made him hard to admire. To Elizabeth's credit, when she finally grasped what Essex really was and what a danger he posed, she took swift and vigorous action. Having been a favorite did not save him from the queen's justice.

Taking her reign as a whole, I think we can clear Elizabeth of the charge of "favoritism" in the pejorative sense of the word. A few men could be called "favorites"; but, for the most part, she needed good, loyal men and had the intelligence and judgment to pick them.

CHAPTER ELEVEN

RELIGION

LOOKING BACK OVER ELIZABETH'S RECORD on religious matters we can draw two fundamental conclusions. First, she presided over a gradual shift in the religion of the capital and, ultimately, of the nation. For the most part, it was a balanced and nuanced shift that has been called her *via media*, her middle road. Second, following that prudent and gradual approach, rather than a radical and traumatic reversal of Mary's policies, she may have saved England from the devastating holy wars that ravaged France, parts of Germany, the lowlands, and, to a more limited extent, Scotland.

Perhaps Elizabeth's views on the severe religious conflicts that marked the 16th century can best be summed up in her remark to the French Ambassador, de Maisse, that there was only one Jesus Christ and only one faith and "all the rest was a dispute about trifles." Still, as Elizabeth well knew, those "trifles" had caused widespread torture and death in many places and had created threat after threat to her crown and her life.

Elizabeth was raised and educated as a Protestant, as was her brother, Edward VI. She believed in the direct study of the Bible; and her prayers illustrate that she believed in a direct relationship with God, not one based on the intercession of the Virgin Mary, the Saints, the Pope or even a priest. These were fundamental Protestant principles. While she disliked the idea of married priests, prized her crucifix and admired the clerical vestments worn in the Catholic mass, she deplored much of that ceremony, particularly the raising of the host to signify the "Real Presence" of Christ.

We know that, during Mary's reign, Elizabeth feigned Catholicism. But she would have been imprisoned, if not executed, had she not. Simply denying the "Real Presence" would likely have resulted in a death sentence, as it did for many Protestants. Apparently, as Mary neared death, Elizabeth promised her to remain in the old faith. Almost certainly, that was not a pledge she meant to keep.

Once she became queen, however, Elizabeth did not rush to reject Catholicism. Much of the nation, particularly outside of London, remained Catholic. Elizabeth was too prudent to begin her reign by offending a significant part of the nation or by risking a religious war with Spain or France for which she was not prepared.

Nevertheless, she gradually saw Protestantism re-established as the official religion, free of the Pope's dictate and with herself as "Supreme Governor" of the Church of England and "Defender of the Faith." This, in itself, was a compromise. Henry VIII made himself "Supreme Head" of the Church. But Elizabeth's Council persuaded her that "Supreme Head" was too radical a title for a female. They convinced her to be known as the Church's "Supreme Governor."

The Catholic bishops who had served in Mary's reign were called upon to take an Oath of Supremacy, acknowledging Elizabeth as Supreme Governor of the Church of England. When they refused, Elizabeth removed them from office and typically sentenced them to "house arrest" or to comfortable confinement in the home of a compliant prelate or considerate nobleman. Unlike her sister, she did not execute them.

Elizabeth was fortunate in that, on Mary's death, five bishoprics were vacant, another bishop died at the same time as Mary and four more bishops died in the next year. This enabled Elizabeth to appoint ten Protestant bishops without having to remove their Catholic predecessors.

John Knox, a Scotsman and a staunch Protestant, would ordinarily have been one of the ten new bishops. But, shortly before Elizabeth's accession, Knox had the bad luck (or bad judgment) to publish a tract entitled *The First Blast of the Trumpet Against the Monstrous Regiment of Women*. For example he wrote, "I am assured that God hath revealed to some in this our age that it is more than a monster in nature that a woman should reign and bear empire above men." Knox was attacking Elizabeth's sister, Mary, as well as Mary Stuart and her mother, Mary of Guise.

But Elizabeth, who certainly didn't consider her reign "a monster in nature," saw Knox's book as an attack on the entire concept of female rule. He was not appointed.

As we have seen, Elizabeth dismissed a number of Catholic Council members, but appointed others. Over the years, Catholic peers served on her Council, as did men with a Puritan outlook.

Elizabeth was generally tolerant on religious matters — at least tolerant for that age. Until later in her reign, Catholics could practice their faith in private, so long as they appeared publicly to conform to the established Church. As she put it, she had no desire to construct a "window into men's souls."

Elizabeth hoped that, with her gradual and permissive approach, English Catholicism would slowly wither away, that Catholics would grow comfortable with the Protestant services they were required to attend; and, finding it difficult to locate a Catholic mass and dangerous to participate in it, they would ultimately give up the old religion.

To narrow the chasm between Catholics and Protestants and to retain as much of the comforting drama and pageantry of the old faith as she could, Elizabeth favored the form of Protestantism closest to Catholic practice. The English *Book of Common Prayer* and the English Bible were used, and services were conducted in English, rather than Latin. Images and relics were eliminated, as were rosary beads. And, of course, there was no place for the Pope or the doctrine of transubstantiation. But there continued to be bishops and, while clergymen could now marry, they continued to wear clerical vestments reminiscent of priestly garb. And the queen retained her crucifix and continued to burn candles on her alter.

Later in Elizabeth's reign, there was strong pressure from the Puritans to rid the church of every vestige of Catholic practice — to eliminate stained glass, the wearing of capes and surplices, kneeling at communion and, of course, to do without bishops. In many towns, stained glass church windows were smashed and replaced by clear glass. The Puritans pushed not only to eliminate bishops as administrators of the Church, but even to replace the monarch as its "Head" or "Governor." Basically, the Puritans wanted a church structured on Presbyterian lines, governed by officers and ministers elected by the public and acting through regional and national synods. As a learned prelate put it, authority over the English church "was justly taken from the Pope" and "given to the Prince." Now the Puritans want to "take it from the Prince and give it unto themselves."

Some of Elizabeth's Councilors had strong Puritan leanings. At first, Elizabeth was tolerant of their views, but, as time went on, her concerns about the Puritans grew. At bottom, those concerns were more political than religious. She saw in the militant Puritan movement the potential for a system that could seriously threaten the power and position of the monarch. Expressing her concern to the French Ambassador, she told him that ultimately the Puritans would recognize "neither God nor king." She also feared that, in the long run, adopting the radical Puritan agenda would lead to an unwise and unhealthy attempt to regulate the lives and thoughts of her subjects.

While the Pope and the forces of the Catholic powers remained a far more dangerous threat, the queen could not ignore the growth of the Puritan movement and the growing strength of the more radical wing of that movement. Comparing the menace of the Catholic powers with the threat posed by the Puritans, she said

From mine enemy (i.e., the Pope and the Catholic rulers) *let me defend myself; from a pretensed friend* (her Puritan Councilors), *good Lord deliver me.*

The Puritans may have been troublesome; but the Catholic problem was far more serious, even lethal. Many Englishmen remained Catholic, at least privately and some not so privately. This was particularly true in the north, where powerful peers, such as the Earls of Northumberland and Westmoreland, remained Catholic in their sympathies. In 1570, encouraged by the Duke of Norfolk, the two Earls led the unsuccessful Northern Rebellion to replace Elizabeth with Mary Stuart. Had they succeeded, Elizabeth would almost surely have been put to death.

Still, for most of her reign, Elizabeth was generally tolerant of Catholics who privately practiced their faith. The penal laws were not rigorously enforced. The law provided for a fine of £20 per month for not attending Protestant services; but, like other penal laws affecting religion, it was generally ignored. Records show that for a two year period from 1581 to 1583, out of the multitude of Catholics who stayed home on Sunday, only 200 paid the fine.

Catholics who didn't draw attention to themselves or rant about politics or religion had little serious trouble and could successfully pursue their lives and careers. Edmund Plowden, for example, was a well-known and successful Catholic lawyer. He published reports of legal decisions that were widely used and are cited even today. He became Treasurer of the Middle Temple and, despite his Catholicism, was generally honored and respected. On his death, William Camden wrote:

> In England died this year no man more worthy to be remembered than Edmund Plowden, who as he was singularly well learned in the common laws of England whereof he deserved well by his writings, so for Integrity of Life, he was second to no man of his profession.

As we have seen, Elizabeth's tolerant attitude toward Catholics, who were discreet about their faith, hardened somewhat in and after 1570. There were several reasons. One was the Northern Rebellion. Another was the papal bull *Regnans in Excelsis* issued in February 1570 excommunicating Elizabeth, that "servant of wickedness," declaring her no longer queen and authorizing or even directing Catholics to kill her. She correctly realized that her danger had increased significantly, and that there was reason to fear the extremists among her own Catholic subjects.

Still, Elizabeth rejected the proposal put forth by some members of her Council that all Catholics be required to take a loyalty oath or face criminal penalties. She vetoed a bill passed by Parliament that would have imposed a heavy fine on anyone not taking Protestant communion. And, even though Parliament passed legislation making it treasonous to bring the papal bull into England or to describe the queen as a "heretic," she prevented passage of a rider that would have eliminated Mary Stuart from the succession by threatening to reject the entire bill.

In 1572, news of the St. Bartholomew's Day Massacre was received with horror and anger in England and by Elizabeth herself. From 1574 on, over 100 militant Catholic priests trained in the English seminaries at Douai or Rome were smuggled into England. These men were highly trained, educated and motivated. Most were ready to die for their faith. They were typically sheltered by Catholic families. Often they were hidden in "priest holes" in the homes of those families where they could be concealed in the event of a search or even the arrival of Protestant visitors.

Some of these priests forcefully reminded English Catholics of the papal bull and argued that they were not only free, but directed by the Pope to overthrow Elizabeth and even to kill her.

The Jesuits among the missionary priests, such as Edmund Campion, took a somewhat different and more effective line. Most were instructed to avoid violating English laws by carrying papal bulls or similar documents and to focus on religion, rather than political issues. The papal bull issued by Pius V, freeing and possibly obligating Englishmen to overthrow and kill Elizabeth, had never been popular with most English Catholics. Most Jesuits sought to excuse them from that radical obligation, merely reminding them that, if someone did rid England of its heretical queen, they must do everything in their power to restore the true religion. Some Jesuits may have asked for more — that, if Elizabeth's overthrow appeared likely, Catholics must assist in bringing it about.

Meanwhile, in Spain, the officials of the Inquisition were arresting English sailors captured at sea or otherwise in Spanish control, whenever they appeared to be Protestants. Some were burned at the stake. Most were "mercifully" sentenced to long years as galley slaves in the Spanish navy. When Elizabeth complained, Philip's attitude was "It's not me. It's the Inquisition." Finally, Elizabeth was able to lessen the danger to her sailors by threatening to impose the same punishments on Spanish subjects who happened to be in England.

By this time, Elizabeth had become much more strict in dealing with Catholic priests and those who harbored them. Priests and their Catholic hosts were faced with "the Bloody Question," i.e., if the Pope sent an army to overthrow Elizabeth would you support the Pope or the Queen? If the answer was "the Pope," the speaker was confessing treason.

Ultimately, even the highly respected Campion was executed, along with two fellow Jesuits. His death had to be with Elizabeth's concurrence, if not her order. As we have seen, Campion had been brutally tortured, although that may have been without the queen's knowledge.

And Parliament wanted more serious punishments for various crimes related to religious speech. Formerly, the penalty for repeating a slander of the queen, such as an attack on her being "Supreme Governor" of the Church, was a month in prison and loss of an ear, with the option of paying a fine and keeping the ear. Now, Parliament eliminated the option; and, if the crime was inventing, rather than just repeating the slander, it was both ears. The Puritans opposed this change, since they favored a church run by committee, not a "Supreme Governor," and they tended to be less guarded in their speech than the Catholics. As historian J. E. Neale put it, the Puritans "had visions of an earless elite of Godly men languishing for years in prison."

By the end of 1585, Gregory XIII, a militantly anti-Elizabeth Pope, had died. His successor was Sixtus V, who was far less hostile and who disapproved of assassination.

The death of Mary Stuart also relieved some of the threat to Elizabeth, since the Scottish Queen had long been the focal point of Catholic plots. With her execution and the likelihood that her Protestant son, James, would be the heir to the English throne, there was less incentive on the part of Catholics to assassinate Elizabeth. Still, the menacing power of Catholic Spain remained real for many years. With the threat of pro-French Mary Stuart taking the throne eliminated, the likelihood of a Spanish attack to remove England's heretical queen significantly increased.

As the years passed, English Catholicism was gradually becoming associated primarily with the older aristocracy. The new nobility and gentry tended to be Protestant. The great universities had long tended to separate on this issue. Cambridge had bred a cadre of active Protestant scholars, such as the men who had educated Edward, Elizabeth and Jane Grey. Oxford, on the other hand, seemed to favor the old Church. Like Edmund Campion, many of the priests trained at the English Seminary at Douai were Oxford graduates.

Elizabeth's concern with the apparent success of Catholicism in France remained real, particularly when the former Protestant leader Henri IV converted to Catholicism in order to enter Paris and be accepted as King. The French may have been pleased at their king's dramatic and cynical conversion. Elizabeth was not. On receiving the news in July of 1593, she wrote Henri expressing her feelings in no uncertain terms.

Oh what griefs, O what regrets, O what groanings felt I in my soul at the sound of such news . . . can we with any reason expect a good sequel from an act so iniquitous? . . . And where you promise me all friendship and fidelity, I confess I have dearly merited it, and I will not repent it provided you do not change your Father. Otherwise I will be only a bastard sister, at least not your sister by the Father . . . .

Elizabeth signed the letter

Your most assured sister, if it be after the old fashion (i.e., you still a Protestant); *with the new* (i.e., you now a Catholic) *I have nothing to do.*

And the Puritans remained a problem. In the 1580s, they launched a campaign to convert the Church to their Presbyterian model and to lobby members of Parliament to that end. In response, Archbishop Whitgift demanded that every clergyman sign an oath to support the established practices and tenets of the Anglican Church, and to recognize Elizabeth as the Church's Supreme Governor. A clergyman refusing to sign was to be removed from his office and imprisoned.

Elizabeth backed Whitgift and announced that she would not permit Parliament to "meddle" in church matters. As to those members of her own Council who might agree with militant Puritan goals, she invented a new verb, "We will redress [that]" she said, "or else uncouncil some."

At the same time, Elizabeth realized that there were things about the Church of England that needed reform. Just as she was ready to "uncouncil" Puritan extremists among her Council members, she unambiguously threatened her Anglican bishops,

If you my lords of the clergy do not amend, I mean to depose you.

By 1587, a bill was actually introduced in the House of Commons to change the established form of religion to that envisioned by the Puritans. The bill made no progress, because Elizabeth had ordered that Parliament neither pass nor consider any law affecting the religion of the realm. Her representatives convinced the majority of members that the bill would work too drastic and fundamental a change in English institutions, and, in defying the queen's will, might even be considered treasonous. When a Puritan member questioned Elizabeth's right to impose such a veto, and a group of Puritans met to plan opposition to her stand, their leaders were sent to the Tower.

Whitgift and the queen prevailed, and the Puritan movement lost its momentum for the balance of her reign. But the Puritans had grasped the concept that Parliament could be an instrument to bring about important changes and that its members could be influenced (we would say "lobbied") to support or reject those changes. That concept would have a dramatic and fundamental impact on English government. But that lay in the future – in the reign of other monarchs.

In Elizabeth's reign, Catholics, Anglicans and Puritans were not the only groups creating issues of conscience or belief. There were atheists and agnostics in England, but they met, if at all, in secret and dared not openly espouse their views. Sir Walter Raleigh maintained a group called the "School of Night" in which free thinkers like Raleigh, the brilliant poet and playwright, Christopher Marlowe, Thomas Harriot and Henry Percy, the "Wizard Earl" of Northumberland, met in secret to smoke their pipes and ponder such forbidden topics as the existence of God and the origin of man.

Heretical and atheistic papers were found in the possession of the playwright Thomas Kyd, who, under torture, attributed them to Marlowe. Marlowe had been a valued spy for Walsingham, going undercover in France to ferret out English priests who were training for a return to England. The Crown had even intervened with Cambridge University to see that, despite his long absences, Marlowe received his degree.

But espousing heresy and atheism was a serious crime. Given Kyd's testimony, Marlowe was ordered to report to the Star Chamber. He faced the possibility of torture, possibly even execution. But, a remarkable event intervened. Dining with friends — former operatives of Walsingham — Marlowe was reportedly stabbed in the eye and killed during a sudden fight over the bill. After an inquest, Marlowe's assailant was found to have acted in self-defense and acquitted.

Was Marlowe's death faked, so that he could escape torture and execution? Was some other corpse buried in his place? Was this charade carried out with the connivance of the queen? Did Marlowe go on to write the remaining works of William Shakespeare from a villa in the Tuscan hills?

What would Elizabeth have done had she believed that, despite espousing atheism, Marlowe was the man writing "Shakespeare's" poems and plays or, even if not the Bard, that he was simply a fine poet and playwright who had rendered valuable and dangerous service as a spy? Would she have signed his death warrant for atheism and heresy or allowed him to run? It would be nice to think the latter, but I'm not sure. She had little sympathy for atheists, but considerable sympathy for good poets. And she might have enjoyed fooling some pompous judges of the Star Chamber. Atheist or not, perhaps she would have been content to see him flee the country and to rely on the report of his death. We have no answers. For all we know, poor Marlowe may really have been fatally stabbed for refusing to pick up the check.

While it may have seemed to the average Englishman that Catholics and Protestants were the principal contenders for men's souls, outside of England another great religion — Islam — had millions of adherents and exercised vast power. The potential uses of that power were not lost on Elizabeth.

The Pope's excommunication led the Queen to consider new and radical measures to protect the nation and her throne. Among those measures was fostering closer and stronger relationships with the Muslim powers, Morocco, Persia and most significant of all, the Ottoman Empire, whose capital, Constantinople, was then one of the largest and most beautiful cities in the world.

Those relationships with the Islamic powers had begun with successful trade; but that trade carried with it the potential of military alliances, particularly against Spain.

Reaching out to the Muslims was treated by the Catholic nations as a betrayal of Christianity. But Elizabeth could tell herself that Muslims and Protestants were not so very different in their beliefs and the origins of their religions and that Catholicism was really the religious deviant.

And, putting aside that rationalization, Elizabeth recognized that she and England faced grave dangers from the Catholic powers — notably Spain. To save England she was prepared to bring the powers of Islam down upon her Christian enemies.

The vision of an Anglo-Islamic alliance did not occur only to Elizabeth. The Sultan of Morocco dreamed of employing a military alliance with England to reconquer

"Andalusia," the Islamic Spain lost to the Catholic monarchs, Ferdinand and Isabella, a century before. With potential English help the "Reconquista" no longer seemed impossible.

But, while English trade with the Muslim countries generally prospered, and Elizabeth carried on a correspondence with the Ottoman Sultan, Murad III, for many years and maintained a generally good relationship with Al Mansur, who ruled Morocco for much of her reign, the Muslim rulers never seemed prepared to move forward with a full and open military alliance.

When the Armada threatened to overcome England, Walsingham still hoped for a powerful Ottoman attack on the Spanish coast. The attack never materialized, but the threat of it may have forced the Spanish to keep troops and ships in or near Spain, lest such an attack occur.

Did the relationship with the forces of Islam engineered and fostered by Elizabeth save England from invasion? No. But it certainly illustrated the queen's ultimate "flexibility" in matters of religion.

Chapter Twelve

Health

ELIZABETH WAS GENERALLY HEALTHY and physically active most of her life. In an age of gastronomic excess, she ate and drank sparingly; and she rode, hunted and danced, even in her later years.

She had some ailments that are difficult to diagnose in hindsight. This is particularly true of her youth. Sometimes these ailments are dismissed as the psychosomatic symptoms of a neurotic and highly stressed young female. But Elizabeth did not manifest the signs of hypochondria. She exhibited no particular fear of disease. She regularly touched subjects who were inflicted with scrofula, since it was believed that the disease could be cured by the "King's touch." Nor did she appear to panic at the signs of plague, a terrifying thing to many, and for good reason.

In her youth, Elizabeth was stricken, from time to time, with a debilitating swelling of her arms, legs and even her face. This occurred, for example, when she was commanded by her sister Mary to return to London, perhaps to face a trial or even death for involvement in a Protestant plot. What was this strange swelling? Was it the product of stress? If so, why did it not appear in her later years, when she certainly faced periods of enormous stress? Perhaps it was lymphodema, which often occurs in young women, but can disappear later in life. Or, it may have been interstitial nephritis, which, if untreated, would more likely have continued. We do not know.

There were times, particularly during Mary's reign, when Elizabeth's normally white skin took on an olive hue, probably due to jaundice; but the problem appeared to have little effect on her ability to function normally.

As we've seen, Elizabeth had a serious case of smallpox. But, like so much about the queen, her smallpox did not follow the ordinary course. Typically, those afflicted with "the pox" ran a high fever, which, if they lived, broke in a few days and was followed by disfiguring sores and scars. But Elizabeth's fever continued on and on, without breaking, until it appeared she would surely die of the infection. Yet, in a few more days, the fever finally broke, and she recovered fully with far less scarring then most.

In her later years, the queen's earlier health problems seemed to disappear, and she remained hard working and vigorous. Perhaps her general good health is attributable to a reluctance to call upon English doctors, whose "treatments" were often likely to increase the chances of death or disability, rather than to effect a cure. For example, the use of leeches to "bleed" the patient was a remedy they commonly used for many disorders; and the rate of death in childbirth was much higher among the upper classes, who could afford English doctors, than among ordinary women who were attended by experienced midwives or dealt with the process on their own.

Elizabeth did, however, have various odd afflictions. At one point, she was troubled by a severe pain in her hip; and, like her father, she suffered from an ulcer in her leg. This led one potential suitor to make the unchivalrous remark that she was just "an old woman with a sore leg." She was always reluctant to take medication to dull pain and, generally, would try to continue working, ignoring any pain.

There are indications that, in her later years, Elizabeth exhibited sensitivity to heat. There was the episode of her complaining of the heat and opening the front of her dress in an audience with the French Ambassador. Was this really heat sensitivity or an attempt to attract? Probably the former. If so, we are unaware of the cause. Elizabeth was too old at the time to have been suffering from the hot flashes of menopause.

But none of these ailments kept Elizabeth from living, working, even thriving to her 70th year, a ripe old age in the 16th century when the average life expectancy was in the 30s. Even in her later years, she continued to dance, ride and hunt. She also continued to go on progress, although it was always an arduous undertaking. Only two years before her death, when there were complaints about the annual progress and suggestions that it be cancelled or at least curtailed, Elizabeth responded, "Let the old stay behind and the young and able go with me."

We do not know the cause of Elizabeth's death. She had caught what seems to have been a cold. Or, perhaps, it was flu, since her head and bones ached. She could no longer sleep. She suffered a swelling in her throat, which apparently became ulcerated. Of course, antibiotics were centuries in the future; and no effective treatment was available. The ulcer broke open, choking her with fluid. She could no longer eat solid food, and, finally, she seemed unable to speak (despite Robert Cecil's claim that she whispered to him that the Scottish king was to succeed her).

Was this pneumonia or a strep infection or some other kind of sepsis spreading from an ulcerated throat? Or was it just the ravages of old age? It's difficult to know. Whatever the cause of her death, it would be nice to think that, as the announcement phrased it, the great queen "departed this lyfe, mildly like a lamb, easily like a ripe apple from the tree."

SUMMING UP

WAS ELIZABETH I England's greatest monarch? Let's quickly explore the other candidates. William I (the "Conqueror") successfully invaded the island and was highly efficient in establishing Norman rule. Henry II was an intelligent and effective monarch who regretted making his friend Thomas Becket Archbishop of Canterbury and regretted even more that two moronic knights slaughtered Becket in the mistaken belief that this was their king's wish. And, putting it mildly, Henry had a serious problem with his wife, Eleanor of Aquitaine, and their rebellious sons. Edward I was a strong ruler who accomplished a great deal in his reign. Never mind that he expelled the Jews from the realm. Richard I (the "Lion-heart") led a crusade, but did little else. Despite his remarkable victory at Agincourt, Henry V was not a particularly effective or admirable king. The same could be said for Edward IV, despite his military prowess. Richard III showed great promise; but, between his defeat at Bosworth Field and his nasty portrayal by Shakespeare, he can't be considered a serious contender. Victoria's long reign was marked by the success of the British Empire; but, for the most part, the accomplishments of her reign were attributable initially to her capable husband, Prince Albert, and later to the men who served her, such as Disraeli and Gladstone.

Considering everything — the state of the realm when she took the throne, its enormously improved position at her death and the monumental challenges she faced successfully in the interim — Elizabeth seems to surpass them all.

Modern historians tend to say that history is not really shaped by individuals, but by economic and social forces. If so, the Elizabethan age would seem an exception. Certainly, economic and social forces played a rule. But it would be difficult to deny that such influential actors as Burghley, Walsingham, Leicester, Essex, Drake and, most importantly, Elizabeth herself had a profound impact on English and European history of the period.

Most of the problems Elizabeth had faced over the forty-four years of her reign — from ominous threats to more manageable issues — had finally resolved themselves by the time of her death. The Spanish seemed no longer likely to mount an invasion. Philip was gone, and their landing in Ireland had been soundly defeated in 1602, as had the troublesome Tyrone. Ireland itself appeared more controllable than in the past, thanks to the policies of the queen and the military efforts of Lord Mountjoy. With James I on the throne of both England and Scotland, the threat of a Franco-Scottish invasion from the north was no longer a significant concern.

Moreover, France itself was far less menacing under Henri IV, an effective, sensible and generally impressive ruler. Despite his becoming a Catholic, Henri showed little or no interest in overthrowing Elizabeth. On the contrary, he sensibly pressed for three-way peace talks between England, France and Spain.

The Dutch were succeeding in freeing themselves from the Spanish in the northern part of the lowlands; and, although the Spanish and Imperial forces still maintained their grip on the Catholic southern provinces, there was less of a threat to English commercial interests. At least, the French and Spanish could be played off against each other, as Elizabeth had successfully done for many years.

In England, the religious controversy appeared to have lost much of its fury. Elizabeth's generally tolerant "centrist" policies had been effective. The extensive Catholic pressure of the 1580s had diminished. Most English Catholics were resistant to extreme papal or Spanish views and, essentially, desired to be allowed to practice their faith privately without fear of imprisonment or death.

Radical Puritanism and the savage Puritan attacks on the Anglican Church had faded for the moment. Although a Puritan movement remained, it was less aggressive and vituperative at the time of Elizabeth's death. Later, that changed.

In her dealings with Parliament, Elizabeth had hewed unswervingly to the proposition that she governed — not they — and that Parliament must not intrude upon the governance decisions that were hers alone to make. Nevertheless, she was prepared to show flexibility when the Commons raised the issue of the monopolies granted to favored individuals. Elizabeth announced that the most egregious monopolies would be ended, but made it clear that this was a matter of grace, based on her concern for her subjects, and should not be taken as a lessening of her royal authority to govern as she pleased.

This is what led to her magnificent "Golden Speech"; and, despite her reservation of the royal prerogatives, Parliament was thrilled and relieved. The vast majority of its members wanted no part of invading those prerogatives, even though it was becoming more and more evident that, in the ability to grant or withhold subsidies, Parliament had a powerful card to play.

In Elizabeth's reign, however, Parliament did not exert its latent power or even think of seriously challenging the monarch's right to govern without interference. It did not do so until the reign of Charles I, and, when it did, the result was civil war and the beheading of the king.

During Elizabeth's reign, England became a thriving center of international trade and finance. Its ships and trading companies were already spreading its commercial and political interests throughout the globe.

All in all, this slim, regal, passionate woman had devoted her life to governing the realm and defending her subjects, sacrificing her own wealth and, perhaps, her personal happiness in the process. She had managed to handle her male councilors and had outmaneuvered the great powers of the time, playing one off against the other. She had held the country together at a time when, like France, it could have been shattered with religious warfare. She left England in a far better and stronger place than when, in her youth, she took on the burden of governing a weak and troubled nation faced with grave threats of all kinds from every side.

The historian William Camden said:

> *Though beset by divers nations, her mortal enemies, she held the most stout and warlike nation of the English four and fourty years and upwards, not only in awe and duty, but even in peace also. Insomuch as, in all England, for so many years, never any mortal man heard the trumpet sound the charge to battle.*

Even Pope Sixtus V voiced his grudging respect for Elizabeth:

> *She certainly is a great Queen,*

he proclaimed.

Were she only a Catholic she would be our dearly beloved. Just look how well she governs! She is only a woman, only mistress of half an island, and yet she makes herself feared by Spain, by France, by the Empire, by all.

Burghley, who was in a good position to know, pronounced Elizabeth

the wisest woman that ever was, for she understood the interests and dispositions of all the princes in her time, and was so perfect in her knowledge of her own realm that no councilor could tell her anything she did not know before.

Perhaps 20th century historians Will and Ariel Durant said it best. Elizabeth, they wrote,

found England bankrupt and despised, and left it rich and powerful; and the sinews of learning and literature grew strong in the wealth of her people She continued the despotism of her father, but moderated it with humanity and charm. Denied husband and child, she mothered England, loved it devotedly, and used herself up serving it. She was the greatest ruler that England has ever known.

Elizabethan Time Line

- 1533 -
Elizabeth born

Robin Dudley born

- 1536 -
Anne Boleyn executed

- 1537 -
Edward VI born

- 1542 -
Mary Queen of Scots born

- 1547 -
Henry VIII dies

Edward VI becomes King

- 1549 -
Admiral Seymour executed

- 1553 -
Edward VI dies

Mary Tudor becomes Queen

- 1554 -
Wyatt's Rebellion

Elizabeth imprisoned in the Tower

Mary Tudor marries Philip II of Spain

- 1558 -

Mary Queen of Scots marries the French Dauphin

Queen Mary dies

Elizabeth becomes Queen

- 1559 -

Mary Queen of Scots' husband becomes King of France

- 1560 -

Amy Robsart dies

- 1561 -

Mary Queen of Scots' French husband dies

She returns to Scotland

- 1562 -

Elizabeth suffers from smallpox

- 1564 -

Robin Dudley made Earl of Leicester

- 1566 -

Mary Queen of Scots' son, James, born

Robert Devereux, Earl of Essex, born

- 1567 -

Mary Queen of Scots abdicates in favor of her son

- 1568 -

Mary Queen of Scots flees to England

Cecil employs Walsingham

Elizabeth seizes the Spanish treasure ship

- 1569 -

The Northern Rebellion

- 1570 -

The Pope excommunicates Elizabeth

Walsingham made Ambassador to France

- 1571 -

Cecil made Lord Burghley

The Ridolfi Plot

- 1572 -

Burghley made Lord Treasurer

Duke of Norfolk executed

St. Bartholomew's Day Massacre

- 1573 -

Walsingham made Councilor and Joint Principal Secretary

- 1574 -

Charles IX of France dies

His brother, Henri III, becomes king

- 1576 -

Leicester secretly marries Lettice Knollys

- 1579 -

Jean de Simier comes to England

Elizabeth learns of Leicester's marriage

Alençon visits England

- 1580 -

Spain annexes Portugal

- 1581 -

Edmund Campion executed

Alençon returns to England. They kiss. Elizabeth reneges

- 1582 -

Alençon leaves for good

- 1583 -

Throckmorton Plot

- 1584 -

Mendoza expelled

Alençon dies

William of Orange assassinated

The "Bond of Association"

Dr. Parry's Plot

Leicester brings young Essex to court

- 1585 -

Leicester commands Netherlands Expedition

- 1586 -

Leicester made Governor General of Netherlands

Babington Plot

Mary Queen of Scots tried, convicted

- FEBRUARY 1, 1587 -

Elizabeth signs Mary's death warrant

- FEBRUARY 8, 1587 -

Mary Queen of Scots executed

- 1587 -

Drake's raid on Cádiz

- 1588 -

The Spanish Armada defeated

Leicester dies

- 1589 -

Henri III assassinated

Henry IV next in line

- 1590 -

Walsingham dies

- 1591 -

Hatton dies

- 1591-2 -

Essex commands English forces in France

- 1593 -

Henri IV converts, takes Paris

Essex appointed to Council

- 1594 -

Dr. Lopez executed

- 1596 -

Essex and Howard raid Cádiz

Robert Cecil made Principal Secretary

– 1597 –

Essex's "Islands Voyage" fiasco

– 1598 –

Burghley dies

Philip II dies

Essex turns his back on the Queen

– MARCH 1599 –

Essex leads army to Ireland

– SEPTEMBER 1599 –

Truce with Tyrone – Essex returns to London

– 1601 –

Essex's rebellion, trial, execution

Elizabeth's "Golden Speech"

– 1603 –

Elizabeth dies

James I becomes King

ACKNOWLEDGEMENTS

There would be no book without the skill and dedication of Bobby Woods, the efforts of Roberta Dunner, and the patience of my dear wife, Barbara.

ABOUT THE AUTHOR

Bertram Fields was born in Los Angeles. A practicing lawyer, he graduated *magna cum laude* from Harvard Law School, where he was an Editor of the Harvard Law Review. After serving as a First Lieutenant in the U.S. Air Force during the Korean War, he began the general practice of law. Since then, he has tried many of the landmark cases in the entertainment, sports and communications industries and has been the subject of numerous personal profiles in magazines and newspapers. He teaches at Stanford Law School and lectures annually at Harvard.

Mr. Fields is the author, under a pseudonym, of two prior novels, *The Sunset Bomber*, published by Simon and Schuster, and *The Lawyer's Tale*, published by Random House.

Under his own name, he has written *Royal Blood*, a biographical work on Richard III and *Players*, an analysis of the Shakespeare authorship question. Both non-fiction books were published by HarperCollins.

His recent books, *Destiny: A Novel Of Napoleon & Josephine* and *Shylock: His Own Story* are also available from Marmont Lane Books.

He lives in Malibu, California with his wife, Barbara Guggenheim, a nationally known art consultant.

MARMONT LANE BOOKS WOULD LIKE TO THANK TOM ANDRE, ELLEN BASKIN, AND ROBERTA DUNNER FOR THEIR ASSISTANCE IN THE MAKING OF THIS BOOK.

MARMONT LANE

BOOKS

MARMONTLANE.COM